The Summa Theologiæ ranks among the greatest documents of the Christian Church, and is a landmark of medieval western thought. It provides the framework for Catholic studies in systematic theology and for a classical Christian philosophy, and is regularly consulted by scholars of all faiths and none, across a range of academic disciplines. This paperback reissue of the classic Latin/English edition first published by the English Dominicans in the 1960s and 1970s, in the wake of the Second Vatican Council, has been undertaken in response to regular requests from readers and librarians around the world for the entire series of 61 volumes to be made available again. The original text is unchanged, except for the correction of a small number of typographical errors.

The original aim of this edition was not narrowly ecclesiastical. It sought to make this treasure of the Christian intellectual heritage available to theologians and philosophers of all backgrounds, including those who, without claiming to be believers themselves, appreciate a religious integrity which embodies hardbitten rationalism and who recognise in Thomas Aquinas a master of that perennial philosophy which forms the bedrock of European civilisation. Because of this the editors worked under specific instructions to bear in mind not only the professional theologian, but also the general reader with an interest in the 'reason' in Christianity. The parallel English and Latin texts can be used successfully by anybody with a basic knowledge of Latin, while the presence of the Latin text has allowed the translators a degree of freedom in adapting their English version for modern readers. Each volume contains a glossary of technical terms and is designed to be complete in itself to serve for private study or as a course text.

NIHIL OBSTAT

IGNATIUS O'BRIEN O.P., S.T.M.
die 23 Novembris 1964

IMPRIMI POTEST

LUDOVICUS COFFEY O.P.
Prior Provincialis Hiberniæ

die 26 Novembris 1964

NIHIL OBSTAT

PAULUS GIGLIO
Censor Deputatus

IMPRIMATUR

SALVATORE ASTA
Administrator Apostolicus Archidioceseos
Isfahanensis Latinorum
Tehran, die 23 Novembris 1964

ST THOMAS AQUINAS

SUMMA THEOLOGIÆ

ST THOMAS AQUINAS

SUMMA THEOLOGIÆ

Latin text and English translation,
Introductions, Notes, Appendices
and Glossaries

NON NISI TE

PIÆ MEMORIÆ

JOANNIS

PP. XXIII

DICATUM

ALLOCUTIO

PAULI

PP. VI

MCMLXIII

HIS HOLINESS POPE PAUL VI

WAS PLEASED to grant an audience, on 13 December 1963, to a group, representing the Dominican Editors and the combined Publishers of the new translation of the *Summa Theologiæ* of St Thomas, led by His Eminence Michael Cardinal Browne, of the Order of Preachers, and the Most Reverend Father Aniceto Fernandez, Master General of the same Order.

AT THIS AUDIENCE

THE HOLY FATHER made a cordial allocution in which he first welcomed the representatives of a project in which he found particular interest. He went on to laud the perennial value of St Thomas's doctrine as embodying universal truths in so cogent a fashion. This doctrine, he said, is a treasure belonging not only to the Dominican Order but to the whole Church, and indeed to the whole world; it is not merely medieval but valid for all times, not least of all for our own.

His Holiness therefore commended the enterprise of Dominicans from English-speaking Provinces of the Order and of their friends; they were undertaking a difficult task, less because the thought of St Thomas is complicated or his language subtle, than because the clarity of his thought and exactness of language is so difficult to translate. Yet the successful outcome of their efforts would undoubtedly contribute to the religious and cultural well-being of the English-speaking world.

What gave him great satisfaction was the notable evidence of interest in the spread of divine truth on the part of the eminent laymen concerned, members of different communions yet united in a common venture.

For these reasons the Holy Father wished it all success, and warmly encouraged and blessed all those engaged. He was happy to receive the first volume presented to him as a gesture of homage, and promised that he would follow with interest the progress of the work and look forward to the regular appearance of all the subsequent volumes.

VOLUMES

PRIMA PARS

1 Theology (1a. 1)
2 Existence and Nature of God (1a. 2–11)
3 Knowing and Naming God (1a. 12–13)
4 Knowledge in God (1a. 14–18)
5 The Will and Power of God (1a. 19–26)
6 The Trinity (1a. 27–32)
7 Father, Son, and Holy Ghost (1a. 33–43)
8 Creation (1a. 44–9)
9 Angels (1a. 50–64)
10 Cosmogony (1a. 65–74)
11 Man (1a. 75–83)
12 Human Intelligence (1a. 84–9)
13 Man Made to God's Image (1a. 90–102)
14 Divine Government (1a. 103–9)
15 The World Order (1a. 110–19)

PRIMA SECUNDÆ

16 End Happiness (1a2æ. 1–5)
17 Human Acts (1a2æ. 6–17)
18 Principles of Morality (1a2æ. 18–21)
19 Love and Desire (1a2æ. 22–30)
20 Pleasure (1a2æ. 31–9)
21 Fear and Anger (1a2æ. 40–8)
22 Dispositions for Human Acts (1a2æ. 49–54)
23 Virtues (1a2æ. 55–67)
24 Gifts and Beatitudes (1a2æ. 68–70)
25 Sin (1a2æ. 71–80)
26 Original Sin (1a2æ. 81–5)
27 Effects of Sin (1a2æ. 86–9)
28 Law (1a2æ. 90–7)
29 The Old Law (1a2æ. 98–105)
30 The Gospel of Grace (1a2æ. 106–14)

SECUNDA SECUNDÆ

31 Faith (2a2æ. 1–7)
32 Consequences of Faith (2a2æ. 8–16)
33 Hope (2a2æ. 17–22)
34 Charity (2a2æ. 23–33)

35 Consequences of Charity (2a2æ. 34–46)
36 Prudence (2a2æ. 47–56)
37 Justice (2a2æ. 57–62)
38 Injustice (2a2æ. 63–79)
39 Religion and Worship (2a2æ. 80–91)
40 Consequences of Religion (2a2æ. 92–100)
41 The Social Virtues (2a2æ. 101–22)
42 Courage (2a2æ. 123–40)
43 Temperance (2a2æ. 141–54)
44 Parts of Temperance (2a2æ. 155–70)
45 Mysticism and Miracle (2a2æ. 171–8)
46 Activity and Contemplation (2a2æ. 179–84)
47 The Pastoral and Religious Lives (2a2æ. 185–9)

TERTIA PARS

48 The Incarnate Word (3a. 1–6)
49 The Grace of Christ (3a. 7–15)
50 The One Mediator (3a. 16–26)
51 Our Lady (3a. 27–30)
52 The Childhood of Christ (3a. 31–7)
53 The Life of Christ (3a. 38–45)
54 The Passion of Christ (3a. 46–52)
55 The Resurrection (3a. 53–9)
56 The Sacraments (3a. 60–5)
57 Baptism and Confirmation (3a. 66–72)
58 The Eucharistic Presence (3a. 73–8)
59 The Eucharist (3a. 79–83)
60 Penance (3a. 84–90

GENERAL PREFACE

BY OFFICIAL APPOINTMENT THE SUMMA PROVIDES THE FRAMEWORK for Catholic studies in systematic theology and for a classical Christian philosophy. Yet the work, which is more than a text-book for professional training, is also the witness of developing tradition and the source of living science about divine things. For faith seeks understanding in the contemplation of God's Logos, his wisdom and saving providence, running through the whole universe.

The purpose, then, of this edition is not narrowly clerical, but to share with all Christians a treasury which is part of their common heritage. Moreover, it consults the interests of many who would not claim to be believers, and yet appreciate the integrity which takes religion into hard thinking.

Accordingly the editors have kept in mind the needs of the general reader who can respond to the reasons in Christianity, as well as of technical theologians and philosophers.

Putting the Latin text alongside the English is part of the purpose. The reader with a smattering of Latin can be reassured when the translator, in order to be clear and readable, renders the thought of St Thomas into the freedom of another idiom without circumlocution or paraphrase.

There are two more reasons for the inclusion of the Latin text. First, to help the editors themselves, for the author's thought is too lissom to be uniformly and flatly transliterated; it rings with analogies, and its precision cannot be reduced to a table of terms. A rigid consistency has not been imposed on the editors of the different volumes among themselves; the original is given, and the student can judge for himself.

Next, to help those whose native tongue is not English or whose duty it is to study theology in Latin, of whom many are called to teach and preach through the medium of the most widespread language of the world, now becoming the second language of the Church.

The Latin is a sound working text, selected, paragraphed, and punctuated by the responsible editor. Important variations, in manuscripts and such major printed editions as the Piana and Leonine, are indicated. The English corresponds paragraph by paragraph and almost always sentence by sentence. Each of the sixty volumes, so far as is possible, will be complete in itself, to serve as a text for a special course or for private study.

THOMAS GILBY O.P.
T. C. O'BRIEN O.P.

ST THOMAS AQUINAS

SUMMA THEOLOGIÆ

VOLUME 58

THE EUCHARISTIC PRESENCE

(3a. 73–78)

Latin text. English translation, Introduction, Notes, Appendices & Glossary

WILLIAM BARDEN O.P.

CAMBRIDGE UNIVERSITY PRESS
Cambridge, New York, Melbourne, Madrid, Cape Town, Singapore, São Paulo

Cambridge University Press
The Edinburgh Building, Cambridge CB2 2RU, UK

Published in the United States of America by Cambridge University Press, New York

www.cambridge.org
Information on this title: www.cambridge.org/9780521394055

This digitally printed first paperback version 2006

A catalogue record for this publication is available from the British Library

ISBN-13 978-0-521-39405-5 hardback
ISBN-10 0-521-39405-8 hardback

ISBN-13 978-0-521-02966-7 paperback
ISBN-10 0-521-02966-X paperback

CONTENTS

EDITORIAL NOTES

THE LATIN TEXT

THE TRANSLATION has used the text of *ms. 15801 Bibliothèque Nationale*, written towards the end of the thirteenth century or during the first years of the fourteenth, and printed in the Latin-French *Summa* of the *Editions du Cerf* (*L'Eucharistie* I, Paris, 1960). In the present volume the punctuation has been modified and some variant readings found in the *Editio Piana* and *Editio Leonina* have been noted. The differences are trifling, and the Latin here given is a sound working text.

FOOTNOTES

Those signified by a superior number are the references given by St Thomas, with the exception of no. 1 to each article which refers to parallel texts in his writings. Those signified alphabetically are editorial references and explanatory remarks.

REFERENCES

Biblical references are to the Vulgate, bracketed numbers to the Psalms are those of versions based on the Hebrew text. Patristic references are to Migne (PG, Greek Fathers; PL, Latin Fathers). Abbreviations to St Thomas's works are as follows:

Summa Theologiæ, without title. Part, question, article, reply; e.g. 1a. 3, 2 ad 3. 1a2æ. 17, 6. 2a2æ. 180, 10. 3a, 35, 8.

Summa Contra Gentiles, *CG*. Book, chapter; e.g. *CG* 1, 28.

Scriptum in IV Libros Sententiarum, *Sent.* Book, distinction, question, article, solution or *quæstiuncula*, reply; e.g. III *Sent.* 25, 2, 3, ii ad 3.

Compendium Theologiæ, *Compend. Theol.*

Commentaries of Scripture (*lecturæ*, *expositiones*): Job, *In Job*; Psalms, *In Psal.*; Isaiah, *In Isa.*; Jeremiah, *In Jerem.*; Lamentations, *In Thren.*; St Matthew, *In Matt.*; St John, *In Joan.*; Epistles of St Paul, e.g. *In Rom.* Chapter, verse, *lectio* as required.

Philosophical commentaries: On the *Liber de Causis*, *In De causis*. Aristotle: *Peri Hermeneias*, *In Periherm.*; Posterior Analytics, *In Poster.*; Physics, *In Physic.*; *De Cælo et Mundo*, *In De Cæl.*; *De Generatione et Corruptione*, *In De gen.*; *Meteorologica*, *In Meteor.*; *De Anima*, *In De anima*;

De Sensu et Sensato, *In De sensu*; *De Memoria et Reminiscentia*, *In De memor.*; Metaphysics, *In Meta.*; Nicomachean Ethics, *In Ethic.*, Politics, *In Pol.* Book, chapter, *lectio* as required, also for Expositions on Boethius, *Liber de Hebdomadibus* and *Liber de Trinitate*, *In De hebd.* and *In De Trin.*, and on Dionysius, *De Divinis Nominibus*, *In De div. nom.* References to Aristotle give the Bekker annotation.

Quæstiones quodlibetales (*de quolibet*), *Quodl.*

Main titles are given in full for other works, including the 10 series of *Quæstiones Disputatæ*.

The views represented in the footnotes and appendices, which are those of the Editor of this volume, are in some cases not shared by the Editorial Board and other collaborators.

INTRODUCTION

THIS TREATISE does not offer a complete Eucharistic theology. The Church has existed for a mere two thousand years and it is unlikely that a complete theology—in any field of dogma—will ever be achieved. There are many approaches to the great dogmas of the faith and no one generation and no one mind can hope to combine them all.

In entering into the world of Revelation in the Scriptures the very turns of thought found there will always prove the happiest and most rewarding. But they are not enough. Behind all the modes and shapes of expression—many of them highly imaginative and poetical—in the writings of the Old and New Testaments there are always the fundamental categories of human intelligence as such. Behind all the great symbolic categories according to which man—the unconscious metaphysician—struggles to give expression to his insights into existence lies the power of rational intelligence. The Greek miracle was the achieved awareness of reason by itself. If God's revelation of himself and of his dealings with us has been made supremely in a life lived amongst us, and then recorded in words uttered or written, not of Greek philosophy but of poetry or rabbinic exegesis, the faith that receives that revelation will eventually have somehow to think itself out in terms of pure reason. That will have to be done. And indeed to a great extent it has already been done. It is not everything. It is not the first thing. It is not the most important thing. But it is a vital necessity for the sane faith of the Church which is composed of rational men, some of whom will always find the need to ask questions.

In the central field of theology, concerned with the mystery of God in himself, the understanding of essence and existence, of potentiality and act, of person and nature, will largely be developed by the tools of the metaphysical theologian. In the field of Christology the concepts of person and nature will be in control all the time. In sacramental theology the metaphysical theory of principal and instrumental causality will be most fruitfully applied; Christ, our great high-priest, is present in all the sacramental mysteries, as the principal cause of our sanctification and as the principal offerer of our sacrifice, and the human priest plays an instrumental role. It is in the Eucharistic theology of the presence of Christ as victim under the appearances of bread and wine that the Aristotelean doctrine of substance and accident proves most helpful. When theologians veer away from it they do so to the impoverishment of their thought. Like all satisfying philosophical insights it is at once something very simple and very profound. The implicit metaphysics of the ordinary man is constantly employing it. To attempt to come to terms with the mystery

of the Real Presence on the plane of mere physicism is to have missed the point.

Here, too, the Aristotelean hylomorphic theory is drawn on by St Thomas; to a great extent, indeed, to show what the Eucharistic change of bread into Christ's body and of wine into his blood is not. Here again we have a philosophical view of the constitution of matter which is independent of what one would nowadays call physical views. The hylomorphic theory that every bodily thing is composed of primal matter and substantial form (pure potentiality and first actuation) can retain its validity through all the vicissitudes of physical theories. It is a philosophical view, a basic intuition of the meaning of bodily things; it is concerned with things on the noumenal and not on the phenomenal plane, and there unsophisticated experience provides quite a sufficient context for intuitions of abiding worth.

This Greek philosophical approach to the great mysteries of God, of the Trinity, of Christ, of his presence in the worshipping Church, will not be particularly congenial to all minds, nor perhaps to the men of this or that period in the history of the Church. But it is an approach which in the nature of things has to be made. In the theology of St Thomas it has been made—magnificently. Here in his theology of the Eucharist we have the thought of a strong, dedicated intelligence raising great questions fearlessly and confronting them with humility and confidence. To allow him to guide one is to feel the presence of a light-filled intelligence, to share somehow in its feel for the truth, and to know the exhilaration of its entry into that which is.

He was steeped in the Biblical sources of theology—no arid speculator he!—and in all the known Patristic sources of his time; he had an infinite respect for the usage of the Church as a norm of doctrine; he loved Christ in his Eucharistic presence with his whole heart, and to him, indeed, he dedicated all the poetry of his nature. If he speaks to us in the language of what we like to think of as the *philosophia perennis*, he does so in the Church, with the revealed Word of God speaking to the docile faith of his angelic intelligence, and the Eucharistic presence of the risen Christ who died for us bringing all the joy he could ever look for to his heart: this last it is that brings a subtle flavour, a particular humanity, to what otherwise would be a piece of pure thought.

This treatise is concerned with that sacrament to which all the others are ordered and which is their end and their crown. St Thomas treats of it immediately after Baptism and Confirmation, the sacraments of Christian initiation, because it is the sacrament for the everyday life of all Christians; the other sacraments—Penance, Unction of the sick, Orders, Matrimony—envisage a particular person or a particular situation.

St Thomas devotes eleven questions (84 articles) to his discussion. In this volume we have the first six of these questions; these are divided into 44 articles. Speaking generally, we might say that he has four topics, in his discussions of both the sacraments in general and of each sacrament in particular. First, the sacrament as the sign and cause of grace, the *locus* or place of encounter with Christ; second, the effect or gift of grace; third, the liturgical minister and the rite of celebrating the mystery; fourth, the recipient or liturgical initiate and his mode of entering into the mystery. We may represent this common scheme diagrammatically thus:

Sacrament

Minister → *Recipient*

Effect

The order of discussion of these topics varies in each case. In the treatise on the Eucharist it is as follows:

1
Sacrament (q. 73)
Matter (qq. 74–77)
Form (q. 78)

4
Minister (q. 82)
Rite of Celebration (q. 83)

3
→ *Recipient* (qq. 80–81)

2
Effect (q. 79)

It will be seen then that this volume, although it contains six of the total of eleven questions, is concerned only with the first topic. St Thomas felt compelled to write at length on the 'matter' of the sacrament. It was because here we have something unique; in the other sacraments the matter and form become charged with the power of God and of Christ. In the Eucharist the matter and form are not just filled with the power of God (as, for example, the words and water in Baptism); the substance of the bread and wine disappear (how, we shall see later) and their *place* (to speak very loosely) is taken by the substance of the body of Christ, indeed by the whole Christ. To the mind of St Thomas this was a completely staggering thing. It was a mystery second only to the overwhelming mystery of God's taking a human nature into personal union with himself. If it is true that there is nothing greater than that God should become man (*Contra Gentes* IV, 27), the wonder of transubstantiation is not considerably less. Divine love, for its own purposes, is doing what to reason

must seem almost a mad and impossible thing, in the Eucharistic change as well as in the hypostatic union.

There is a real presence of Christ, the priest and the sanctifier, in the celebration of all the sacraments. There is a real presence of Christ the priest in the first Eucharistic moment which is the sacrifice of the Mass. In all these cases the reality of the presence is explained in terms of the presence of a higher to a subordinate efficient cause. That is a close union, a real presence surely; but in comparison with the presence of Christ's body and blood to the enveloping shell of the appearances of bread and wine, it is something which does not leave our reason in amaze. Christ's body and blood are as near to the accidental forms or the sense-phenomena of bread and wine as was the very substance of the bread and wine to them before. Before what? Before the unique and wonderful change which the Church calls 'transubstantiation', and which St Thomas will regard as the passing of the complete reality of the substance of the bread and wine, remaining, as it were, *where* it was, into the body and blood of Christ, thus bringing it about that the living Christ, not ceasing to be where he was, now begins to be present to the accidents of the bread and wine, and contained by them, just as up to then was the substance of the bread and wine.[1]

It is his teaching on the real presence of the body and blood of Christ in the Eucharist and on the nature of transubstantiation that reveals his power as a speculative theologian. The work that he did in this particular field was something that had to be done eventually in the life of the intelligence of the believing Church. St Thomas has done it, once for all.

The very success of his achievement, however, in this field, and the degree of his preoccupation with this theme, does perhaps mean that other areas of Eucharistic thought have not been so closely explored, nor perhaps has their importance been sufficiently stressed. The criticism might be made that the sacrifice of the Mass does not occupy the commanding place it should, and that its nature has not been illuminated. We might feel today that the emphasis given to the abiding real presence of the body and the blood (and of the whole Christ) has left the wonder of the Eucharistic sacrifice rather in the corner. A piety which would express the theological interest of St Thomas might find its centre rather in the tabernacle and in the monstrance than on the stone of sacrifice. There is, perhaps, some truth in this. All the elements, however, for a fruitful study of what happens at the Mass will be found in that part of the treatise which appears in the next volume (particularly in qq. 79 and

[1]'contained': used hereafter not in the sense of 'confined' or 'restricted', but for a definite special presence within the sacramental appearances. See Appendix 3 (10–11).

83). There also the Eucharist as Holy Communion will be studied (in q. 79), together with its effect as the food of our souls.

The present volume then is predominantly St Thomas's teaching on the Real Presence, though the great commanding lines for all Eucharistic thinking are also laid down. This great directive vision is that of all his sacramental thinking, namely of the three levels of reality—what we can see and hear, what that points to, and the further ultimate reality into which we are introduced. To enter into this teaching, on each of the sacraments and especially on the sacramental sacrifice of the Mass, is to taste the characteristic flavour of the Augustinian contribution to the thought of St Thomas and to share in the exhilaration of a catholic intelligence that felt the pull of sympathy not only to Aristotle but to Plato too. But the secret sap of the whole thing is the love of Christ.

Consequenter considerandum est de sacramento Eucharistiæ. Et

primo, de ipso sacramento;
secundo, de materia;
tertio, de forma;
quarto, de effectu;
quinto, de recipientibus hoc sacramentum;
sexto, de ministro;
septimo, de ritu.

Quæstio 73. de sacramento Eucharistiæ

Circa primum quæruntur sex:

1. utrum Eucharistia sit sacramentum;
2. utrum sit unum vel plura;
3. utrum sit de necessitate salutis;
4. de nominibus ejus;
5. de institutione ipsius;
6. de figuris ejus.

articulus 1. *utrum Eucharistia sit sacramentum?*

AD PRIMUM sic proceditur:[1] 1. Videtur quod Eucharistia non sit sacramentum. Ad idem enim non debent ordinari duo sacramenta; quia unumquodque sacramentum efficax est ad suum effectum producendum. Cum ergo ad perfectionem ordinetur Confirmatio et Eucharistia, ut Dionysius dicit,[2] videtur Eucharistia non esse sacramentum, cum Confirmatio sit sacramentum, ut prius habitum est.[3]

2. Præterea, in quolibet sacramento Novæ Legis id quod visibiliter subjicitur sensui efficit invisibilem effectum sacramenti: sicut ablutio aquæ causat et characterem baptismalem et ablutionem spiritualem, ut supra dictum est.[4] Sed species panis et vini, quæ subjiciuntur sensui in hoc sacramento, non efficiunt neque ipsum corpus Christi verum, quod est res et sacramentum, neque corpus mysticum, quod est res tantum in Eucharistia. Ergo videtur quod Eucharistia non sit sacramentum Novæ Legis.

---

[1] cf 3a. 65, 1; 79, 5, 7. IV *Sent.* 8, 1, 1, i. *In* 1 *Cor.* 11, *lect.* 5. *CG* IV, 61
[2] *Ecclesiastical Hierarchy* 4. PG 3, 472
[3] 3a. 65, 1; 72, 1
[4] 3a. 63, 6; 66, 1, 3, 7

At this juncture it is natural to consider the sacrament of the Eucharist:

first, the sacrament itself;
then, its matter;
thirdly, its form;[a]
fourthly, its effects;
fifthly, those who receive this sacrament;
sixthly, its minister;
seventhly, its rite.

Question 73. the sacramentality of the Eucharist

Under the first of these questions there are six points of inquiry:

1. is the Eucharist a sacrament at all?
2. is it one sacrament or many?
3. is it necessary for salvation?
4. what are its names?
5. who instituted it?
6. was it prefigured?

article 1. is the Eucharist a sacrament?[b]

THE FIRST POINT:[1] 1. It would seem that the Eucharist should not be regarded as a sacrament. Every sacrament is quite sufficient in itself for its proper purpose; there are not then two sacraments for the same purpose. Now both Confirmation and the Eucharist are ordered to perfection, as Dionysius teaches,[2] and for this Confirmation is the sacrament, as we have already seen.[3] Hence it would seem that the Eucharist is not a sacrament.

2. Moreover, in all the sacraments of the New Law that which strikes our senses is what brings about the hidden effect of the sacrament. As we have seen,[4] washing with water causes the baptismal character and cleanses us spiritually. But in the Eucharist the accidents of bread and wine do not bring about either Christ's actual body and blood or Christ's mystical body, which are respectively the first thing and the ultimate thing[c] of which the Eucharist is the sign. Therefore it is not properly a sacrament in the New Law.

---

[a]These are the three headings taken in the present volume; the remaining four will be taken in the following volume (59).

[b]St Thomas takes the teaching of the Church that the Eucharist is a sacrament for granted. This was later defined at Trent (Denz. 844). As a speculative theologian he is concerned to show how it fulfils the conditions required to be a sacrament.

[c]For the 'thing' of the sacrament see Appendix 1.

3. Præterea, sacramenta Novæ Legis habentia materiam in usu materiæ perficiuntur; sicut Baptismus in ablutione et Confirmatio in chrismatis consignatione. Si ergo Eucharistia sit sacramentum, perficeretur in usu materiæ, non in consecratione ipsius materiæ. Quod patet esse falsum, quia forma hujus sacramenti sunt verba quæ in consecratione materiæ dicuntur, ut infra patebit.[5] Ergo Eucharistia non est sacramentum.

SED CONTRA est quod in collecta dicitur, *Hoc tuum sacramentum non sit nobis reatus ad pœnam.*[6]

RESPONSIO: Dicendum quod sacramenta ecclesiæ ordinantur ad subveniendum homini in vita spirituali. Vita autem spiritualis vitæ corporali conformatur, eo quod corporalia spiritualium similitudinem gerunt. Manifestum est autem quod sicut ad vitam corporalem requiritur generatio per quam homo vitam accipit, et augmentum quo homo perducitur ad perfectionem vitæ, ita etiam requiritur alimentum quo homo conservatur in vita. Et ideo sicut ad vitam spiritualem oportuit esse Baptismum qui est spiritualis generatio et Confirmationem quæ est spirituale augmentum. Ita oportuit esse sacramentum Eucharistiæ quod est spirituale alimentum.

1. Ad primum ergo dicendum quod duplex est perfectio. Una quæ est in ipso homine ad quam perducitur per augmentum. Et talis perfectio competit Confirmationi. Alia autem est perfectio quam homo consequitur ex adjunctione cibi vel indumenti vel alicujus hujusmodi. Et talis perfectio competit Eucharistiæ, quæ est spiritualis refectio.

2. Ad secundum dicendum quod aqua Baptismi non causat aliquem spiritualem effectum propter ipsam aquam, sed propter virtutem Spiritus Sancti in aqua existentem: unde Chrysostomus dicit super illud *Joan.* v, '*Angelus Domini secundum tempus*, etc.', *In baptizatis non simpliciter aqua operatur, sed cum Spiritus Sancti susceperit gratiam tunc omnia solvit peccata.*[7] Sicut autem se habet virtus Spiritus Sancti ad aquam baptismi, ita se habet corpus Christi verum ad species panis et vini. Unde species panis et vini non efficiunt aliquid nisi virtute corporis Christi veri.

3. Ad tertium dicendum quod sacramentum dicitur ex eo quod continet aliquid sacrum. Potest autem aliquid esse sacrum dupliciter; scilicet

---

[5]3a. 78, 1

[6]Post-communion prayer for the Living and the Dead in the Roman Missal

[7]*In Joan.* Homily 36. On *John* 5, 4. PG 59, 204

[d]Both nutrition and growth are vital processes having their spring in man himself. And both require food. But in the case of nutrition the part played by food is immediate, obvious and continuous. The perfection of growth, of full maturity is not so consciously linked up with the thought of something external. Here is the point of St Thomas's analogy which must not be pressed too far. It is only a suggestion

3. Again, in the sacraments of the New Law in which a material element is employed, the sacrament is fully established only at the moment when the physical element is being used: for example, in Baptism only at the moment of the actual washing and in Confirmation only at the moment of actually signing the candidate with chrism. Hence, if the Eucharist were a sacrament it would be fully established when the matter is being used, and not at the consecration of the matter. But this is not the case, because the form which establishes this sacrament is the actual words of the consecration of the matter, as will be shown later on.[5] Therefore the Eucharist is not a sacrament.

ON THE OTHER HAND, we say in a post-communion prayer, *May this sacrament of thine not be an occasion of our deserving to be punished.*[6]

REPLY: The sacraments of the Church have for their purpose to serve man's need in his spiritual life. Now the spiritual life runs parallel to that of the body, since bodily things are shadows of spiritual realities. But it is obvious that in the life of the body the first requirement is generation by which a man receives the gift of life; then comes growth by which he is brought to maturity; so likewise food is also required that a man may be kept alive. Well then in the spiritual life there is Baptism which is spiritual birth and Confirmation which is spiritual growth. Likewise the Eucharist is needed; it is our spiritual food.

Hence: 1. There are two kinds of perfection. One has its spring in man himself; he attains it by growth. Confirmation envisages a perfection of this kind.[d] But there is another perfection which is brought about by our being fed and clothed and helped in other external ways. It is here that the Eucharist comes in. It is our spiritual refreshment.

2. It is not because of the natural power of the water that any spiritual effect is caused in Baptism, but because of the power of the Spirit which is in the water. Hence Chrysostom, commenting on *John*, '*An angel of the Lord went down at certain times into the pool*, etc.', observes, *It is not mere water which acts on the baptized; it is water in which the grace of the Holy Spirit is found that washes sins away.*[7] But what the power of the Spirit is to the water of Baptism, that the very body of Christ is to the appearances of bread and wine. These are operative only because of the very body of Christ that they contain.

3. A sacrament is so called because it contains something sacred. A thing can be sacred in two ways; in itself absolutely, and in relation to

to help our theological thinking. In the Eucharist, more than in any other sacrament, the external element makes an overwhelming impact. It contains Christ himself, and not merely some power deriving from him.

absolute, et in ordine ad aliud. Hæc est autem differentia inter Eucharistiam et alia sacramenta habentia materiam sensibilem: quod Eucharistia continet aliquid sacrum absolute, scilicet ipsum Christum; aqua vero baptismi continet aliquid sacrum in ordine ad aliud, scilicet virtutem ad sanctificandum; et eadem ratio est de chrismate et similibus. Et ideo sacramentum Eucharistiæ perficitur in ipsa consecratione materiæ: alia vero sacramenta perficiuntur in applicatione materiæ ad hominem sanctificandum.

Et ex hoc etiam consequitur alia differentia. Nam in sacramento Eucharistiæ id quod est res et sacramentum est in ipsa materia; id autem quod est res tantum est in suscipiente, scilicet gratia quæ confertur. In baptismo autem utrumque est in suscipiente, et character, qui est res et sacramentum; et gratia remissionis peccatorum, quæ est res tantum. Et eadem ratio est de aliis sacramentis.

articulus 2. utrum Eucharistia sit unum sacramentum vel plura?

AD SECUNDUM sic proceditur:[1] 1. Videtur quod Eucharistia non sit unum sacramentum sed plura. Dicitur enim in collecta, *Purificent nos, quæsumus, Domine, sacramenta quæ sumpsimus*:[2] quod quidem dicitur propter Eucharistiæ sumptionem. Ergo Eucharistia non est unum sacramentum, sed plura.

2. Præterea, impossibile est, multiplicato genere, non multiplicari speciem: sicut quod unus homo sit plura animalia. Sed signum est genus sacramenti, ut supra dictum est.[3] Cum igitur in Eucharistia sint plura signa, scilicet panis et vini, videtur consequens esse quod sint plura sacramenta.

3. Præterea, hoc sacramentum perficitur in consecratione materiæ, sicut dictum est.[4] Sed in hoc sacramento est duplex materiæ consecratio. Ergo est duplex sacramentum.

SED CONTRA est quod Apostolus dicit 1 *Cor.* x, *Unus panis et unum corpus multi sumus, omnes qui de uno pane et uno calice participamus.*[5] Ex quo patet quod Eucharistia sit sacramentum ecclesiasticæ unitatis. Sed sacramentum similitudinem gerit rei cujus est sacramentum. Ergo Eucharistia est unum sacramentum.

---

[1]cf 3a. 78, 6 ad 2. IV *Sent.* 8, 1, 1, ii
[2]Post-communion prayer for the Living and the Dead in the Roman Missal
[3]3a. 60, 1
[4]3a. 73, 1 ad 3
[5]1 *Corinthians* 10, 17

[e]The Eucharist is fully established as a sacrament when the matter (the bread and wine) is consecrated. cf 3a. 72, 3; 74, 2 ad 3; 78, 1. The real presence of Christ is

something else. The difference between the Eucharist and other sacraments having a material element is this: whereas the Eucharist contains something that is sacred in itself absolutely, namely, Christ, the water of Baptism contains something that is sacred in relation to something else, that is, it contains the power of sanctifying us; and we can say the same of chrism and suchlike. The Eucharist is fully established when the matter is consecrated;[e] the other sacraments are fully established only at the moment when the matter is being applied to the person who is receiving the sacrament.

And another difference follows on this one. In the sacrament of the Eucharist what we call the 'thing and sign' is in the very matter, but that which is the 'thing only', namely the grace bestowed, is in the person who receives. In Baptism both of these are to be found in the person who receives the sacrament, namely the character which is the 'thing and sign' and the grace of the forgiveness of sins which is the 'thing only'. The same holds good of the other sacraments.

article 2. is the Eucharist one sacrament or several?

THE SECOND POINT:[1] 1. It would appear that the Eucharist is not one sacrament, but several. We say in a post-communion prayer, *May the sacraments which we have received purify us, O Lord.*[2] And this on account of having received the Eucharist. Therefore, it is not one sacrament, but many.

2. Moreover, you cannot pluralize a genus without simultaneously pluralizing species: one man (the species) could not be two animals (the genus). But under the generic aspect all the sacraments are signs, as we said above.[3] Now in the Eucharist there are two signs, the bread and the wine, and consequently two sacraments seem to be there.

3. Furthermore, this sacrament is established when the matter is consecrated, as we have just said.[4] But there are two consecrations (of bread and of wine). There is, then, a double sacrament.

ON THE OTHER HAND, the Apostle says, *For we being many are one bread, one body, all that partake of one bread and one chalice.*[5] This text shows clearly that the Eucharist is the sacrament of the Church's unity. But a sacrament bears the likeness of that of which it is a sacrament. Therefore, the Eucharist itself should be one.

---

already brought about before the actual communion. This is the dogmatic basis for the Catholic cult of Christ in the Eucharist outside the moment of Holy Communion. See Denzinger 886.

RESPONSIO: Dicendum quod, sicut dicitur *Meta.*[6] unum dicitur non solum quod est indivisibile vel quod est continuum, sed etiam quod est perfectum: sicut cum dicitur una domus, et unus homo. Est autem unum perfectione ad cujus integritatem concurrent omnia quæ requiruntur ad finem ejusdem: sicut homo integratur ex omnibus membris necessariis operationi animæ, et domus ex partibus quæ sunt necessariæ ad inhabitandum. Et sic hoc sacramentum dicitur unum. Ordinatur enim ad spiritualem refectionem, quæ corporali conformatur. Ad corporalem autem refectionem duo requiruntur: scilicet cibus, qui est alimentum siccum; et potus, qui est alimentum humidum. Et ideo etiam ad integritatem hujus sacramenti duo concurrunt, scilicet spiritualis cibus et spiritualis potus: secundum illud *Joan.* vi, *Caro mea vere est cibus, et sanguis meus vere est potus.*[7] Ergo hoc sacramentum multa quidem materialiter est, sed unum formaliter et perfective.

1. Ad primum ergo dicendum quod in collecta eadem et pluraliter dicitur primo, *Purificent nos sacramenta quæ sumpsimus*; et postea singulariter subditur, *Hoc tuum sacramentum non sit nobis reatus ad pœnam*: ad ostendendum quod hoc sacramentum quodammodo est multa, simpliciter autem unum.

2. Ad secundum dicendum quod panis et vinum materialiter quidem sunt plura signa, formaliter vero et perfective unum, inquantum ex eis perficitur una refectio.

3. Ad tertium dicendum quod ex hoc quod est duplex consecratio hujus sacramenti, non potest plus haberi nisi quod hoc sacramentum materialiter est multa, ut supra dictum est.[8]

articulus 3. utrum hoc sacramentum sit de necessitate salutis?

AD TERTIUM sic proceditur:[1] 1. Videtur quod hoc sacramentum sit de necessitate salutis. Dicit enim Dominus, *Joan.* vi, *Nisi manducaveritis carnem Filii hominis et biberitis ejus sanguinem, non habebitis vitam in vobis.*[2] Sed in hoc sacramento manducatur caro Christi et bibitur sanguis ejus. Ergo sine hoc sacramento non potest homo habere salutem spiritualis vitæ.

2. Præterea, hoc sacramentum est quoddam spirituale alimentum. Sed alimentum corporale est de necessitate corporalis salutis. Ergo etiam hoc sacramentum est de necessitate salutis spiritualis.

3. Præterea, sicut Baptismus est sacramentum Dominicæ passionis, sine qua non est salus, ita et Eucharistia: dicit enim Apostolus, 1 *Cor.* xi, *Quotiescumque manducaveritis panem hunc et calicem biberitis, mortem*

---

[6] *Metaphysics* IV, 6. 1015b36. 1016a17, b9
[7] *John* 6, 56
[8] In this article

REPLY: According to Aristotle[6] we predicate oneness not merely of that which is undivided or continuous, but also of that which is perfect, when, for example, we say that a house is one or that a man is one. A thing is said to be one in its perfection when it is integral, and has all the elements required in order to attain its purpose: a man is thus complete when he has all the members needed for his vital actions, and a house when it has all the parts needed for dwelling in it. In this sense we say that the sacrament is one. Its purpose is to refresh us spiritually, as bodily nourishment does physically. Now this last consists of food which is dry sustenance and of drink which is wet. Just so, two things combine to make this sacrament complete—a spiritual food and a spiritual drink, according to our Lord's words in *John, My flesh is food indeed and my blood is drink indeed.*[7] It follows then that this sacrament is several in a material sense, but in a formal and complete sense it is one.

Hence: 1. In the prayer referred to we first speak in the plural when we say, *May the sacraments which we have received purify us*; but then we go on to say in the singular, *May thy sacrament not be the occasion of our deserving to be punished.* This shows that this sacrament, although in some measure many, is simply speaking one.

2. The bread and the wine are different signs in a material sense; but taken formally and with regard to what they achieve they are one, and taken together they make a single meal.

3. From the fact that there is a double consecration nothing more follows than that this sacrament is many in a material sense, as we have just said.[8]

article 3. is this sacrament required for salvation?

THE THIRD POINT:[1] 1. It would appear that this sacrament is required for salvation. Our Lord says, *Unless you eat the flesh of the Son of Man and drink his blood, you will not have life in you.*[2] But it is in this sacrament that Christ's flesh is eaten and his blood is drunk. Therefore, this sacrament is required in order for us to be saved by being spiritually alive.

2. Moreover, this sacrament is a kind of spiritual food. But food is a necessity for our bodily life. Therefore, this sacrament is needed for our spiritual health.

3. Also, Baptism is the sacrament of our Lord's passion, which is the indispensable source of salvation. But the Eucharist is also its sacrament; St Paul says, *as often as you eat this bread and drink this cup, you show*

---

[1]cf 3a. 80, 11. Also IV *Sent.* 9, 1, 2; 12, 3, 2, i ad 1. *In Joan.* 6, *lect.* 7
[2]*John* 6, 54

Domini annuntiabitis, donec veniat.[3] Ergo sicut baptismus est de necessitate salutis, ita et hoc sacramentum.

SED CONTRA est quod scribit Augustinus Bonifacio, contra Pelagianos, *Nec id cogitetis, parvulos vitam habere non posse, qui sunt expertes corporis et sanguinis Christi.*[4]

RESPONSIO: Dicendum quod in hoc sacramento duo est considerare, scilicet ipsum sacramentum, et rem sacramenti. Dictum est autem quod res sacramenti est unitas corporis mystici, sine qua non potest esse salus:[5] nulli enim patet aditus salutis extra Ecclesiam, sicut nec in diluvio absque arca Noe, quæ significat Ecclesiam, ut habetur 1 *Pet.*[6] Dictum est autem supra[7] quod res alicujus sacramenti haberi potest ante perceptionem sacramenti, ex ipso voto sacramenti percipiendi. Unde ante perceptionem hujus sacramenti, potest homo habere salutem ex voto percipiendi hoc sacramentum: sicut et ante Baptismum ex voto Baptismi, ut supra dictum est.[8]

Tamen est differentia quantum ad duo. Primo quidem, quia Baptismus est principium spiritualis vitæ, et janua sacramentorum. Eucharistia vero est quasi consummatio spiritualis vitæ, et omnium sacramentorum finis, ut supra dictum est:[9] per sanctificationes enim omnium sacramentorum fit præparatio ad suscipiendam vel consecrandam Eucharistiam. Et ideo perceptio Baptismi est necessaria ad inchoandam spiritualem vitam, perceptio autem Eucharistiæ est necessaria ad consummandam ipsam: non ad hoc quod simpliciter habeatur, sed sufficit eam habere in voto, sicut et finis habetur in desiderio et intentione.

Alia differentia est, quia per Baptismum ordinatur homo ad Eucharistiam. Et ideo ex hoc ipso quod pueri baptizantur, ordinantur per Ecclesiam ad Eucharistiam. Et sic, sicut ex fide Ecclesiæ credunt, sic ex intentione

---

[3] 1 *Corinthians* 11, 26

[4] *Against the Pelagians* 1, 22. PL 44, 570

[5] 3a. 73, 1

[6] 1 *Peter* 3, 20, 21

[7] 3a. 68, 2

[8] 3a. 68, 2

[9] 3a. 63, 6

[a] This unity of the mystical body of Christ is charity. Here we might ask what is meant by the mystical body of Christ. It is the solidarity of all those who are baptized and who are subject to the bishops and the pope. This solidarity is an external, an impersonal union. Its whole purpose is to engender and safeguard the inner, spiritual, personal union of charity. The Church, the mystical body, in and through which Christ operates, is the proper *locus*, the connatural zone, in which the life of charity is lived. This is not to say that charity is not found outside this zone, among the unbaptized or among the baptized who do not accept the Catholic hierarchy. It is found; among men of goodwill who are invincibly ignorant of the

forth the death of the Lord, until he come.[3] Therefore, the Eucharist is just as necessary for salvation as Baptism is.

ON THE OTHER HAND, we have Augustine writing to Boniface against the Pelagians, *you must not think that infants who have not received the body and blood of Christ cannot have spiritual life.*[4]

REPLY: We have two things to consider in this sacrament—the sacramental sign itself and the thing which is signified by it. We have already said[5] that the thing signified is the unity of the mystical body of Christ which is an absolute requisite for salvation, because outside the Church there is no salvation; it is like Noah's ark at the time of the flood.[6a] We said earlier[7] that the thing signified by a sacrament may already be possessed before the sacrament is received by reason of one's desiring the sacrament. Hence, before actually receiving this sacrament a man can be saved through his very desire to receive it. We affirmed this earlier in regard to Baptism.[8]

Yet in this matter there are two differences to be noted between these two sacraments: first, Baptism is the beginning of the spiritual life[b] and opens the door into the sacramental world; the Eucharist is the summit of the spiritual life and all the sacraments are ordered to it, as we said above.[9] They sanctify us and prepare us to receive the Eucharist or to consecrate it. Baptism is required in order to begin this spiritual life; the Eucharist is necessary in order to bring it to its culmination. It is not therefore needed for basic Christian living; for that it is enough to will the Eucharist, to desire and intend it as the natural culmination to Baptism.

The second difference is this. Infants receive Baptism, and because Baptism is ordered towards the Eucharist, they are thus set by the Church in the direction of the Eucharist. Just as they believe with the faith of

---

Church or of her divine character and who in good faith are unaware of or reject her claims. *Deus non alligatur sacramentis*, and we might add *Deus non alligatur ecclesiæ*. God can sanctify men outside the sacramental system and outside the zone we have indicated. But such men are not completely outside the Church; they are in it by desire, an implicit one, no doubt. Charity seeks the safeguarding shell of the sacraments and of the Church. In this sense there is no salvation outside the Church. He who is in charity is in the Church by desire. He has the ultimate *thing* of which the Church and the sacraments are the *sign*.

[b]The spiritual life here means the sacramental life of the Church in time. It is the life of the Church at worship and receiving the grace of God in and through the sacraments. It is Christ, the high-priest, really present (with varying degrees of *real presence*) among his baptized people, leading their worship and mediating the grace of the Spirit sent to them by the Father.

Ecclesiæ desiderant Eucharistiam: et per consequens recipiunt rem ipsius. Sed ad Baptismum non ordinantur per aliud præcedens sacramentum. Et ideo, ante susceptionem baptismi, non habent pueri aliquo modo baptismum in voto, sed soli adulti. Unde rem sacramenti percipere non possunt sine perceptione sacramenti. Et ideo hoc sacramentum non hoc modo est de necessitate salutis sicut baptismus.

1. Ad primum ergo dicendum quod, sicut Augustinus dicit, exponens illud verbum Joannis, '*Hunc cibum et potum*', scilicet carnis suæ et sanguinis, *societatem vult intelligi corporis et membrorum suorum, quod est Ecclesia, in prædestinatis et vocatis et justificatis sanctis et fidelibus ejus.*[10] Unde, sicut ipse dicit, in Epistola *ad Bonifacium, nulli est aliquatenus ambigendum tunc unumquemque fidelium corporis sanguinisque Domini participem fieri, quando in baptismate membrum corporis Christi efficitur; nec alienari ab illius panis calicisque consortio, etiam si, antequam panem illum comedat et calicem bibat, de hoc sæculo in unitate corporis Christi constitutus abscedat.*[11]

2. Ad secundum dicendum quod hæc est differentia inter alimentum corporale et spirituale, quod alimentum corporale convertitur in substantiam ejus qui nutritur; et ideo non potest homini valere ad vitæ conservationem alimentum corporale nisi realiter sumatur. Sed alimentum spirituale convertit hominem in seipsum: secundum illud quod Augustinus dicit, quod quasi audivit vocem Christi dicentis, '*Nec tu me mutabis in te, sicut cibum carnis tuæ, sed tu mutaberis in me*'.[12] Potest autem aliquis in Christum mutari et ei incorporari voto mentis, etiam sine hujus sacramenti perceptione. Et ideo non est simile.

3. Ad tertium dicendum quod baptismus est sacramentum mortis et passionis Christi prout homo regeneratur in Christo virtute passionis ejus. Sed Eucharistia est sacramentum passionis Christi prout homo perficitur in unione ad Christum passum. Unde, sicut baptismus dicitur 'sacramentum fidei', quæ est fundamentum spiritualis vitæ; ita Eucharistia dicitur 'sacramentum caritatis' quæ est *vinculum perfectionis*, ut dicitur *Coloss*. iii.[13]

---

[10]*In Joan.* 6, 55. *Tract.* 26. PL 35, 1614

[11]Pseudo-Bede, *In 1 Cor.* 10, 17. cf Gratian, *Decretum* 3, 4, 131 *Nulli est.* Richter-Friedberg 1, 1404

[12]*Confessions* 7, 10. PL 32, 742

[13]*Colossians* 3, 14

[c]The body of Christ and its members are analogous terms which can be understood in many senses. Since the encyclical of Pius XII, *Mystici Corporis,* we know that the Catholic Church and its members are the first to which the terms are attributed. This is formally because of the sacramental character engraved upon the soul at baptism, which unites each baptized person to Christ the Priest and King and Teacher, present in and working through the pope, bishops and clergy of the Church. But there are other groupings of souls on which the Spirit is acting in various degrees, beginning with faith (even implicit) and going on to the full light of glory. Here we can legitimately apply the terms 'body of Christ' and 'members

the Church, so by the intention of the Church they desire the Eucharist, and, as a result, they receive the *thing signified* by the Eucharist. But there is no prior sacrament to turn them towards Baptism; hence before they receive that sacrament there is no sense in which they can be said to desire it. That is possible only for adults. Hence infants cannot receive the *thing signified* by the sacrament (of Baptism and of the Eucharist) unless they actually receive the sacrament (of Baptism). So this sacrament is not required for salvation in the same way as Baptism is.

Hence: 1. As Augustine, commenting on a text of John, '*by this food and drink*', i.e. his flesh and his blood, says *our Lord gives us to understand the society of his body and its members,*[c] *which is the Church of the predestined, who are called by God to faith and holiness, to justification and glorification.*[10] Hence, as he writes in a letter to Boniface, *no one should have any doubt that all the faithful share in the body and blood of the Lord when they become members of the body of Christ at Baptism; nor are they deprived of their share in this bread and this cup, even if they should leave this world before eating this bread and drinking this cup, but in the unity of the body of Christ.*[11]

2. There is a difference between bodily and spiritual food. Bodily food is changed into the substance of the person who eats it and, therefore, is of no help in conserving life unless it is physically consumed. But spiritual food changes man into itself. This is the teaching of Augustine in his *Confessions*. He heard, as it were, the voice of Christ saying to him, '*you will not change me into yourself as you would the food of your flesh; but you will be changed into me.*'[12] A man can be changed into Christ and be incorporated into him by his mind's earnest devotion, even though he does not actually receive this sacrament. There is then no parity.

3. Baptism is the sacrament of the death and passion of Christ in that by it a man is re-born in Christ. But the Eucharist is the sacrament of the passion of Christ because in it a man is brought to spiritual perfection in being closely united to Christ who suffered for us. Hence, just as Baptism is called 'the sacrament of faith', which is the beginning of spiritual life, so the Eucharist is called 'the sacrament of charity',[d] which *is the bond of perfectness*, as we read in *Colossians*.[13]

---

of the body' in a less proper but analogous and valid sense. The solidarity of all souls in charity is the *thing signified* by the Eucharist. The mystical body of the Catholic Church at Mass and Communion is the *sacrament* of that. The lines of these two solidarities do not exactly coincide, though there is a natural order of one to the other. In its own way and in a less proper sense, the *thing signified* by the Eucharist can be called 'the body of Christ'. St Augustine is fond of speaking in this way and St Thomas sometimes follows him.

[d]All the sacraments look back to Christ on the cross and allow us to appropriate in

Footnote d continued on page 14

articulus 4. utrum convenienter hoc sacramentum pluribus nominibus nominetur

AD QUARTUM sic proceditur:[1] 1. Videtur quod inconvenienter hoc sacramentum pluribus nominibus nominetur. Nomina enim debent respondere rebus. Sed hoc sacramentum est unum, ut dictum est.[2] Ergo non debet pluribus nominibus nominari.

2. Præterea, species non notificatur convenienter per id quod est commune toti generi. Sed Eucharistia est sacramentum Novæ Legis. Omnibus autem sacramentis commune est quod in eis confertur gratia: quod significat nomen 'eucharistia', quod est idem quod 'bona gratia'. Omnia etiam sacramenta remedium nobis afferunt in via præsentis vitæ: quod pertinet ad rationem 'viatici'. In omnibus etiam sacramentis fit aliquid sacrum: quod pertinet ad rationem 'sacrificii'. Et per omnia sacramenta sibi invicem fideles communicant: quod significat hoc nomen 'synaxis' in græco, vel 'communio' in latino. Ergo hæc nomina non convenienter adaptantur huic sacramento.

3. Præterea, hostia videtur idem esse quod sacrificium. Sicut ergo non proprie dicitur 'sacrificium', ita nec proprie dicitur 'hostia'.

SED CONTRA est quod usus fidelium habet.

RESPONSIO: Dicendum quod hoc sacramentum habet triplicem significationem. Unam quidem respectu præteriti: inquantum scilicet est commemorativum Dominicæ passionis, quæ fuit verum sacrificium, ut supra dictum est.[3] Et secundum hoc nominatur 'sacrificium'.

Aliam autem significationem habet respectu rei præsentis, scilicet ecclesiasticæ unitatis, cui homines congregantur per hoc sacramentum. Et secundum hoc nominatur 'communio' vel 'synaxis': dicit enim Damascenus, quod *dicitur 'communio', quia communicamus per ipsam Christo; et quia participamus ejus carne et deitate; et quia communicamus et unimur ad invicem per ipsam.*[4]

Tertiam significationem habet respectu futuri: inquantum scilicet hoc

---

different ways the moral worth of his redeeming act—his merit, his satisfaction, his propitiation. All the sacraments look up to the risen Christ and make him in varying degrees *really present* to us. But the Eucharist is pre-eminently the sacrament of the union of love, because in it *real presence* goes to the very limit of possibility outside natural real presence. It looks up to *Christus passus gloriosus* in a unique way.

[1]cf 3a. 79, 2 ad 1

[2]3a. 73, 2

[3]3a. 48, 3

[4]*De Fide Orthodoxa* 4, 13. PG 94, 1153

[a]True is here contrasted, not with false, but with figurative or sacramental. The patriarchal and mosaic sacrifices were types or figures of the sacrifice of Christ. His

article 4. is it right to give this sacrament many names?

THE FOURTH POINT:[1] 1. It seems that it is not desirable to give this sacrament many names. Names should correspond to realities. But we have just said[2] that this sacrament is one. It should not then be given many names.

2. Moreover, a species is not suitably signified by a name that belongs to the genus. Now the Eucharist is a sacrament of the New Law. All the sacraments of the New Law have this in common, they confer grace. But the word 'eucharist', which is translated 'good grace', means just this. Also, all the sacraments act as restoratives as we journey through this present life, and this is precisely what a 'viaticum' does. Likewise, in all the sacraments something sacred is made: so they have the nature of 'sacrifice'. Finally, in all the sacraments the faithful enter into union with one another; this is signified by the name '*synaxis*' in Greek or '*communio*' in Latin. Therefore, it is not right to restrict these names to this sacrament.

3. Also, victim and sacrifice seem to be the same thing. Therefore, the term 'victim' should be ruled out just as much as the term 'sacrifice'.

ON THE OTHER HAND stands the usage of the faithful.

REPLY: This sacrament signifies three things. It looks back to the past: in this sense it commemorates the passion of our Lord, which was the true[a] sacrifice, as we saw earlier.[3] Because of this it is called 'sacrifice'.

In regard to the present, there is another thing to which it points. This is the unity[b] of the Church, into which men are drawn together through this sacrament. Because of this it is called '*communio*' or '*synaxis*'. As Damascene says, *it is called 'communion' because by it we are joined to Christ and because we share his flesh and his godhead, and because we are joined and united to one another through that.*[4]

It has a third significance with regard to the future. It prefigures that

---

sacrifice is the reality, the substance, of which they are the shadow. It is the truth, the antitype, of which they are the type. The Eucharistic sacrifice of the Mass is also an antitype of the true sacrifice of the cross, but in a fuller sense than the Old Testament sacrifices. It contains in a mysterious way what they merely signified.

[b]This unity of the Church is not precisely the being together of the baptized, by reason of their common baptismal character, or their coming together at the Eucharist, but their spiritual solidarity in charity, of which their Baptism and their common Eucharist are signs and causes. The proper *locus* of charity is the Church. All in charity should be in the Church; all in the Church should be in charity. Charity is Church-unity in the deepest sense.

sacramentum est præfigurativum fruitionis Dei, quæ erit in patria. Et secundum hoc dicitur 'viaticum', quia hoc præbet nobis viam illuc perveniendi. Et secundum hoc etiam dicitur 'eucharistia', id est 'bona gratia', quia *gratia Dei est vita æterna*, ut dicitur *Rom.* vi;[5] vel quia realiter continet Christum, qui est plenus gratia.

Dicitur etiam in græco '*metalepsis*', id est 'assumptio', quia, ut Damascenus dicit, *per hoc Filii deitatem assumimus.*[6]

1. Ad primum ergo dicendum quod nihil prohibet idem pluribus nominibus nominari secundum diversas proprietates vel effectus.

2. Ad secundum dicendum quod id quod est commune omnibus sacramentis, attribuitur antonomastice ei, propter ejus excellentiam.

3. Ad tertium dicendum quod hoc sacramentum dicitur 'sacrificium', inquantum repræsentat ipsam passionem Christi. Dicitur autem 'hostia', inquantum continet ipsum Christum, qui est *hostia suavitatis,** ut dicitur *Ephes.*[7]

articulus 5. utrum fuerit conveniens institutio istius sacramenti

AD QUINTUM sic proceditur:[1] 1. Videtur quod non fuerit conveniens institutio istius sacramenti. Ut enim Philosophus dicit, *ex eisdem nutrimur ex quibus sumus.*[2] Sed per baptismum, qui est spiritualis regeneratio, accipimus esse spirituale, ut Dionysius dicit.[3] Ergo per baptismum etiam nutrimur. Non ergo fuit necessarium instituere hoc sacramentum quasi spirituale nutrimentum.

2. Præterea, per hoc sacramentum homines Christo uniuntur sicut membra capiti. Sed Christus est caput omnium hominum, etiam qui fuerunt ab initio mundi, ut supra dictum est.[4] Ergo non debuit institutio hujus sacramenti differri usque ad Cenam Domini.

3. Præterea, hoc sacramentum dicitur esse memoriale Dominicæ passionis: secundum illud *Matth.* xxvi, *Hoc facite in meam commemorationem.*[5] Sed memoria est præteritorum. Ergo hoc sacramentum non debuit institui ante Christi passionem.

4. Præterea, per baptismum aliquis ordinatur ad Eucharistiam, quæ

---

*Piana and all mss.: *hostia salutaris,* a saving victim

[5]*Romans* 6, 23

[6]*De Fide Orthodoxa,* loc cit

[7]*Ephesians* 5, 2

[1]cf 3a. 83, 2 ad 3. IV *Sent.* 8, 1, 3. *De Ven. Sacramento Altaris* 1. *In Matt.* 26. *In* 1 *Cor.* 11, *lect.* 4, 5

[2]*De Generatione et Corruptione* II, 8. 335a10

[3]*Ecclesiastical Hierarchy* 2. PG 3, 392

[4]3a. 8, 3, 6

enjoyment of God which will be ours in heaven. That is why it is called '*viaticum*', because it keeps us on the way to heaven. For the same reason it is called 'eucharist', that is, 'desirable gift or grace', because *the free gift of God is eternal life*,[5] as we read in *Romans*, or because it really contains Christ, who is full of grace.

It is also called in Greek '*metalepsis*', i.e. a 'taking to oneself', because as Damascene says, through this sacrament *we take to ourselves the Godhead of the Son.*[6]

Hence: 1. There is nothing against the same thing having many names according to its different powers or effects.

2. That which is common to all the sacraments is attributed *par excellence* to this one; it is supreme.

3. This sacrament[c] is called a 'sacrifice', because it represents the passion of Christ. It is called victim, because it contains Christ himself, who, in the words of *Ephesians*, is a *fragrant victim.*[7]

article 5. was the institution of this sacrament a wise arrangement?

THE FIFTH POINT:[1] 1. There are reasons for thinking that the institution of this sacrament was not a wise thing. As the philosopher says, *we are nourished on those very elements which give us our being.*[2] But it is in our baptism, which is our spiritual re-birth, that we receive our spiritual being, as Dionysius teaches.[3] Therefore we are nourished also by baptism. The institution then of this sacrament as a spiritual nourishment was not called for.

2. Moreover, it is through this sacrament that men are united to Christ as members to their head. But Christ is the head of all men, even of those who lived at the beginning of the world as we saw earlier on.[4] Therefore, the institution of this sacrament should not have been delayed until the time of the Last Supper.

3. Again, this sacrament is called the memorial of the passion of our Lord, according to the text of *Matthew*, *Do this for a commemoration of me.*[5] Now remembrance is concerned with what is already past. Therefore, this sacrament should not have been instituted before the passion of Christ.

4. Also, Baptism puts a man in a position to receive the Eucharist,

---

[5]*Luke* 22, 19 (the text is actually in *Luke*, not in *Matthew*)

[c]Note how for St Thomas the idea of sacramentality covers both the sacrifice of the Mass as well as the consecrated species. This is the key to the doctrine of the Eucharist. Representing, re-presenting and containing are the ideas in sacramental theology which find their fullest verification in the Eucharist, as sacrifice and as sacrament (in the narrower sense).

nonnisi baptizatis dari debet. Sed baptismus institutus fuit post Christi passionem et resurrectionem, ut patet *Matth.* ult.[6] Ergo inconvenienter hoc sacramentum fuit ante passionem Christi institutum.

SED CONTRA est quod hoc sacramentum institutum est a Christo, de quo dicitur *Marc.* vii, *Bene omnia fecit.*[7]

RESPONSIO: Dicendum quod convenienter hoc sacramentum institutum fuit in Cena, in qua scilicet Christus ultimo cum discipulis suis fuit conversatus. Primo quidem, ratione continentiæ hujus sacramenti. Continetur enim ipse Christus in Eucharistia sicut in sacramento. Et ideo, quando ipse Christus in propria specie a discipulis discessurus erat, in sacramentali specie seipsum eis reliquit; sicut in absentia imperatoris exhibetur veneranda ejus imago. Unde Eusebius dicit, *Quia corpus assumptum ablaturus erat ab oculis et illaturus sideribus, necesse erat ut die Cenæ sacramentum corporis et sanguinis sui consecraret nobis, ut coleretur jugiter per mysterium quod semel offerebatur in pretium.*[8]

Secundo, quia sine fide passionis Christi nunquam potuit esse salus: secundum illud *Rom.* iii, *Quem proposuit Deus propitiatorem per fidem in sanguine ipsius.*[9] Et ideo oportuit omni tempore apud homines esse aliquod repræsentativum Dominicæ passionis. Cujus in veteri quidem Testamento præcipuum sacramentum erat agnus paschalis: unde et Apostolus dicit, 1 *Cor.* v, *Pascha nostrum immolatus est Christus.*[10] Successit autem ei in novo Testamento Eucharistiæ sacramentum, quod est rememorativum præteritæ passionis, sicut et illud fuit præfigurativum futuræ. Et ideo conveniens fuit, imminente passione, celebrato priori sacramento, novum sacramentum instituere, unde Leo Papa dicit, *ut umbræ cederent corpori, antiqua observantia novo excluditur sacramento; hostia in hostiam transit; sanguine sanguis aufertur; et legalis festivitas, dum mutatur, impletur.*[11]*

Tertio, quia ea quæ ultimo dicuntur, maxime ab amicis recedentibus, magis memoriæ commendantur, præsertim quia tunc magis inflammatur affectus ad amicos; ea vero ad quæ magis afficimur, profundius animo

---

*Leonine omits quotation

Matthew 28, 19

[7] *Mark* 7, 37

[8] cf Gratian, *Decretum* 3, 2, 35 *Quia corpus.* In PL the text is attributed to Pseudo-Jerome, ep. 38 (PL 30, 281), and to Pseudo-Isidore, *Sermones* 4 (PL 83, 1225). Actually, it belongs to Faustus, Bishop of Riez in Provence, France, d. 490

[9] *Romans* 3, 25

[10] 1 *Corinthians* 5, 7

[11] *Sermones* 58, 1. PL 54, 332

[a] The word 'image' is an analogical term. It is capable of ascending degrees of verification. At the lowest level we speak of someone's picture or statue; at the highest level we speak of Christ as being *the image of the invisible God* (*Colossians* 1, 15). The

which should be given only to the baptized. But Baptism was instituted after Christ's passion and resurrection, as is clear from the last chapter of *Matthew*.[6] Therefore, it was unwise to institute this sacrament before the passion of Christ.

ON THE OTHER HAND, this sacrament has been instituted by Christ; and *he did all things well*, as we read in *Mark*.[7]

REPLY: This sacrament was wisely instituted at the Last Supper when Christ was spending his last hours with his disciples. First, look at what this sacrament contains. Christ himself is sacramentally contained in the Eucharist. And so at the moment of his departure from his disciples in his natural presence, he left himself among them in a sacramental presence; as when the emperor is absent his image[a] is set up for homage. As Eusebius puts it, *because he was about to take away from their bodily sight and to bring to heaven that body which he had hypostatically united to himself, he felt he had to consecrate for us the sacrament of his body and blood on the day of the Last Supper, so that we would be always able to reverence in a sacrament the price then being paid for our salvation*.[8]

Secondly, salvation, according to *Romans*, was never possible without faith in the passion of Christ, *whom God put forward as a propitiation by his blood, to be received by faith*.[9] Hence at all times men had to have something which was a sign of our Lord's passion. The principal figure of this in the Old Testament was the paschal lamb. As St Paul says, *Christ our paschal lamb has been sacrificed*.[10] In the New Covenant its place has been taken by the Eucharist, which commemorates the passion as being over, just as the paschal lamb prefigured it as yet to come. It was then just the right moment when the passion was about to begin and after the celebration of the older sacrament that he instituted the new one. As Pope Leo puts it, *so that the shadow would yield to the substance, the old observance is eliminated by the new sacrament; the one victim is fulfilled in the other; the one blood yields to the other; the festivity of the mosaic law in being changed is fulfilled*.[11]

Thirdly, the last words said, especially by friends when parting, are best remembered; particularly at the parting of friends is the affection of love most sensitive; and the more our affections are involved the more

---

sacrament of the Eucharist is the *image* of Christ, in the full sense of containing what it signifies. In the epistle to the *Hebrews*, and in the thought of St Ambrose, the sequence of shadow, image, truth (reality) is an important motif. St Thomas uses it passim in his Eucharistic theology and very explicitly in his discussion of the liturgy of the Old Law, 1a2æ. 101, 2.

imprimuntur. Quia igitur, ut beatus Alexander Papa dicit, *nihil in sacrificiis majus esse potest quam corpus et sanguis Christi, nec ulla oblatio hac potior est*,[12] ideo, ut in majori veneratione haberetur, Dominus in ultimo discessu suo a discipulis hoc sacramentum instituit. Et hoc est quod Augustinus dicit, in libro *Responsionum ad Januarium*, *Salvator, quo vehementius commendaret mysterii illius altitudinem, ultimum hoc voluit infigere cordibus et memoriæ discipulorum, a quibus ad passionem discessurus erat.*[13]

1. Ad primum ergo dicendum quod *ex eisdem nutrimur ex quibus sumus*, non tamen eodem modo nobis advenientibus. Nam ea ex quibus sumus nobis adveniunt per generationem; eadem autem, inquantum ex eis nutrimur, nobis adveniunt per manducationem. Unde et sicut per baptismum regeneramur in Christo, ita per Eucharistiam manducamus Christum.

2. Ad secundum dicendum quod Eucharistia est sacramentum perfectum Dominicæ passionis, tanquam continens ipsum Christum passum. Et ideo non potuit institui ante incarnationem: sed tunc habebant locum sacramenta quæ erant tantum præfigurativa Dominicæ passionis.

3. Ad tertium dicendum quod sacramentum illud fuit institutum in Cena ut in futurum esset memoriale Dominicæ passionis, ea perfecta. Unde signanter dicit, *Hæc quotiescumque feceritis*, de futuro loquens.

4. Ad quartum dicendum quod institutio respondet ordini intentionis. Sacramentum autem Eucharistiæ, quamvis sit posterius baptismo in perceptione, est tamen prius in intentione. Et ideo debuit prius institui.

Vel potest dici quod baptismus jam erat* institutus in ipso Christi baptismo. Unde et jam aliqui ipso Christi baptismo erant baptizati, ut legitur *Joan.*[14]

articulus 6. utrum agnus paschalis fuerit præcipua figura hujus sacramenti

AD SEXTUM sic proceditur.[1] 1. Videtur quod agnus paschalis non fuerit præcipua figura hujus sacramenti. Christus enim dicitur *sacerdos secundum ordinem Melchisedech*,[2] propter hoc quod Melchisedech gessit figuram sacrificii Christi, *offerens panem et vinum*.[3] Sed expressio similitudinis facit quod unum ab alio denominetur. Ergo videtur quod oblatio Melchisedech fuerit potissima figura hujus sacramenti.

---

*Piana: *aliqualiter*, by some way or other

[12]cf Gratian, *Decretum* 3, 2, 8 *Nihil in sacrificiis*. Richter-Friedberg I, 1317

[13]*Epistle* 54, 6. PL 33, 203 [14]*John* 3, 22

[1]cf 3a. 61, 3 ad 3; 80, 10 ad 2. IV *Sent*. 8, 1, 2 [2]*Psalm* 109, 4 [3]*Genesis* 14, 18

[b]St Thomas is actually quoting from the Canon of the Mass. But the text is equivalently in 1 *Corinthians* 11, 25.

[c]In the order of planning or intention we first intend the end. Then we desire the means to it. In the order of carrying out the plan, we first accomplish the means and then we obtain the end. Baptism is the means to the Eucharist which is the end of all the sacraments.

things are deeply impressed upon our soul. Since, therefore, as Pope St Alexander says, *there can be no sacrifice greater than that of the body and blood of Christ, nor is there any better offering,*[12] our Lord instituted this sacrament when making his last farewell to his disciples in order that it might be held in the greater regard. Augustine had the same idea when he wrote, *our Saviour, in order the more strongly to impress on us the value of this sacrament, wished it to be the last thing he would fix in the hearts and memory of his disciples when he was leaving them to go to his passion.*[13]

Hence: 1. It is true that *we are nourished on those very elements that give us our being*, but they come to us in different ways. The things that give us our being come to us by generation, and in so far as we are nourished by them they come to us by our eating them. So it is that as we were re-born in Christ through Baptism, we eat Christ through the Eucharist.

2. The Eucharist is the perfect sacrament of our Lord's passion, because it contains Christ himself who endured it. Hence it could not have been instituted before the Incarnation; that was the time for sacraments which were merely prefigurative of our Lord's passion.

3. This sacrament was instituted at the Last Supper that it might in the future be a memorial of the passion when that had been accomplished. Hence the text expressly says, *when you shall do these things,*[b] speaking of the future.

4. The institution corresponds to the order of intention.[c] Although the sacrament of the Eucharist is received only after Baptism, it comes before it in intention. Therefore, it was right to institute it first.

Or one might say that Baptism was already instituted when Christ was baptized. Some had already been baptized in the Baptism of Christ, as we read in *John.*[14]

article 6. was the paschal lamb the most important figure of this sacrament?

THE SIXTH POINT:[1] 1. It would seem that it was not. Christ is said to be *a priest according to the order of Melchizedek,*[2] because Melchizedek *offering bread and wine*[3] prefigured the sacrifice of Christ. Now if we call one thing after another it is in order to express a resemblance. It seems then that the oblation made by Melchizedek[a] was the most important figure of this sacrament.

---

[a]It was not precisely because he offered bread and wine that Melchizedek is regarded by the author of the *Epistle to the Hebrews* as being the figure of Christ the priest. It is because he appears in history without precursors and without successors and makes but one recorded oblation that he resembles Christ, the one mediator, the unique priest in the full sense, who made one all-sufficient oblation on the cross. The Eucharistic oblation is the *sacrament* of that. Melchizedek is a type of Christ offering the Eucharistic oblation only in a secondary sense.

2. Præterea, transitus maris rubri fuit figura baptismi: secundum illud 1 *Cor*. x, *Omnes baptizati sunt in nube et in mari*.[4] Sed immolatio agni paschalis præcessit transitum maris rubri: quem subsecutum est manna, sicut Eucharistia sequitur baptismum. Ergo manna est expressior figura hujus sacramenti quam agnus paschalis.

3. Præterea, potissima virtus hujus sacramenti est quod introducit nos in regnum cælorum, sicut quoddam viaticum. Sed hoc maxime figuratum fuit in sacramento expiationis, quando *pontifex intrabat semel in anno cum sanguine in sancta sanctorum*, sicut Apostolus probat, *Heb*. ix.[5] Ergo videtur quod illud sacrificium fuerit expressior figura hujus sacramenti quam agnus paschalis.

SED CONTRA est quod Apostolus dicit, 1 *Cor*. v, *Pascha nostrum immolatus est Christus. Itaque epulemur in azymis sinceritatis et veritatis*.[6]

RESPONSIO: Dicendum quod in hoc sacramento tria considerare possumus: scilicet id quod est sacramentum tantum, scilicet panis et vinum; et id quod est res et sacramentum, scilicet corpus Christi verum; et id quod est res tantum, scilicet effectus hujus sacramenti. Quantum igitur ad id quod est sacramentum tantum, potissima figura fuit hujus sacramenti oblatio Melchisedech, qui *obtulit panem et vinum*. Quantum autem ad ipsum Christum passum, qui continetur in hoc sacramento, figuræ ejus fuerunt omnia sacrificia veteris Testamenti; et præcipue sacrificium expiationis, quod erat solemnissimum. Quantum autem ad effectum, fuit præcipua ejus figura manna, quod *habebat in se omnis saporis suavitatem*, ut dicitur *Sap*. xvi,[7] sicut et gratia hujus sacramenti quantum ad omnia reficit mentem.

Sed agnus paschalis quantum ad hæc tria præfigurabat hoc sacramentum. Quantum enim ad primum, quia manducabatur cum panibus azymis: secundum illud *Exod*. xii, *Edent carnes et azymos panes*.[8] Quantum vero ad secundum, quia immolabatur ab omni multitudine filiorum Israel quartadecima luna: quod fuit figura passionis Christi, qui propter innocentiam dicitur agnus. Quantum vero ad effectum, quia per sanguinem agni paschalis protecti sunt filii Israel, a devastante angelo, et educti de Ægyptiaca servitute. Et quantum ad hoc, ponitur figura hujus sacramenti præcipua agnus paschalis, quia secundum omnia ipsum repræsentat.

Et per hoc patet responsio ad objecta.

---

[4] 1 *Corinthians* 10, 2
[5] *Hebrews* 9, 7
[6] 1 *Corinthians* 5, 7, 8
[7] *Wisdom* 16, 20

2. Moreover, the passage through the Red Sea was a type or figure of Baptism, *They were all baptized in the cloud and in the sea.*[4] But the immolation of the paschal lamb happened before the passage through the Red Sea and the manna fell afterwards, as the Eucharist comes after Baptism. Therefore, the manna is a much better figure of this sacrament than is the paschal lamb.

3. Furthermore, the greatest thing that this sacrament does is to bring us into heaven; it keeps us going on that road. But what chiefly prefigured this was the sacrament of expiation when the high-priest went once a year with blood into the holy of holies, as the apostle shows.[5] It seems then that that sacrifice was a much more vivid figure of this sacrifice than the paschal lamb.

ON THE OTHER HAND, St Paul says, *Christ, our paschal lamb, has been sacrificed; let us then celebrate the festival . . . with the unleavened bread of sincerity and truth.*[6]

REPLY: There are three things we can think of in this sacrament: that which is the *sign only*, the bread and the wine; that which is *thing and sign*; that which is *thing only*, namely, the spiritual effect. Looking at the *sign only*, the most obvious figure of this sacrament was the sacrifice of Melchizedek *who offered bread and wine*. When we consider Christ who suffered for us, who is contained in this sacrament, then all the sacrifices of the Old Testament, and especially the most solemn sacrifice of expiation, were figures of the Eucharist. With regard to the effect of this sacrament, it was especially prefigured by the manna, which *had in itself the sweetness of every taste* as we read in *Wisdom*,[7] just as the grace of this sacrament brings every possible refreshment to the soul.

But the paschal lamb prefigured this sacrament under all these three aspects; under the first aspect, because it was eaten with unleavened bread, as the book of *Exodus* states, *They shall eat the flesh with unleavened bread*;[8] under the second aspect, because it was immolated on the fourteenth day of the month by the whole assembly of the children of Israel—that was a prefiguring of the passion of Christ, who because of his innocence is called the lamb; under the third aspect, because it was through the blood of the paschal lamb that the children of Israel were preserved from the destroying angel and delivered from the Egyptian captivity. For this reason the paschal lamb is regarded as the outstanding type or figure of this sacrament, seeing that it represents it under all its aspects.

The replies to the objections should now be clear.

[8] *Exodus* 12, 8

Deinde considerandum est de materia hujus sacramenti:

et primo, de specie materiæ;
secundo, de conversione panis et vini in corpus Christi;
tertio, de modo existendi corporis Christi in hoc sacramento;
quarto, de accidentibus panis et vini quæ in hoc sacramento remanent.

Quæstio 74. de materia hujus sacramenti

Circa primum quæruntur octo:

1. utrum panis et vinum sint materia hujus sacramenti;
2. utrum ad materiam hujus sacramenti requiratur determinata quantitas;
3. utrum materia hujus sacramenti sit panis triticeus;
4. utrum sit panis azymus vel fermentatus;
5. utrum materia hujus sacramenti sit vinum de vite;
6. utrum sit admiscenda aqua;
7. utrum aqua sit de necessitate hujus sacramenti;
8. de quantitate aquæ quæ apponitur.

articulus 1. utrum materia hujus sacramenti sit panis et vinum

AD PRIMUM sic proceditur:[1] 1. Videtur quod materia hujus sacramenti non sit panis et vinum. Hoc enim sacramentum perfectius debet repræsentare passionem Christi quam sacramenta Veteris Legis. Sed carnes animalium, quæ erant materia sacramentorum Veteris Legis, expressius repræsentant passionem Christi quam panis et vinum. Ergo materia hujus sacramenti magis debent esse carnes animalium quam panis et vinum.

2. Præterea, hoc sacramentum est ubique celebrandum. Sed in multis terris non invenitur panis, et in aliquibus non invenitur vinum. Ergo panis et vinum non est conveniens materia hujus sacramenti.

3. Præterea, hoc sacramentum competit sanis et infirmis. Sed vinum nocet quibusdam infirmis. Ergo videtur quod vinum non debeat esse materia hujus sacramenti.

SED CONTRA est quod Alexander Papa dicit, *In sacramentorum oblationibus panis tantum et vinum aqua permixtum in sacrificium offerantur.*[2]

RESPONSIO: Dicendum quod circa materiam hujus sacramenti aliqui multipliciter erraverunt. Quidam enim, qui dicuntur 'Artotyritæ', ut Augustinus

[1]cf IV *Sent.* 11, 2, 1, i & ii. *CG* IV, 61. *De Sacramento Altaris* 9, 29. *In* 1 *Cor.* 11, *lect.* 5

We now come to consider the matter of this sacrament:

first, the matter itself;
then, the change of the bread and wine into the body and blood of Christ;
thirdly, the way Christ's body exists in this sacrament;
fourthly, the accidents of bread and wine which remain.

Question 74. the matter of this sacrament

Under the first of these questions there are eight points of inquiry:

1. are bread and wine the matter of this sacrament?
2. is a fixed quantity necessary for the matter of this sacrament?
3. is the matter of this sacrament wheaten bread?
4. is it unleavened or leavened bread?
5. is the matter of this sacrament wine of the grape?
6. should water be mixed with it?
7. is the mixing of water required for validity?
8. how much water should be added?

article 1. are bread and wine the matter of this sacrament?

THE FIRST POINT:[1] 1. It seems that the matter of this sacrament is not bread and wine. This sacrament is meant to represent Christ's passion more fully than did the sacraments of the Old Law. But animal flesh, which was the matter of the sacraments of the Old Law, represents Christ's passion much more vividly than does bread and wine. Therefore, the matter of this sacrament should be animal flesh rather than bread and wine.

2. Moreover, this sacrament is meant to be celebrated everywhere. But in many countries bread is not found and in some there is no wine. Therefore, bread and wine are not suitable matter for this sacrament.

3. Furthermore, this sacrament is meant for all, for those who are well and for those who are ill. But wine is bad for some who are ill. Therefore, it ought not to be the matter of this sacrament.

ON THE OTHER HAND, Pope Alexander says, *in the sacramental oblations only bread and wine mixed with water should be offered in sacrifice.*[2]

REPLY: With regard to the matter of this sacrament people have held many mistaken views. Some who are called 'Artotyrites', as Augustine says in his

[2]Alexander I. cf Gratian, *Decretum* 3, 2, 1 *In sacramentorum.* Richter-Friedberg 1, 1314

dicit, *offerunt panem et caseum* in hoc sacramento, *dicentes a primis hominibus oblationes de fructibus terræ et ovium fuisse celebratas.*[3] Alii vero, scilicet 'Cataphrygæ' et 'Pepuziani', *de infantis sanguine, quem de toto ejus corpore minutis punctionum vulneribus extorquent, quasi Eucharistiam suam conficere perhibentur, miscendo eum farinæ, panem inde facientes.*[4] Quidam vero, qui dicuntur 'Aquarii', aquam solam, sub specie sobrietatis, in hoc sacramento offerunt.[5]

Omnes autem hi errores, et similes, excluduntur per hoc quod Christus hoc sacramentum sub specie panis et vini instituit, sicut patet *Matth.* xxvi.[6] Unde panis et vinum sunt materia conveniens hujus sacramenti. Et hoc rationabiliter. Primo quidem, quantum ad usum hujus sacramenti, qui est manducatio. Sicut enim aqua assumitur in sacramento baptismi ad usum spiritualis ablutionis quia corporalis ablutio communiter fit in aqua, ita panis et vinum, quibus communius homines reficiuntur, assumuntur in hoc sacramento ad usum spiritualis manducationis.

Secundo, quantum ad passionem Christi, in qua sanguis a corpore est separatus. Et ideo in hoc sacramento, quod est memoriale Dominicæ passionis, seorsum sumitur panis ut sacramentum corporis, et vinum ut sacramentum sanguinis.

Tertio, quantum ad effectum consideratum in unoquoque sumentium. Quia, ut Ambrosius dicit,[7] *super Epistolam ad Corinthios*, hoc sacramentum *valet ad tuitionem corporis et animæ*: et ideo *caro Christi* sub specie panis *pro salute corporis, sanguis vero* sub specie vini *pro salute animæ offertur*, sicut dicitur *Levit.* xvii, quod animalis *anima* in sanguine est.*[8]

Quarto, quantum ad effectum respectu totius Ecclesiæ, quæ constituitur ex diversis fidelibus, sicut *panis conficitur ex diversis granis, et vinum fluit ex diversis uvis*, ut dicit Glossa super illud 1 *Cor.* x, *Multi unum corpus sumus*, etc.[9]

1. Ad primum ergo dicendum quod, licet carnes animalium occisorum expresse† repræsentent Christi passionem, tamen minus competunt ad communem usum hujus sacramenti, et ad ecclesiasticam unitatem significandam.

2. Ad secundum dicendum quod, licet non in omnibus terris nascatur triticum et vinum, tamen de facili ad omnes terras deferri potest quantum

---

*Piana: for *animalis anima* read *anima carnis*, the soul of flesh

†Piana: *expressius*, would more expressly represent

[3] *De Haeresibus* 28. PL 42, 31

[4] ibid, 26, 27. PL 42, 30

[5] cf ibid, 64. PL 42, 42

[6] *Matthew* 26, 26

[7] Ambrosiaster, *In* 1 *Cor.* 11, 20. PL 17, 256

[8] *Leviticus* 17, 14

book *On Heresies*, *offer bread and cheese* in this sacrament, *affirming that at the beginning men offered sacrifices from the fruits of the earth and of sheep.*[3] Others, called 'Cataphrygians' and 'Pepuzians', *are said to make their Eucharist from the blood of an infant. They gather it from tiny pricks all over the infant's body and mix it with flour and make bread in this way.*[4] Some, who are called 'Aquarians', in their cultivation of sobriety use only water in this sacrament.[5]

All these and similar errors are ruled out by the fact that Christ instituted this sacrament using bread and wine, as is evident from *Matthew*.[6] Hence bread and wine are suitable matter for this sacrament. We can see many reasons for this. First, look at the way this sacrament is used as fare for us. Just as water is employed in the sacrament of Baptism for our spiritual cleansing because water is commonly used for washing our bodies, so bread and wine, which are the most common food of mankind, are employed in this sacrament to be used as spiritual food.

Second, consider the passion of Christ in which his blood was separated from his body. Now this sacrament is the commemoration of our Lord's passion, and the bread is taken as the sacrament of his body and the wine of his blood.

Third, look at the effect of this sacrament on each individual. As Ambrose says,[7] commenting on the first *Epistle to the Corinthians*, this sacrament *protects* both body and soul; hence *the flesh of Christ* under the form[a] of bread *is offered for the well-being of the body*, *the blood* under the form of wine *for the well-being of the soul*. As we read in *Leviticus*, the animal's *soul is in the blood*.[8]

Fourth, consider the effect of this sacrament in terms of the whole Church. The Church is the gathering together of all the different baptized faithful;[b] in the same way *bread is made of different grains of wheat and wine flows together from different grapes*, as the Gloss on 1 *Corinthians* 10, 17 puts it.[9]

Hence: 1. I agree that the flesh of animals that have been slain would be a vivid representation of the passion of Christ. But it would not be suitable for the widespread use of this sacrament or for signifying the unity of the Church.

2. Although wheat and wine are not native to all lands, the amount

---

[9]*Glossa Ordinaria*, Augustine, *In Joan.* 6, 56. *Tract.* 26. PL 35, 1614

[a]The Latin word '*species*', here translated *form*, means first the inner nature of a thing; it then means the outer appearance, the accidents of a thing.

[b]'The faithful', a technical term for those who have professed their faith by being baptized.

sufficit ad usum hujus sacramenti. Nec propter defectum alterius, est unum tantum sine altero consecrandum: quia non esset perfectum sacrificium.*

3. Ad tertium dicendum quod vinum in modica quantitate sumptum non potest ægrotanti multum nocere. Et tamen, si nocumentum timeatur, non est necesse quod omnes accipientes corpus Christi, etiam sanguinem accipiant, ut infra dicetur.[10]

articulus 2. utrum requiratur determinata quantitas panis et vini ad materiam hujus sacramenti

AD SECUNDUM sic proceditur.[1] 1. Videtur quod requiratur determinata quantitas panis et vini ad materiam hujus sacramenti. Effectus enim gratiæ non sunt minus ordinati quam effectus naturæ. Sed, sicut dicitur in *De Anima*, *omnium natura constantium positus est terminus et ratio magnitudinis et augmenti*,[2] Ergo multo magis in hoc sacramento, quod dicitur 'eucharistia', id est 'bona gratia', requiritur determinata quantitas panis et vini.

2. Præterea, ministris Ecclesiæ non est a Christo data potestas ad ea quæ pertinent ad irrisionem fidei et sacramentorum ejus; secundum illud II *Cor.* x, *Secundum potestatem quam dedit mihi Deus in ædificationem, et non in destructionem.*[3] Sed hoc esset ad irrisionem sacramenti, si sacerdos vellet consecrare totum panem qui venditur in foro, et totum vinum quod est in cellario. Ergo hoc facere non potest.

3. Præterea, si aliquis baptizetur in mari, non tota aqua maris sanctificatur per formam baptismi, sed sola illa aqua qua corpus baptizati abluitur. Ergo nec in hoc sacramento superflua quantitas panis† consecrari potest.

SED CONTRA est quod multum opponitur pauco et magnum parvo. Sed nulla est ita parva quantitas panis aut vini quæ non possit consecrari. Ergo nulla est ita magna quæ consecrari non possit.

RESPONSIO: Dicendum quod quidam[4] dixerunt quod sacerdos non posset consecrare immensam quantitatem panis aut vini, puta totum panem qui venditur in foro, aut totum vinum quod est in dolio. Sed hoc non videtur

---

*Piana: *sacramentum*, sacrament
†Piana: *et vini*, and wine

[10]3a. 80, 12
[1]cf IV *Sent.* 11, 2, 1, iii
[2]Aristotle, *De Anima*, IV, 8. 416a16

needed for this sacrament can easily be transported anywhere. Were one of the elements not available it would not be right to consecrate; the sacrifice would be unfinished.[c]

3. A little wine could not do much harm to a sick person. However, if there is reason for anxiety, there is no need for all who receive the body of Christ to take his blood also, as we shall see later.[10]

article 2. is a fixed quantity of bread and wine necessary for the matter of this sacrament?

THE SECOND POINT:[1] 1. There are reasons for thinking that a fixed quantity of bread and wine is required for the matter of this sacrament. Effects in the realm of grace are not less well ordered than in the realm of nature. But, as it is stated in the *De Anima*, *there is a fixed term to the size and growth of all natural things*.[2] Much more then should there be in this sacrament, which is called Eucharist or good grace, a fixed quantity of bread and wine.

2. Moreover, Christ did not give the ministers of the Church a power which would allow them to expose the faith or the sacraments to ridicule: as we read in II *Corinthians*, *our authority, which the Lord gave for building you up and not for destroying you*.[3] Now it would be a mockery were a priest to decide to consecrate all the bread in the market or all the wine in the cellar. Therefore, he could not do so.

3. Again, if anyone were to be baptized in the sea, all the water of the sea would not be sanctified because of baptism, but only that amount which washed the body of such a one. Hence also in this sacrament an unnecessary amount of bread cannot be consecrated.

ON THE OTHER HAND, many corresponds to few and great corresponds to little. But no quantity of bread or wine is too small to be consecrated. Therefore, no amount is too great.

REPLY: Some[4] have maintained that a priest could not consecrate a huge amount of bread and wine, for example, all the bread now in the market or all the wine in a cask. But this does not seem to be true. In all things made

---

[3]II *Corinthians* 10, 8

[4]Alexander of Hales, *Summa Theologica* 4, 34, 1, 3. Bonaventure, *In* IV *Sent.* 10, 2, 1. Peter of Tarantaise, *In* IV *Sent.* 10, 4, 2

[c]The sacramental sacrifice of the Mass requires the double consecration—of the bread and of the wine. In virtue of the consecration as such all you have directly under the appearances of bread is the body of Christ and under the form of wine there is only his blood. The body and blood are thus separated sacramentally (though never again really as on Calvary). This is the sacramental (not natural) immolation of the Mass.

esse verum. Quia in omnibus habentibus materiam, ratio determinationis materiæ sumitur ex ordine ad finem; sicut materia serræ est ferrum ut sit apta sectioni. Finis autem hujus sacramenti est usus fidelium. Unde oportet quod quantitas materiæ hujus sacramenti determinetur per comparationem ad usum fidelium. Non autem potest esse quod determinetur per comparationem ad usum fidelium qui nunc occurrunt: alioquin sacerdos habens paucos parochianos non posset consecrare multas hostias. Unde relinquitur quod materia hujus sacramenti determinetur per comparationem ad usum fidelium absolute. Numerus autem fidelium est indeterminatus. Unde non potest dici quod quantitas materiæ hujus sacramenti sit determinata.

1. Ad primum ergo dicendum quod cujuslibet rei naturalis materia accipit determinatam quantitatem secundum comparationem ad formam determinatam. Sed numerus fidelium, ad quorum usum ordinatur hoc sacramentum, est indeterminatus. Unde non est simile.

2. Ad secundum dicendum quod potestas ministrorum ecclesiæ ad duo ordinatur; primo quidem, ad effectum proprium, secundo, ad finem effectus. Secundum autem non tollit primum. Unde, si sacerdos intendat consecrare corpus Christi propter aliquem malum finem, puta ut irrideat vel veneficia faciat, propter intentionem mali finis peccat, nihilominus tamen, propter potestatem sibi datam, perficit sacramentum.

3. Ad tertium dicendum quod baptismi sacramentum perficitur in usu materiæ. Et ideo per formam baptismi non plus de aqua sanctificatur quam quantum venit in usum. Sed hoc sacramentum perficitur in consecratione materiæ. Et ideo non est simile.

articulus 3. *utrum requiratur ad materiam hujus sacramenti quod sit panis triticeus*

AD TERTIUM sic proceditur.[1] 1. Videtur quod non requiratur ad materiam hujus sacramenti quod sit panis triticeus. Hoc enim sacramentum est rememorativum Dominicæ passionis. Sed magis videtur esse consonum Dominicæ passioni panis hordeaceus, qui est asperior, et de quo etiam turbas pavit in monte, ut dicitur *Joan.* vi,[2] quam panis triticeus. Ergo non est propria materia hujus sacramenti panis triticeus.

2. Præterea, figura est signum speciei in rebus naturalibus. Sed quædam frumenta sunt quæ habent similem figuram grano tritici, sicut far et spelta: de qua etiam in quibusdam locis panis conficitur ad usuam hujus sacramenti. Ergo panis triticeus non est propria materia hujus sacramenti.

3. Præterea, permixtio speciem solvit. Sed vix invenitur farina triticea quæ alterius frumenti permixtionem non habeat: nisi forte electis granis

of matter the criterion which determines the material is its fitness for the purpose envisaged; for example, a saw is made of steel which is good for cutting. The purpose of this sacrament is its use by the faithful. Its matter is not reckoned with reference to the use of those faithful present then and there: otherwise a priest who had only a few parishioners could not consecrate many hosts. It remains, then, that the matter of this sacrament is to be reckoned in terms of its use by the faithful without restriction. Their number is not fixed. Hence it should not be affirmed that the amount of the matter of this sacrament is fixed.

Hence: 1. The matter of any natural thing has quantity determinate by relation to a defined form. But the number of the faithful for whose use this sacrament is ordained is indefinite. Therefore there is no parity.

2. The power of Church ministers has two purposes: the first is the immediate effect, the second is what can follow on the immediate effect. The second purpose does not invalidate the first. Hence if a priest intends to consecrate the body of Christ for some ulterior evil motive, as, for example, to make a mockery or to administer poison, his sacramental act is valid.

3. The sacrament of Baptism is completed when the matter is actually being used. Hence by the form of Baptism only that amount of water is sanctified which is actually being used. But this sacrament is established in the prior consecration of the matter. Hence there is no parity.

article 3. is wheaten bread required for the matter of this sacrament?

THE THIRD POINT:[1] 1. It seems that the matter of this sacrament does not require that the bread should be wheaten bread. This sacrament is a memorial of our Lord's passion. Yet barley bread seems more in keeping with the passion of our Lord than wheaten bread; in the first place, it is rougher; and then it was with barley bread that our Lord fed the crowds on the mountain, as we read in *John*.[2] Therefore, the proper matter of this sacrament is not wheaten bread.

2. Again, in natural things the shape is the sign of the specific nature. But some cereals have the same shape as wheat, thus maize and spelt, from which in certain regions altar bread is made. Therefore, wheaten bread is not the only matter for this sacrament.

3. Furthermore, if you mix a thing with something else you no longer have one specific nature. But it is scarcely possible to have pure wheaten flour without some admixture of some other meal, unless one most

[1]cf IV *Sent.* 11, 2, 2, i; 19, 1, 2, iii ad 1. *CG* IV 69. *De Sacramento Altaris* 10
[2]*John* 6, 9 ff.

studiose fiat. Non ergo videtur quod panis triticeus sit propria materia hujus sacramenti.

4. Præterea, illud quod est corruptum, videtur esse alterius speciei. Sed aliqui conficiunt ex pane corrupto, qui jam non videtur esse panis triticeus. Ergo videtur quod talis panis non sit propria materia hujus sacramenti.

SED CONTRA est quod in hoc sacramento continetur Christus, qui se grano frumenti comparat, *Joan.* xii, *Nisi granum frumenti, cadens in terram, mortuum fuerit, ipsum solum manet.*[3] Ergo panis frumentinus, sive triticeus, est materia hujus sacramenti.

RESPONSIO: Dicendum quod, sicut dictum est,[4] ad usum sacramentorum assumitur talis materia quæ communius apud homines in talem usum venit. Inter alios autem panes communius homines utuntur pane triticeo: nam alii panes videntur esse introducti in hujus panis defectum. Et ideo Christus creditur in hujus panis specie hoc sacramentum instituisse. Qui etiam panis confortat hominem, et ita convenientius significat effectum hujus sacramenti. Et ideo propria materia hujus sacramenti est panis triticeus.

1. Ad primum ergo dicendum quod panis hordeaceus competit ad significandam duritiam veteris legis. Tum propter duritiem panis. Tum quia etiam, ut Augustinus dicit, *hordei medulla, quæ tenacissima palea tegitur, vel ipsam legem significat, quæ ita data erat ut in ea vitale animaæ alimentum corporalibus sacramentis obtegeretur: vel ispum populum, nondum expoliatum carnali desiderio, quod tanquam palea cordi ejus inhærebat.*[5] Hoc autem sacramentum pertinet ad *suave jugum* Christi, et ad veritatem jam manifestatam, et ad populum spiritualem. Unde non esset materia conveniens hujus sacramenti panis hordeaceus.

2. Ad secundum dicendum quod generans generat sibi simile in specie: fit tamen aliquando aliqua dissimilitudo generantis ad genitum quantum ad accidentia, vel propter materiam vel propter debilitatem virtutis generativæ. Et ideo, si qua frumenta sunt quæ ex semine tritici generari possunt, sicut ex grano seminato in malis terris nascitur siligo, ex tali frumento panis confectus potest esse materia hujus sacramenti. Quod tamen non videtur habere locum neque in hordeo, neque in spelta, neque etiam in farre, quod inter omnia est grano tritici similius. Similitudo autem figuræ in talibus magis videtur significare propinquitatem quam identitatem speciei: sicut ex similitudine figuræ manifestatur quod canis et lupus sunt propinquæ speciei, non autem ejusdem. Unde ex talibus frumentis, quæ

---

[3] *John* 12, 24–5
[4] 3a. 74, 1; 60, 7 ad 2

carefully selects the grains. It does not seem then that wheaten bread is the proper matter for this sacrament.

4. Besides, when a thing becomes corrupt its nature is changed. Now, there are some who consecrate with bread that has become corrupted, which would then no longer seem to be wheaten bread. Hence it would appear that such bread is not the necessary matter of this sacrament.

ON THE OTHER HAND, in this sacrament Christ is contained who compares himself to a grain of wheat, *unless a grain of wheat falls into the earth and dies it remains alone.*[3] Therefore wheaten bread is the matter of this sacrament.[a]

REPLY: As we have already said,[4] in the sacraments that kind of matter is employed which men commonly use for like purposes. Of all kinds of bread men most commonly use wheaten bread; other breads seem to be only a substitute for it. Hence we believe that Christ used this bread when he instituted this sacrament. This bread is also the more strengthening, and for this reason it more suitably signifies the effect of this sacrament. Therefore, its proper matter is wheaten bread.

Hence: 1. Barley bread serves to signify the hardness of the Old Law. First, because of its harshness. Then again, because, as Augustine says, *the pith of the barley grain which has a shell most difficult to remove, signifies either the Law itself, which was so given that in it the vital nourishment of the soul was covered over by corporeal signs; or the people itself, which had not yet been freed from fleshly desire, which like a shell stuck close to its heart.*[5] But this sacrament pertains to the *easy yoke* of Christ and to the truth which is already made manifest and to a spiritual people. Hence barley bread would not be suitable matter for this sacrament.

2. A living thing, in reproducing, reproduces something specifically the same as itself; occasionally, however, there is an unlikeness between them with regard to accidental qualities owing to the material or to some weakness in generative power. Hence, if there are cereals which can grow from wheat seed, as for example wild wheat from seed sown in poor land, the bread made from such wheat can be the matter of this sacrament. This, however, does not seem to be the case with barley or spelt or even maize, which of all seeds is most like wheat. Their resemblance in shape seems to spell closeness rather than identity of species; just as this in the case of the dog and the wolf goes to show they are of allied but not the

---

[5]*Octog. Tria Quæst.* 61. PL 40, 48

[a]As so often, the thought of the '*sed contra*' is meant merely to give us pause. It is not offered as an argument, but merely as a suggestion.

nullo modo possunt ex semine grani generari, non potest confici panis qui sit debita materia hujus sacramenti.

3. Ad tertium dicendum quod modica permixtio non solvit speciem; quia id quod est modicum, quodammodo absumitur a plurimo. Et ideo, si sit modica admixtio alterius frumenti ad multo majorem quantitatem tritici, poterit exinde confici panis qui est materia hujus sacramenti. Si vero sit magna permixtio, puta ex æquo vel quasi, talis commixtio speciem mutat. Unde panis inde confectus non erit materia debita hujus sacramenti.

4. Ad quartum dicendum quod aliquando est tanta corruptio panis quod solvitur species panis: sicut cum continuitas solvitur, et sapor et color et alia accidentia mutantur. Unde ex tali materia non potest confici corpus Christi. Aliquando vero non est tanta corruptio quæ speciem solvat, sed est aliqua dispositio ad corruptionem: quod declarat aliqualis immutatio saporis. Et ex tali pane potest confici corpus Christi: sed peccat conficiens, propter irreverentiam sacramenti.

Et quia amidum est ex tritico corrupto, non videtur quod panis ex eo confectus possit fieri corpus Christi: quamvis quidam[6] contrarium dicant.

articulus 4. utrum hoc sacramentum debeat confici ex pane azymo

AD QUARTUM sic proceditur:[1] 1. Videtur quod hoc sacramentum non debeat confici ex pane azymo. Debemus enim in hoc sacramento imitari institutionem Christi. Sed Christus videtur hoc sacramentum instituisse in pane fermentato: quia, sicut legitur *Exod.* xii,[2] Judæi secundum legem incipiebant uti azymis in die Paschæ, quod celebratur quartadecima luna; Christus autem instituit hoc sacramentum in Cena, quam celebravit *ante diem Paschæ*, ut habetur *Joan.* xiii.[3] Ergo et nos debemus hoc sacramentum celebrare in pane fermentato.

2. Præterea, legalia non sunt observanda tempore gratiæ. Sed uti azymis fuit quædam legalis cæremonia: ut patet *Exod.* xii.[4] Ergo in hoc sacramento gratiæ non debemus azymis uti.

3. Præterea, sicut supra dictum est,[5] Eucharistia est 'sacramentum caritatis', sicut baptismus fidei. Sed fervor caritatis significatur per fermentum: ut patet in glossa, super illud *Matth.* xiii, *Simile est regnum cælorum fermento, etc.*[6] Ergo hoc sacramentum debet confici de pane fermentato.

---

[6]cf Albert the Great, *In* IV *Sent.* 12, 7 ad 8
[1]cf IV *Sent.* 11, 2, 2, iii. *CG* IV, 69
[2]*Exodus* 12, 12
[3]*John* 13, 1, 4
[4]*Exodus* 12, 15
[5]3a. 73, 3 ad 3
[6]*Matthew* 13, 33. Interlinear gloss (v. 45)

same species. Hence from cereals which cannot be grown from wheat grain bread cannot be baked which would be the right matter for this sacrament.

3. A light mixture does not change the species; because that which is of a little quantity is, as it were, absorbed by that of a greater. Hence if a slight amount of some other cereal be added to a much larger part of wheat, bread can be made of the type required for this sacrament; however, if the amount added is considerable, so that the mixture is half-and-half or thereabouts, then the type of bread is changed, and it will not be the right matter for this sacrament.

4. Sometimes the corruption is such that the specific nature of bread is no longer there, as when the consistency, the taste, the colour and other accidents are changed. Hence from such matter the body of Christ cannot be made.[b] Sometimes, however, the corruption is not such as to change the specific nature, but is only beginning, as the slight change in taste shows. From such bread the body of Christ can be made, but it would be a sin to use such bread, as it would show irreverence for the sacrament.

And because starch comes from wheat that has become corrupt, it does not seem that from bread made from it the body of Christ could be made, although some[6] hold the contrary.

article 4. should this sacrament be made from unleavened bread?

THE FOURTH POINT:[1] 1. It would seem that it should not. In this sacrament we should follow the example of what Christ did when he instituted it. But he seems to have instituted this sacrament with leavened bread. We read in *Exodus*[2] that the Jews according to the Law began to use unleavened bread only on the paschal feast itself which is kept on the fourteenth day of the month. But Christ instituted this sacrament at the Last Supper, which he celebrated *on the day before the paschal feast*, as we have from *John*.[3] Therefore we also should celebrate this sacrament with leavened bread.

2. Moreover, we who live in the time of grace should not keep the Old Law observances. But the use of unfermented bread was an Old Law prescription, as is clear from *Exodus*.[4] Therefore in this time of grace it is not right to use unleavened bread.

3. Besides, as we have said earlier,[5] the Eucharist is the sacrament of charity just as Baptism is the sacrament of faith. But the fervour of charity is signified by leaven, as we read in a gloss on *Matthew*, *the kingdom of heaven is like unto leaven*.[6] Therefore this sacrament should be made with leavened bread.

---

[b]This way of stating the Eucharistic change is not the happiest. St Thomas later in 75, 8 will explain in what sense it can be justified.

4. Præterea, azymum et fermentatum sunt accidentia panis, non variantia ejus speciem. Sed in materia baptismi nulla discretio adhibetur circa differentiam accidentium aquæ: puta si sit salsa vel dulcis, calida vel frigida. Ergo in hoc sacramento aliqua discretio adhiberi non debet utrum panis sit azymus vel fermentatus.

SED CONTRA est quod *Extra, de Celebrat. Missar.*, cap. *Litteras*, punitur sacerdos qui *in pane fermentato et scypho ligneo missarum solemnia celebrare præsumpsit.*[7]

RESPONSIO: Dicendum quod circa materiam hujus sacramenti duo possunt considerari: scilicet quid sit necessarium, et quid conveniens. Necessarium quidem est ut sit panis triticeus, sicut dictum est:[8] sine quo non perficitur sacramentum. Non est autem de necessitate sacramenti quod sit azymus vel fermentatus: quia in utroque confici potest.

Conveniens autem est ut unusquisque servet ritum suæ ecclesiæ in celebratione sacramenti. Super hoc autem sunt diversæ ecclesiarum consuetudines. Dicit enim beatus Gregorius in *Registro*:[9] *Romana ecclesia offert azymos panes: propterea quod Dominus sine ulla commixtione suscepit carnem. Sed certæ** *ecclesiæ offerunt fermentatum: pro eo quod Verbum Patris indutum est carne, sicut et fermentum miscetur farinæ.* Unde, sicut peccat sacerdos in ecclesia Latinorum celebrans de pane fermentato, ita peccaret presbyter græcus in ecclesia Græcorum celebrans de azymo pane, quasi pervertens ecclesiæ suæ ritum.

Et tamen consuetudo de pane azymo celebrandi rationabilior est. Primo quidem, propter institutionem Christi, qui hoc sacramentum instituit *prima die azymorum*, ut habetur *Matth.* xxvi et *Marc.* xiv et *Luc* xxii,[10] qua die nihil fermentatum in dimibus Judæorum esse debebat, ut habetur *Exod.* xii.[11] Secundo, quia panis est proprie sacramentum corporis Christi, quod sine corruptione conceptum est, magis quam divinitatis ipsius, ut infra patebit.[12] Tertio, quia hoc magis competit sinceritati fidelium, quæ requiritur ad usum hujus sacramenti: secundum illud I *Cor.* v, *Pascha nostrum immolatus est Christus: itaque epulemur in azymis sinceritatis et veritatis.*[13]

Habet tamen hæc consuetudo Græcorum aliquam rationem: et propter significationem, quam tangit Gregorius; et in detestationem hæresis Nazaræorum, qui legalia Evangelio miscebant.

---

*Leonine: *ceteræ*, other

[7]Decretals of Gregory IX. III, 41, 14. Richter-Friedberg II, 643

[8]3a. 74, 3

[9]Treatise *Contra Errores Græcorum* by a Dominican author A.D. 1252. PG 140, 524

[10]*Matthew* 26, 17. *Mark* 14, 12. *Luke* 22, 7

4. Again, being leavened or unleavened is an accidental difference; it does not change the specific nature of the bread. In the water which is the matter for Baptism we do not bother about accidental differences, whether the water is salty or sweet, hot or cold. Likewise in this sacrament we should not be concerned as to whether the bread is leavened or unleavened.

ON THE OTHER HAND, the Decretal *on the celebration of the mass* says the priest is to be punished who dares to celebrate the mass *with fermented bread or with a wooden chalice.*[7]

REPLY: With regard to the matter of this sacrament we can consider what is necessary or what is also desirable. It is absolutely required that the bread be wheaten, as we have just said;[8] without that there is no sacrament. But it is not necessary that the bread be leavened or unleavened; the Eucharist can be made with either.

But it is desirable that each one should follow the rite of his own church when he celebrates this sacrament. In this matter the different churches have different customs. St Gregory writes, *the Roman church offers unleavened bread, because the Lord united human nature to himself without any mixture of the divine and human natures. But certain churches offer leavened bread, because the Word of the Father clothed himself with our nature, as the leaven is mixed with the flour.*[9] So, just as a priest of the Latin church sins if he celebrates with leavened bread, a priest of the Greek church would be at fault if he celebrated with unleavened bread; he would be corrupting the rite of his church.

All the same, the custom of celebrating with unleavened bread has more in its favour. First of all, because Christ instituted the Eucharist thus. It was on *the first day of the unleavened bread*, as we read in *Matthew*, *Mark*, and *Luke*,[10] that Christ instituted this sacrament and on that day no leavened bread was allowed in Jewish homes, as we can see from *Exodus.*[11] Then again, the bread is more exactly the sacrament of Christ's body than of his divinity, as will be evident later on.[12] Now, Christ's body was conceived without corruption. Thirdly, it corresponds nicely with that sincerity which the faithful should have when they receive this sacrament; as the text of 1 *Corinthians* puts it, *Christ, our paschal lamb, has been sacrificed. Let us therefore celebrate the festival . . . with the unleavened bread of sincerity and truth.*[13]

But the Greek custom has something to be said for it; there is the symbolism that Gregory touches on, and it shows how opposed we are to the heresy of the Nazareans who mixed legal observances with the Gospel.

[11]*Exodus* 12, 15, 19 [12]3a. 76, 1 ad 11 [13]1 *Corinthians* 5, 7, 8

1. Ad primum ergo dicendum quod, sicut legitur *Exod.* xii,[14] solemnitas paschalis incipiebat a vesperis quartædecimæ lunæ. Et tunc Christus, post immolationem agni paschalis, hoc sacramentum instituit. Unde hic dies a *Joanne* dicitur præcedere sequentem diem paschæ, et a tribus aliis Evangelistis dicitur *prima die azymorum*, quando fermentatum in domibus Judæorum non inveniebatur, ut dictum est. Et de hoc supra[15] notatum est plenius in tractatu Dominicæ passionis.

2. Ad secundum dicendum quod conficientes ex azymo non intendunt cæremonias legis servare, sed conformare se institutioni Christi. Et ideo non judaizant. Alioquin et celebrantes in pane fermentato judaizarent: quia Judæi panes primitiarum fermentatos offerebant.

3. Ad tertium dicendum quod fermentum significat caritatem propter aliquem effectum, quia scilicet panem facit sapidiorem et majorem. Sed corruptionem significat ex ipsa ratione suæ speciei.

4. Ad quartum dicendum quod, quia fermentum habet aliquid corruptionis, et ex pane corrupto non potest confici hoc sacramentum, ut dictum est;[16] ideo magis attenditur circa panem differentia azymi et fermentati quam circa aquam baptismi differentia calidi et frigidi. Posset enim tanta esse corruptio fermenti quod ex eo non posset fieri sacramentum.

articulus 5. utrum sit propria materia hujus sacramenti vinum vitis

AD QUINTUM sic proceditur:[1] 1. Videtur quod non sit propria materia hujus sacramenti vinum vitis. Sicut enim aqua est materia baptismi, ita vinum est materia hujus sacramenti. Sed in qualibet aqua potest fieri baptismus. Ergo in quolibet vino, puta malorum granatorum vel mororum aut hujusmodi, potest confici hoc sacramentum: præsertim cum in quibusdam terris vites non crescant.

2. Præterea, acetum est quædam species vini quod de vite sumitur, ut Isidorus dicit.[2] Sed de aceto non potest confici hoc sacramentum. Ergo videtur quod vinum vitis non sit propria materia hujus sacramenti.

3. Præterea, sicut de vite sumitur vinum depuratum, ita et agresta et mustum. Sed de his non videtur confici posse hoc sacramentum: secundum illud quod in Sexta Synodo legitur, *Didicimus quod in quibusdam ecclesiis sacerdotes sacrificio oblationis conjungunt uvas, et sic simul utrumque populo dispensant. Præcipimus igitur ut nullus sacerdos hoc ulterius faciat.*[3]

---

[14] *Exodus* 12, 7, 18
[15] 3a. 46, 9 ad 1
[16] 3a. 74, 3 ad 4
[1] cf IV *Sent.* 11, 2, 3. *CG* IV, 69
[2] *Etymologies* 20, 3. PL 82, 712

Hence: 1. As we read in *Exodus*[14] the feast of the pasch began with the evening of the fourteenth day of the month. It was then that Christ, after the immolation of the paschal lamb, instituted this sacrament. Hence this day is said in *John* to be the day before the pasch, and by the other three evangelists it is said to be the *first day of the unleavened bread*, when there was no leaven to be found in Jewish homes, as we have said. We discussed all this more fully earlier on[15] in the treatise on our Lord's passion.

2. Those who consecrate with unleavened bread have no intention of observing the ceremonial precepts of the Old Law; their only wish is to act in line with what Christ did. They cannot be said, then, to be Judaizers. If they are Judaizers, so then are those who celebrate with leavened bread Judaizers also, for the Jews offered leavened bread as first-fruit offerings.

3. The leaven signifies charity, because of the effect of the leaven, which is to make the bread better tasting and to give it more volume. But by reason of its specific nature it can signify corruption.

4. Because the leaven is a principle of decomposition and because this sacrament cannot be celebrated with bread that has become corrupt, as I have said,[16] the difference between unleavened and leavened bread is much more important than the difference between warm and cold baptismal water. The corruption caused by the leaven could be such that the sacrament could not be performed.

article 5. is the right matter of this sacrament wine of the grape?

THE FIFTH POINT:[1] 1. There are reasons for thinking that the proper matter for this sacrament is not wine of the grape. As water is the matter for Baptism, so is wine the matter for this sacrament. But Baptism can be given with any water at all. Therefore this sacrament can be consecrated with any wine, for example, pomegranate wine or mulberry wine; and especially as in many regions there are no vines.

2. Moreover, vinegar is a certain type of grape-wine, as Isidore says.[2] But this sacrament cannot be consecrated with vinegar. Hence it seems that grape-wine is not the proper matter for this sacrament.

3. Furthermore, just as clarified wine comes from the grape, so too does the juice of the unripe grape and the unfermented juice of the ripe grape. But it would seem that the sacrament cannot be consecrated with these last two, for we gather from the sixth Ecumenical Council, *we have learned that in certain churches the clergy put grapes alongside the sacrificial oblation and dispense both together to the people. We order therefore that no priest do this in future.*[3] And Pope Julius condemns those who use *what*

---

[3]In fact the *Concilium in Trullo*, A.D. 692. Mansi XI, 955. cf Gratian, *Decretum* 3, 2, 6 *Didicimus quod.* Richter-Friedberg I, 1315

Et Julius Papa reprehendit quosdam qui *expressum vinum in sacramento Dominici calicis offerunt.*[4] Ergo videtur quod vinum vitis non sit propria materia hujus sacramenti.

SED CONTRA est quod, sicut Dominus comparavit se grano frumenti, etiam se comparavit viti, dicens, *Joan.* xv, *Ego sum vitis vera.*[5] Sed solus panis de frumento est materia hujus sacramenti, ut dictum est. Ergo solum vinum de vite est propria materia hujus sacramenti.

RESPONSIO: Dicendum quod de solo vino vitis potest confici hoc sacramentum. Primo quidem, propter institutionem Christi, qui in vino vitis hoc sacramentum instituit: ut patet ex eo quod ipse dicit, *Luc.* xxii, circa institutionem hujus sacramenti, *Amodo non bibam de hoc genimine vitis.*[6]

Secundo quia, sicut dictum est,[7] ad materiam sacramentorum assumitur id quod proprie et communiter habet talem speciem. Proprie autem vinum dicitur quod de vite sumitur: alii autem liquores vinum dicuntur secundum quandam similitudinem ad vinum vitis.

Tertio, quia vinum vitis magis competit ad effectum hujus sacramenti, qui est spiritualis lætitia: quia scriptum est quod *vinum lætificat cor hominis.*[8]

1. Ad primum ergo dicendum quod illi liquores non dicuntur proprie vinum, sed secundum similitudinem. Potest autem verum vinum ad terras illas deferri in quibus vites non crescunt, quantum sufficit ad hoc sacramentum.

2. Ad secundum dicendum quod vinum fit acetum per corruptionem: unde non fit reditus de aceto in vinum, ut dicitur *Meta.*[9] Et ideo, sicut de pane totaliter corrupto non potest confici hoc sacramentum, ita nec de aceto potest confici. Potest tamen confici de vino acescenti, sicut de pane qui est in via ad corruptionem, licet peccet conficiens: ut prius dictum est.[10]

3. Ad tertium dicendum quod agresta est in via generationis, et ideo nondum habet speciem vini. Et propter hoc de ea non potest confici hoc sacramentum.

Mustum autem jam habet speciem vini: nam ejus dulcedo attestatur digestioni, quæ est *completio a naturali calore*, ut dicitur in *Meteor.*[11] Et ideo de musto potest confici hoc sacramentum.

---

[4] cf ibid 3, 2, 7 *Cum omne.* Richter-Friedberg I, 1316. cf Mansi XI, 155
[5] *John* 15, 1
[6] *Luke* 22, 18
[7] 3a. 74, 3
[8] *Psalms* 103, 15
[9] *Metaphysics* VII, 5, 3. 1044b34
[10] 3a. 74, 3 ad 4
[11] *Meteorology* IV, 2, 4. 379b12

has just been pressed from the grape in the sacrament of the chalice of the Lord.[4] Hence it seems that grape-wine is not the proper matter for this sacrament.

ON THE OTHER HAND, just as our Lord compared himself to a grain of wheat, so he also compared himself to a vine, saying *I am the true wine.*[5] But we have said that only wheaten bread is the matter for this sacrament. Therefore only wine of the grape is the proper matter for this sacrament.

REPLY: This sacrament can be consecrated with wine of the grape only. First, because of the way Christ instituted it; he instituted it with grape-wine, as is clear from the words he used in regard to its institution, *from now on I shall not drink of the fruit of the vine.*[6]

Secondly, as I have said,[7] for the material element used in the sacraments we employ the proper and commonly received type of that specific element. Wine of the grape is properly called wine; other liquids are called wine only because of their similarity to wine of the grape.

Thirdly, wine of the grape is more in keeping with the effect of this sacrament which is spiritual joy; as Scripture has it, *wine to gladden the heart of man.*[8]

Hence: 1. These liquids are not called wine in the strict sense of the term, but only because of a certain resemblance. As much real wine as is required for the celebration of this sacrament can always be transported to those regions where vines do not grow.[a]

2. Wine is changed into vinegar by a process of fermentation; hence there is no possibility of the vinegar becoming wine, as Aristotle points out.[9] And, therefore, just as the sacrament cannot be consecrated with bread that has gone bad, so it cannot be consecrated with vinegar. It can however be made with wine that is on the turn, though it would be sinful to do so, as we said earlier.[10]

3. The juice of the unripe grape is on the way to becoming wine; it has not yet the specific nature of wine and therefore it cannot be used to consecrate this sacrament. But the unfermented juice of the ripe grape already has the nature of wine; the sweetness shows that the process of generation *due to the natural heat is complete*, as Aristotle says.[11] But entire grapes ought not to be used in this sacrament; you would then have some-

---

[a]This is a further instance of the *scandal of particularity* which we first meet in the Incarnation itself. God became man, not some sort of universal, undifferentiated man, but a man of a certain race, place, time and culture. Our Lord was a Jew, a man of the Mediterranean world. In the Eucharist he used wheaten bread and wine, the normal food and drink of his time and place. Doubtless, had he been Chinese, he might have used rice and tea.

Non tamen debent uvæ integræ huic sacramento misceri: quia jam esset ibi aliquid præter vinum.

Prohibetur etiam ne mustum statim expressum de uva in calice offeratur: quia hoc est indecens, propter impuritatem musti. Potest tamen in necessitate fieri: dicitur enim ab eodem Julio Papa, *Si necesse fuerit, botrus in calicem prematur.*[12]

articulus 6. *utrum aqua sit vino permiscenda*

AD SEXTUM sic proceditur:[1] 1. Videtur quod aqua non sit vino permiscenda. Sacrificium enim Christi figuratum fuit per oblationem Melchisedech, qui, *Gen.* xiv, non legitur obtulisse nisi *panem et vinum.*[2] Ergo videtur quod in hoc sacramento non debeat adjungi aqua.

2. Præterea, diversorum sacramentorum diversæ sunt materiæ. Sed aqua est materia baptismi. Ergo non debet ad materiam assumi hujus sacramenti.

3. Præterea, panis et vinum sunt materia hujus sacramenti. Sed pani nihil adjungitur. Ergo nec vino debet aliquid adjungi.

SED CONTRA est quod Alexander Papa scribit, *In sacramentorum oblationibus quæ inter missarum solemnia Domino offeruntur, panis tantum et vinum aqua permixtum in sacrificium offerantur.*[3]

RESPONSIO: Dicendum quod vino quod offertur in hoc sacramento debet aqua misceri. Primo quidem, propter institutionem. Probabiliter enim creditur quod Dominus hoc sacramentum instituerit in vino aqua permixto, secundum morem terræ illius: unde et *Proverb.* ix dicitur, *Bibite vinum quod miscui vobis.*[4]

Secundo, quia hoc convenit repræsentationi Dominicæ passionis. Unde dicit Alexander Papa, *Non debet in calice Domini aut vinum solum, aut aqua sola offerri, sed utrumque permixtum: quia utrumque ex latere Christi in passione sua profluxisse legitur.*[5]

Tertio, quia hoc convenit ad significandum effectum hujus sacramenti, qui est unio populi Christiani ad Christum; quia, ut Julius Papa dicit, *videmus in aqua populum intelligi, in vino vero ostendi sanguinem Christi. Ergo, cum in calice vino aqua miscetur, Christo populus adunatur.*[6]

Quarto, quia hoc competit ad ultimum effectum hujus sacramenti, qui

---

[12]see note 4

[1]cf IV *Sent.* 11, 2, 4, i. *In Matt.* 26. *In* 1 *Cor.* XI, *lect.* 6

[2]*Genesis* 14, 18

[3]cf Gratian, *Decretum* 3, 2, 1 *In sacramentorum.* Richter-Friedberg I, 1314

thing else as well as wine. Moreover, it is not allowed to offer in the chalice juice which has just been pressed from ripe grapes; this would not be fitting as the must is not yet purified. But in case of necessity it could be used. As Pope Julius also says, *in case of necessity one may press a grape in the chalice.*[12]

article 6. should water be mixed with the wine?

THE SIXTH POINT:[1] 1. It would seem that water should not be mixed with the wine. The sacrifice of Christ was prefigured by the offering of Melchizedek and the book of *Genesis* does not mention that he offered else except *bread and wine.*[2] Therefore it seems that water should not be added to the wine in this sacrament.

2. Again, the different sacraments employ different material elements. But water is the matter for the sacrament of Baptism. Therefore it should not be used as the matter for this sacrament.

3. Moreover, bread and wine are the matter for this sacrament. But we add nothing to the bread. Therefore, we should add nothing to the wine.

ON THE OTHER HAND, we have Pope Alexander saying, *in the sacramental oblations made at mass only bread and wine mixed with water is to be offered in sacrifice.*[3]

REPLY: Water should be added to the wine which is offered in this sacrifice. First of all, because that is how the Eucharist was instituted. It is most probable that our Lord in instituting this sacrament used wine mixed with water, as was customary in that country. Hence we read in *Proverbs, drink of the wine I have mixed.*[4]

Then again, this fits in well with representing our Lord's passion. For this reason Pope Alexander writes, *neither wine alone nor water alone should be offered in the chalice of the Lord, but the two mixed together, because we read that both flowed from Christ's side in his passion.*[5]

Thirdly, it helps to bring out the effect of this sacrament which is the union of the Christian people to Christ, because, as Pope Julius says, *in the water we see the people signified and in the wine we see the blood of Christ. Therefore, when water is added in the chalice to the wine, Christ's people are united to him.*[6]

Finally, it harmonizes with the last effect of this sacrament which is our

---

[4]*Proverbs* 9, 5
[5]see note 3
[6]cf Gratian, *Decretum* 3, 2, 7 *Cum omne*. Richter-Friedberg 1, 1316

est introitus ad vitam æternam. Unde Ambrosius dicit, *Redundat aqua in calicem, et salit in vitam æternam.*[7]

1. Ad primum ergo dicendum quod, sicut Ambrosius dicit ibidem, sicut sacrificium Christi significatum est per oblationem Melchisedech, ita etiam significatum est per aquam quæ in eremo fluxit de petra: secundum illud 1 *Cor.* x, *Bibebant autem de spirituali consequente eos petra.*[8]

2. Ad secundum dicendum quod aqua sumitur in baptismo ad usum ablutionis. In hoc autem sacramento assumitur ad usum refectionis: secundum illud Psalmi, *Super aquam refectionis educavit me.*[9]

3. Ad tertium dicendum quod panis ex aqua et farina conficitur. Et ideo, cum vino aqua miscetur, neutrum sine aqua existit.

articulus 7. utrum permixtio aquæ sit de necessitate hujus sacramenti

AD SEPTIMUM sic proceditur:[1] 1. Videtur quod permixtio aquæ sit de necessitate hujus sacramenti. Dicit enim Cyprianus ad Cæcilium, *Sic calix Domini non est aqua sola et vinum solum, nisi utrumque misceatur, quo modo nec corpus Domini potest esse farina sola, nisi utrumque*, scilicet farina et aqua, *fuerit adunatum.*[2] Sed admixtio aquæ ad farinam est de necessitate hujus sacramenti. Ergo, pari ratione, admixtio aquæ ad vinum.

2. Præterea, in passione Domini, cujus hoc sacramentum est memoriale, sicut *de latere ejus exivit sanguis*, ita *et aqua.*[3] Sed vinum, quod est sacramentum sanguinis, est de necessitate hujus sacramenti. Ergo, pari ratione, et aqua.

3. Præterea, si aqua non esset de necessitate hujus sacramenti, non referret quæcumque aqua huic sacramento apponeretur: et ita posset apponi aqua rosacea, vel quæcumque alia hujusmodi aqua. Quod non habet usus ecclesiæ. Aqua ergo est de necessitate hujus sacramenti.

SED CONTRA est quod Cyprianus dicit, *Si quis de antecessoribus nostris ignoranter vel simpliciter non observavit*, ut scilicet aquam vino misceret in sacramento, *potest simplicitati ejus venia concedi.*[4] Quod non esset si aqua esset de necessitate sacramenti, sicut est vinum vel panis. Non ergo aquæ admixtio est de necessitate sacramenti.

RESPONSIO: Dicendum quod judicium de signo sumendum est ex eo quod significatur. Appositio autem aquæ ad vinum refertur ad significandam participationem hujus sacramenti a fidelibus, quantum ad hoc quod per

---

[7]*De Sacramentis* 5, 1. PL 16, 466

[8]1 *Corinthians* 10, 4

[9]*Psalms* 22, 2

entering into eternal life. This leads Ambrose to say, in his book *On the Sacraments, the water is added to the chalice and it leaps up into life eternal.*[7]

Hence: 1. As Ambrose says in the same place, just as the sacrifice of Christ was typified by the offering of Melchizedek, so also it was signified by the water which flowed from the rock in the desert. As St Paul wrote, *for they drank from the supernatural rock which followed them.*[8]

2. Water is used in Baptism for the purpose of cleansing. But in this sacrament it is used as refreshment; as the psalm puts it, *he has led me by waters of refreshment.*[9]

3. Bread is made from water and flour. Consequently, since water is mixed with the wine, neither element is without water.

article 7. is the mixing of the water with the wine necessary for validity in this sacrament?

THE SEVENTH POINT:[1] 1. It seems so. St Cyprian says in a letter to Cæcilius, *thus the chalice of the Lord is neither water alone nor wine alone, but a mixture of both, in the same way as the body of the Lord is not flour alone, but both,*[2] i.e. flour and water. But the mixing of water with the flour is absolutely necessary. Therefore, it is the same for the mixing of water with the wine.

2. Again, in our Lord's passion, of which this sacrament is a memorial, just as *from his side there came forth blood*, so also *water.*[3] But wine, which is the sacrament of the blood, is absolutely necessary in this sacrament. So also then is water.

3. Furthermore, if water were not necessary for validity, it would be of no importance what kind of water was added, and thus rose water or any such could be used. But the Church is careful not to add any but pure water. Therefore water is absolutely necessary.

ON THE OTHER HAND, we have Cyprian saying, *if any of our predecessors, through ignorance or simplicity, did not observe this rule* of mixing water with the wine, *his simplicity can be pardoned.*[4] He would not have said this if water were absolutely necessary, in the same way as wine or bread. I conclude that the mixing of water is not required for validity.

REPLY: A sign is judged in the light of what it signifies. Now the adding of water to the wine has to do with signifying the sharing by the faithful in this sacrament, because, as we have said, in the water mixed with the wine

---

[1]cf I *Sent.* 11, 2, 4, ii, 3. *In* I *Cor.* 11, *lect.* 6
[2] *Ep.* 63. PL 4, 396
[3]*John* 19, 34
[4]*Ep.* 63. PL 4, 399

aquam mixtam vino significatur populus adunatus Christo, ut dictum est. Sed et hoc ipsum quod de latere Christi pendentis in cruce aqua profluxit, ad idem refertur: quia per aquam significabatur ablutio peccatorum, quæ fiebat per passionem Christi. Dictum est autem supra[5] quod hoc sacramentum perficitur in consecratione materiæ: usus autem fidelium non est de necessitate sacramenti, sed est aliquid consequens ad sacramentum. Et ideo consequens est quod appositio aquæ non sit de necessitate sacramenti.

1. Ad primum ergo dicendum quod verbum illud Cypriani est intelligendum secundum quod dicitur illud esse non posse quod convenienter esse non potest. Et sic similitudo illa attenditur quantum ad illud quod debet fieri, non autem quantum ad necessitatem: nam aqua est de essentia panis, non autem de essentia vini.

2. Ad secundum dicendum quod effusio sanguinis directe pertinebat ad ipsam Christi passionem: est enim naturale corpori humano vulnerato quod ex eo profluat sanguis. Sed effusio aquæ non fuit de necessitate passionis, sed ad demonstrandum effectum, qui est ablutio a peccatis et refrigerium contra ardorem concupiscentiæ. Et ideo aqua non seorsum offertur a vino in hoc sacramento, sicut vinum seorsum offertur a pane: sed aqua offertur vino permixta, ut ostendatur quod vinum per se pertinet ad hoc sacramentum, tanquam de ejus necessitate existens, aqua autem secundum quod adjungitur vino.

3. Ad tertium dicendum quod, quia admixtio aquæ ad vinum non est de necessitate sacramenti, non refert quantum ad sacramenti necessitatem, quæcumque aqua misceatur vino, sive naturalis sive artificialis, ut rosacea. Quamvis, quantum ad convenientiam sacramenti, peccet qui aliam aquam miscet nisi naturalem et veram: quia de latere Christi pendentis in cruce vera aqua profluxit, non humor phlegmaticus, ut quidam dixerunt, ad ostendendum quod corpus Christi erat vere compositum ex quatuor elementis; sicut per sanguinem fluentem ostendebatur quod erat compositum ex quatuor humoribus; ut Innocentius III dicit in quadam Decretali.[6] Quia vero admixtio aquæ ad farinam est de necessitate hujus sacramenti, utpote constituens substantiam panis; si farinæ admisceretur aqua rosacea, vel quicumque alius liquor quam vera aqua, non posset ex eo confici sacramentum: quia non est vere panis.

articulus 8. *utrum debeat aqua in magna quantitate apponi*

AD OCTAVUM sic proceditur:[1] 1. Videtur quod debeat aqua in magna quantitate apponi. Sicut enim sanguis de latere Christi sensibiliter fluxit,

---

[5] 3a. 73, 1 ad 3

[6] *Regesta* XII *Ad Ferrariensem episc.* PL 216, 17; *Decretalia Gregorii IX* 3, 41, 8 *In quadam.* Richter-Friedberg II, 641

we see the people united to Christ. The same thing is brought out by the water which flowed from the side of Christ hanging on the cross and which signified that through his passion Christ has washed away our sins. But we saw earlier[5] that this sacrament is fully established at the moment when the matter is consecrated; the use by the faithful of this sacrament is not required for validity, but is something that takes place afterwards. It follows then that the addition of water is not absolutely required in this sacrament.

Hence: 1. We are to understand Cyprian in the same way as when we say a thing cannot be, but what we really mean is that it cannot suitably be. Thus that comparison has to do with what is desirable, not with what is absolutely necessary, because water is a very part of bread but not of wine.

2. The shedding of blood was a part of Christ's actual passion, because it is natural that blood should flow from a wounded human body. But the issue of water did not follow necessarily on the passion; its purpose was to show forth the effect of the passion which is to wash away our sins and to cool us against our concupiscence. Hence in this sacrament water is not offered apart from wine, but water is offered mixed with wine, in order to show that wine belongs to the essence of this sacrament and is required for validity, but water is used only as mixed with wine.

3. Since the mixing of water with the wine is not of the essence of this sacrament, it is of no import, as far as the essentials are concerned, what kind of water is mixed with the wine, whether it be natural water or artificial, as, for example, rose water. Still, suitability demands natural and true water and it would be sinful to add some other kind; because, when Christ was hanging on the cross it was true water that issued from his side, not a lymphatic humour, as some people said. This showed that his body was composed of the four elements, as the issue of blood showed that it was composed of the four humours. This is Innocent III's idea in a certain decretal.[6] But since the mixing of water with the flour is of the essence of this sacrament, because it goes to make the very substance of the bread, if one were to mix rose water or any other liquid other than pure water with the flour, the Eucharist could not be consecrated because it would not be genuine bread.

article 8. *should water be added in a large quantity?*

THE EIGHTH POINT:[1] 1. It would seem that it should. Just as the blood flowed in a visible way from Christ's side, so did the water; hence St John writes,

---

[1]cf IV *Sent.* 11, 2, 4, iv. *In* I *Cor.* 11, *lect.* 6

ita et aqua: unde dicitur *Joan.* xix, *Qui vidit, testimonium perhibuit.*[2] Sed aqua non posset sensibiliter esse in hoc sacramento nisi in magna quantitate poneretur. Ergo videtur quod aqua debeat apponi in magna quantitate.

2. Præterea, parva aqua multo vino admixta corrumpitur. Quod autem corruptum est, non est. Ergo idem est apponere parum de aqua in hoc sacramento, et nihil apponere. Sed non licet nihil apponere. Ergo non licet parum apponere.

3. Præterea, si sufficeret parum apponere, per consequens esset sufficiens quod gutta aquæ in totum dolium projiceretur. Sed hoc videtur ridiculum. Ergo non sufficit quod parva quantitas ponatur.

SED CONTRA est quod *Extra, de Celebrat. Missar.*, dicitur, *Perniciosus in tuis partibus inolevit abusus, videlicet quod in majori quantitate de aqua ponitur in sacrificio quam de vino: cum, secundum rationabilem consuetudinem ecclesiæ generalis, plus in ipso sit de vino quam de aqua ponendum.*[3]

RESPONSIO: Dicendum quod circa aquam adjunctam vino, ut Innocentius III dicit, in quadam *Decretali,*[4] triplex est opinio. Quidam enim dicunt quod aqua adjuncta vino per se manet, vino converso in sanguinem. Sed hæc opinio omnino* stare non potest. Quia in sacramento altaris, post consecrationem, nihil est nisi corpus et sanguis Christi: sicut Ambrosius dicit, in libro *de Officiis, Ante benedictionem alia species nominatur, post benedictionem corpus significatur.*[5] Alioquin non† adoraretur veneratione latriæ.

Et ideo alii dixerunt quod, sicut vinum convertitur in sanguinem, ita aqua convertitur in aquam quæ de latere Christi fluxit. Sed hoc non rationabiliter dici potest. Quia secundum hoc, aqua seorsum consecraretur a vino, sicut vinum a pane.

Et ideo, sicut ipse dicit, aliorum opinio probabilior est, qui dicunt aquam converti in vinum, et vinum in sanguinem. Hoc autem fieri non posset nisi adeo modicum apponeretur de aqua quod converteretur in vinum. Et ideo semper tutius est parum de aqua apponere, et præcipue si vinum sit debile: quia, si tanta fieret appositio aquæ quod solveretur species vini, non posset perfici sacramentum. Unde Julius Papa reprehendit quosdam qui *pannum lineum musto intinctum per totum annum servant, et in tempore sacrificii aqua partem ejus lavant, et sic offerunt.*[6]

---

*Piana omits *omnino*

†Piana: *totum,* the whole would not receive

[2]*John* 19, 35

[3]*Decretalia Gregorii IX* 3, 41, 8, 13 *Perniciosus.* Richter-Friedberg II, 643

[4]ibid 6 *Cum Marthæ.* Richter-Friedberg II, 638

[5]Ambrose, *De Mysteriis* 9. PL 16, 424. cf Gratian, *Decretum* 3, 2, 40 *Ante Benedictionem.* Richter-Friedberg I, 1328

he who saw it has borne witness.[2] But water would not be visible in this sacrament unless a large quantity were used. Hence it seems that it should be added in a large quantity.

2. Again, if a little water is mixed with much more wine it is changed. What is changed no longer is. Hence to add a little is the same as to add nothing. But we are forbidden to add nothing. Therefore it is not right to add only a small quantity.

3. Moreover, if it were sufficient to add a little, it would logically follow that a single drop would be enough for a whole barrel of wine. But this seems laughable. Therefore, it is not sufficient to add a little.

ON THE OTHER HAND, we read in a decretal on the celebration of mass, *in your country a harmful abuse has become customary of using a larger quantity of water than of wine in the sacrifice, against the reasonable tradition of the universal church of using a greater proportion of wine than of water.*[3]

REPLY: In this matter of the water added to the wine, a decretal of Innocent III[4] recognized the existence of three opinions. Some say that the water added to the wine keeps to itself at the change of the wine into the blood. But this opinion is quite unacceptable, because in the sacrament of the altar, after the consecration, there is nothing other than the body and the blood of Christ. As Ambrose puts it, *before* the consecration we speak of another kind of thing, after the consecration it is the *body of Christ that is designated.*[5] If it were not so, the sacrament would not receive the worship of latria.

That is why others held that just as the wine is changed into the blood, so the water is changed into the water that flowed from Christ's side. But this is not a reasonable view, because in this case the water would be consecrated separately from the wine, in the same way as the wine is consecrated separately from the bread.

Hence, as Innocent himself says, the third opinion is the most likely to be true, according to which the water is changed into the wine and the wine into the blood. This could only be if such a small amount of water were added as would be changed into the wine. Hence it is always safer to add a very little water and particularly if the wine is weak. Because if so much water were to be added that the wine were to lose its nature the sacrament could not be effected. Hence Pope Julius I reproves those who *for a whole year keep a piece of linen which has been dipped in wine and at the time of sacrifice wash a part of it in water and make the offering thus.*[6]

---

[6] cf Gratian, *Decretum* 3, 2, 7 *Cum omne.* Richter-Friedberg 1, 1316

1. Ad primum ergo dicendum quod sufficit ad significationem hujus sacramenti quod sentiatur aqua cum apponitur vino: non autem oportet quod sit sensibilis post mixtionem.

2. Ad secundum dicendum quod, si aqua omnino non apponeretur, totaliter excluderetur significatio: sed, cum aqua in vinum convertitur, significatur quod populus Christo incorporatur.

3. Ad tertium dicendum quod, si aqua apponeretur dolio, non sufficeret ad significationem hujus sacramenti: sed oportet aquam vino apponi circa ipsam celebrationem sacramenti.

Hence: 1. The sacramental symbolism[a] is sufficiently evident if the water is seen to be added to the wine; it is not necessary that it should be visible after the mingling has taken place.

2. If no water at all were added the symbolism would be completely excluded; but the fact that the water is changed into the wine symbolizes that the people are incorporated into Christ.

3. If water were to be added to the cask of wine, the sacramental symbolism would not be preserved; the water must be added to the wine when the Eucharist is being celebrated.

---

[a]This sacramental symbolism is not such in the strict sense. It does not cause what it signifies. It is the partaking of the Eucharist—Holy Communion—which causes as well as signifies the incorporation by charity of the people into Christ. Holy Communion is the sacramental sign of the unity of the mystical body of Christ. It is not desirable to make too much of the mingling of the water with the wine.

Quæstio 75. de conversione panis et vini in corpus et sanguinem Christi

Deinde considerandum est de conversione panis et vini in corpus et sanguinem Christi. Et circa hoc quaeruntur octo:

1. utrum substantia panis et vini remaneat in hoc sacramento post consecrationem;
2. utrum annihiletur;
3. utrum convertatur in corpus et sanguinem Christi;
4. utrum remaneant ibi accidentia post conversionem;
5. utrum remaneat ibi forma substantialis;
6. utrum conversio ista fiat subito;
7. utrum sit miraculosior omni alia mutatione;
8. quibus verbis convenienter exprimi possit.

1. utrum in hoc sacramento sit corpus Christi secundum veritatem, vel solum secundum figuram vel sicut in signo;
2. utrum in hoc sacramento remaneat substantia panis et vini post consecrationem;
3. utrum substantia panis, post consecrationem hujus sacramenti, annihiletur, aut in pristinam materiam resolvatur;
4. utrum panis possit converti in corpus Christi;
5. utrum in hoc sacramento remaneant accidentia panis et vini;
6. utrum, facta consecratione, remaneat in hoc sacramento forma substantialis panis;
7. utrum ista conversio fiat in instanti vel fiat successive;
8. utrum haec sit vera, 'ex pane fit corpus Christi'.

articulus 1. *utrum in hoc sacramento sit corpus Christi secundum veritatem, vel solum secundum figuram vel sicut in signo*

AD PRIMUM sic proceditur:[1] 1. Videtur quod in hoc sacramento non sit corpus Christi secundum veritatem, sed solum secundum figuram, vel

[1]cf IV *Sent.* 10, 1. *CG* IV, 61–3. *De Sacramento Altans,* 11. *In Matt.* 26. *In Joan.* 6, *lect.* 6. *In* 1 *Cor.* 11, *lect.* 5

[a]The eight titles here announced do not head the eight articles that follow. The case is unique in the *Summa Theologiæ*. St Thomas first intended to follow the plan of his commentary on the *Sentences* (IV *Sent.* 40). The second series of titles is taken from the articles as he actually set about them.

Question 75. the change of the bread and wine into the body and blood of Christ

We now come to consider the change of the bread and wine into the body and blood of Christ. There are eight points of inquiry:

1. does the substance of the bread and wine remain in this sacrament after the consecration?
2. is it annihilated?
3. is it changed into the body and blood of Christ?
4. do the accidents remain there after the change?
5. does the substantial form remain there?
6. does this change take place instantaneously?
7. is it more miraculous than any other change?
8. what words can be suitably used to express it?[a]

1. is the body of Christ really and truly[b] in this sacrament or only in a figurative way or as in a sign?
2. does the substance of the bread and wine remain in this sacrament after the consecration?
3. is the substance of the bread, after the consecration, annihilated or reduced into one of the four elements?
4. can the bread be changed into the body of Christ?
5. do the accidents of the bread and wine remain?
6. does the substantial form of the bread remain after the consecration?
7. is this change an instantaneous or a successive one?
8. is it true to say, 'The body of Christ comes from the bread'?

article 1. *is the body of Christ really and truly in this sacrament or only in a figurative way or as in a sign?*

THE FIRST POINT:[1] 1. It seems that the body of Christ is not really and truly in this sacrament, but only in a figurative way or as in a sign. For we read

---

[b]It is best to translate '*secundum veritatem*' here as 'really and truly'; 'really'—in contrast to in a figurative way only, and 'truly'—in relation to the types and figures of the Old Testament of which the Eucharist is the fulfilment. Its relationship to them is that of substance to shadow, of truth to type or figure. The Council of Trent (13th session, 11th October, 1551) later defined that the body and blood, soul and divinity of our Lord are contained in the Eucharist, '*vere, realiter et substantialiter*, truly, really and substantially' (Denz. 883).

sicut in signo. Dicitur enim *Joan.* vi quod, cum Dominus dixisset, *Nisi manducaveritis carnem Filii hominis et biberitis ejus sanguinem*, etc., *multi ex discipulis ejus audientes dixerunt, Durus est hic sermo:* quibus ipse, *Spiritus est qui vivificat, caro non prodest quidquam.*[2] Quasi dicat, secundum expositionem Augustini super *quartum Psalmum, Spiritualiter intellige quæ locutus sum. Non hoc corpus quod videtis manducaturi estis, et bibituri illum sanguinem quem fusuri sunt qui me crucifigent. Sacramentum aliquod vobis commendavi. Spiritualiter intellectum vivificabit vos: caro autem non prodest quidquam.*[3]

2. Præterea, Dominus dicit, *Matth.* ult. *Ecce, ego vobiscum sum omnibus diebus usque ad consummationem sæculi:*[4] quod exponens Augustinus dicit, *Donec sæculum finiatur, sursum est Dominus: sed tamen et hic nobiscum est veritas Dominus. Corpus enim in quo resurrexit, uno in loco esse oportet: veritas autem ejus ubique diffusa est.*[5] Non ergo secundum veritatem est corpus Christi in hoc sacramento, sed solum sicut in signo.

3. Præterea, nullum corpus potest esse simul in pluribus locis, cum nec angelo hoc conveniat: eadem enim ratione posset esse ubique. Sed corpus Christi est verum corpus, et est in cælo. Ergo videtur quod non sit secundum veritatem in sacramento altaris, sed solum sicut in signo.

4. Præterea, sacramenta Ecclesiæ ad utilitatem fidelium ordinantur. Sed secundum Gregorium, in quadam homilia, regulus reprehenditur quia *quærebat corporalem Christi præsentiam.*[6] Apostoli etiam impediebantur recipere Spiritum Sanctum propter hoc quod affecti erant ad ejus præsentiam corporalem; ut Augustinus dicit[7] super illud *Joan.* xvi. *Si non abiero, Paracletus non veniet ad vos.*[8] Non ergo Christus secundum præsentiam corporalem est in sacramento altaris.

SED CONTRA est quod Hilarius dicit, *De veritate carnis et sanguinis Christi non est relictus ambigendi locus. Nunc et ipsius Domini professione, et fide nostra, caro ejus vere est cibus et sanguis ejus vere est potus.*[9] Et Ambrosius dicit, *Sicut verus est Dei Filius Dominus Jesus Christus, ita vera Christi caro est quam accipimus, et vere sanguis ejus est potus.*[10]

RESPONSIO: Dicendum quod verum corpus Christi et sanguinem esse in hoc sacramento, non sensu deprehendi potest, sed sola fide, quæ auctoritati

---

[2] *John* 6, 54, 61, 64
[3] *Enarrationes in Psalmos.* On Psalm 98, 5. PL 37, 1265. cf Gratian, *Decretum* 3, 2, 44 *Prima quidem.* Richter-Friedberg 1, 1330
[4] *Matthew* 28, 20
[5] *In Joan. Tract.* 30. PL 35, 1632
[6] *Homilies or the Gospels* 28. PL 76, 1213

in *John* that when our Lord had said, *Unless you eat the flesh of the son of man and drink his blood*, etc., *many of his disciples said this is a hard saying.* He answered them, *it is the spirit that gives life, the flesh is of no avail.*[2] As if he were to say, as Augustine explains it commenting on the fourth *Psalm*, *Take what I have said in a spiritual way. You will not be eating this body which you see, nor will you be drinking that blood which my executioners will shed. I have entrusted a mystery to you. If you take it in a spiritual way it will bring you life; flesh is of no avail.*[3]

2. Moreover, the Lord says, *Lo, I am with you always, to the close of the age.*[4] Augustine, in explaining this, says, *until the close of the age the Lord is above*, but at *the same time the Lord is here with us as the truth (on which our minds feed). The body in which he rose can be in one place only, but his truth is found everywhere.*[5] The body of Christ then is not really and truly in this sacrament, but only as in a sign.

3. No body can be in several places at once. Not even an angel has that power; if he had he could be everywhere.[a] But the body of Christ is a real body and it is in heaven. Therefore, it seems that it cannot be in the sacrament of the altar in very truth, but only as in its sign.

4. The purpose of the Church's sacraments is to benefit the faithful. Now, according to Gregory, our Lord reproved the official (mentioned in *John* 4, 48) because *he wanted the bodily presence of Christ.*[6] Again, it was because of their attachment to this bodily presence that the Apostles were hindered from receiving the Holy Ghost, as Augustine teaches,[7] commenting on *John*, *If I do not go away, the Counseller will not come to you.*[8] Christ is not then by bodily presence in the sacrament of the altar.

ON THE OTHER HAND, Hilary says, *there is no room for doubt about the reality of the body and blood of Christ. Our Lord taught and our faith accepts that his flesh is really our food and his blood is really our drink.*[9] And Ambrose says, *just as our Lord Jesus Christ is the real son of God, so the real flesh of Christ is what we receive, and his blood is really our drink.*[10]

REPLY: We could never know by our senses that the real body of Christ and his blood are in this sacrament, but only by our faith which is based on

---

[7] *In Joan. Tract.* 94. PL 35, 1869
[8] *John* 16, 7
[9] *De Trinitate* VIII, 15. PL 10, 247
[10] *De Sacramentis* VI, 1. PL 16, 473. cf Gratian, *Decretum* 3, 2, 84 *Sicut est verus.* Richter-Friedberg I, 1349

[a] This argument from angelology is very compressed. See 1a. 52, 2. An angel is where he operates. Since his power of operation is finite, there is a definite local limit to the field of his action on bodies. Only God can be everywhere. See 1a. 8, 2–4.

divinæ innititur. Unde super illud *Luc.* xxii, *Hoc est corpus meum quod pro vobis tradetur*, dicit Cyrillus, *Non dubites an hoc verum sit, sed potius suscipe verba Salvatoris in fide: cum enim sit veritas, non mentitur.*[11]

Hoc autem conveniens est, primo quidem, perfectioni Novæ Legis. Sacrificia* enim Veteris Legis illud verum sacrificium passionis Christi continebant solum in figura: secundum illud *Heb.* x, *Umbram habens lex futurorum bonorum, non ipsam rerum imaginem.*[12] Et ideo oportuit ut aliquid plus haberet sacrificium novæ legis a Christo institutum; ut scilicet contineret ipsum passum, non solum in significatione vel figura, sed etiam in rei veritate. Et ideo hoc sacramentum, quod ipsum Christum realiter continet, ut Dionysius dicit, est *perfectivum omnium sacramentorum aliorum*,[13] in quibus virtus Christi participatur.

Secundo, hoc competit caritati Christi, ex qua pro salute nostra corpus verum nostræ naturæ assumpsit. Et quia maxime proprium amicitiæ est *convivere amicis*, ut Philosophus dicit,[14] sui præsentiam corporalem nobis repromittit in præmium, *Matt.* xxiv, *Ubi fuerit corpus, illuc congregabuntur et aquilæ.*[15] Interim tamen nec sua præsentia corporali in hac peregrinatione destituit, sed per veritatem corporis et sanguinis sui nos sibi conjungit in hoc sacramento. Unde ipse dicit, *Joan.* vi, *Qui manducat meam carnem et bibit meum sanguinem, in me manet et ego in eo.*[16] Unde hoc sacramentum est maximæ caritatis signum, et nostræ spei sublevamentum, ex tam familiari conjunctione Christi ad nos.

Tertio, hoc competit perfectioni fidei, quæ sicut est de divinitate Christi, ita est de ejus humanitate: secundum illudi *Joan.* xiv, *Creditis in Deum, et in me credite.*[17] Et quia fides est invisiblium, sicut divinitatem suam nobis exhibet Christus invisibiliter, ita et in hoc sacramento carnem suam nobis exhibet invisibili modo.

Quæ quidam non attendentes, posuerunt corpus et sanguinem Christi non esse in hoc sacramento nisi sicut in signo. Quod est tanquam hæreticum abjiciendum, utpote verbis Christi contrarium. Unde et Berengarius, qui primus inventor hujus erroris fuerat, postea coactus est suum errorem revocare, et veritatem fidei confiteri.[18]

1. Ad primum ergo dicendum quod ex hac auctoritate prædicti hæretici occasionem errandi sumpserunt, male verba Augustini intelligentes. Cum enim Augustinus dicit, *Non hoc corpus quod videtis manducaturi estis,*

---

*Piana reads *sacramenta* for *sacrificia*

[11]*Commentary on Luke* 22, 19. PG 72, 92

[12]*Hebrews* 10, 1

[13]*Ecclesiastical Hierarchy* 3, 1. PG 3, 423

[14]*Ethics* IX, 12. 1171b32

[15]*Matthew* 24, 28

the authority of God. For this reason Cyril, commenting on the text of *Luke*, *this is my body which is given for you*, says, *do not doubt the truth of this, but take our Saviour's word in faith: he is truth itself, he does not lie.*[11]

This is entirely in keeping, first of all with the perfection of the New Law. The sacrifices of the Old Law contained that true sacrifice which was the passion of Christ, only in a figurative way; as we read in *Hebrews*, *the law has but a shadow of the good things to come instead of the true form of these realities.*[12] It was only right that the sacrifice of the New Law instituted by Christ should have something more, that it should contain Christ himself who suffered for us, and contain him, not merely as by a sign or figure, but in actual reality as well. So it is that this sacrament which really contains Christ himself is, as Dionysius says, the *fulfilment of all the other sacraments*,[13] in which a share of Christ's power is to be found.

Secondly, it fits in perfectly with that charity of Christ which led him to take a real body having human nature and unite it to himself in order to save us. And because it is the very law of friendship that *friends should live together*,[14] as Aristotle teaches, he promises us his bodily presence as a reward, in the text of *Matthew*, *wherever the body is, there the eagles will be gathered together.*[15] In the meantime, however, he has not left us without his bodily presence in this our pilgrimage, but he joins us to himself in this sacrament in the reality of his body and blood. For this reason he says, *he who eats my flesh and drinks my blood abides in me and I in him.*[16] Hence this sacrament, because it joins Christ so closely to us, is the sign of the extreme of his love and lifts our hope on high.

Thirdly, this real presence is just what is right for the perfection of our faith, which bears not only on the divinity of Christ, but also on his humanity; as he has said, *believe in God, believe also in me.*[17] Now faith has to do with unseen realities, and just as he offers his divinity to our acceptance as something that we do not see, so in this sacrament he offers his very flesh to us in like manner.

Some people did not pay attention to these points and they declared that Christ's body and blood were only symbolically in this sacrament. But we must reject this position as heretical, because it is contrary to the words of Christ. For this reason Berengarius, who was the first to hold this erroneous view, was compelled to retract and to accept what is a truth of faith.[18]

Hence: 1. It is this very text of Augustine that provided the heretics whom we have just mentioned with the occasion of their errors. They misunderstood his words. When Augustine says, *you will not be eating this*

---

[16]*John* 6, 57
[17]*John* 14, 1
[18]cf Gratian, *Decretum* 3, 2, 42 *Ego Berengarius*. Richter-Friedberg 1, 1328

non intendit excludere veritatem corporis Christi, sed quod non erat manducandum in hac specie in qua ab eis videbatur. Per hoc autem quod subdit, *Sacramentum vobis aliquod commendavi, spiritualiter intellectum vivificabit vos*, non intendit quod corpus Christi sit in hoc sacramento solum secundum mysticam significationem, sed spiritualiter dici, id est invisibiliter et per virtutem spiritus. Unde, super *Joan.*, exponens id quod dicitur, 'Caro non prodest quidquam',[19] dicit, *Sed quo modo illi intellexerunt. Carnem quippe sic intellexerunt manducandam, quo modo in cadavere dilaniatur aut in macello venditur: non quo modo spiritu vegetatur. Accedat spiritus ad carnem, et prodest plurimum: nam, si caro nihil prodesset, Verbum caro non fieret, ut habitaret in nobis.*[20]

2. Ad secundum dicendum quod verbum illud Augustini, et omnia similia, sunt intelligenda de corpore Christi secundum quod videtur in propria specie: secundum quod etiam ipse Dominus dixit, *Matth.* xxvi, *Me autem non semper habebitis.*[21] Invisibiliter tamen sub speciebus hujus sacramenti est ubicumque hoc sacramentum perficitur.

3. Ad tertium dicendum quod corpus Christi non est eo modo in sacramento sicut corpus in loco, quod suis dimensionibus loco commensuratur: sed quodam speciali modo, qui est proprius huic sacramento. Unde dicimus quod corpus Christi est in diversis altaribus, non sicut in diversis locis, sed *sicut in sacramento.* Per quod non intelligimus quod Christus sit ibi solum sicut in signo, licet sacramentum sit in genere signi: sed intelligimus corpus Christi hic esse, sicut dictum est, secundum proprium modum huic sacramento.

4. Ad quartum dicendum quod ratio illa procedit de præsentia corporis Christi prout est præsens per modum* corporis, id est prout est in sua specie visibilis: non autem prout spiritualiter, id est invisibiliter, modo et virtute spiritus. Unde Augustinus dicit, super *Joan.*, *Si intellexisti spiritualiter* verba Christi de carne sua, *spiritus et vita tibi sunt: si intellexisti carnaliter, etiam spiritus et vita sunt, sed tibi non sunt.*[22]

articulus 2. utrum in hoc sacramento remaneat substantia panis et vini post consecrationem

AD SECUNDUM sic proceditur:[1] 1. Videtur quod in hoc sacramento remaneat substantia panis et vini post consecrationem. Dicit enim Damascenus,

---

*Piana reads *motum* for *modum*, present through bodily change

[19] *John* 6, 64 [20] *In Joan. Tract.* 27. PL 35, 1617 [21] *Matthew* 26, 11

[22] *In Joan. Tract.* 27. PL 35, 1618

[1] cf IV *Sent.* 11, 1, 1, i. *CG* IV, 63. *In Matt.* 26. *In* 1 *Cor.* 11, *lect.* 4

[a] This article is a first step in the theology of transubstantiation. The doctrine of *impanation* holds that the substance of the bread is hypostatically united to Christ,

body which you see, he does not intend to exclude the reality of Christ's body; what he does rule out is that they would eat it under the same form in which they were looking at it. When he adds, *I have entrusted a mystery to you. If you take it in a spiritual way it will bring you life*, he does not mean that the body of Christ is in this sacrament only as in a mystical symbol; it is said to be there spiritually, that is, invisibly and by the power of the spirit. For this reason, commenting on the text of *John*, 'the flesh is of no avail',[19] he writes, *it is of no avail, in the way they understood. They thought of eating flesh as if it had been torn from the carcass or sold in the butcher's stall; they did not understand flesh as enlivened by the spirit. When the spirit is united to the flesh, then indeed it is of great avail, for if flesh could never be of avail, the Word would not have been made flesh to dwell among us.*[20]

2. This text of Augustine and all others in the same vein are to be taken as referring to Christ's body in its natural appearance; in this sense our Lord himself said, *you will not always have me.*[21] But wherever this sacrament is celebrated he is present in an invisible way under sacramental appearances.

3. The body of Christ is not in this sacrament in the way a body is in place. The dimensions of a body in place correspond with the dimensions of the place that contains it. Christ's body is here in a special way that is proper to this sacrament. For this reason we say that the body of Christ is on different altars, not as in different places, but as in the sacrament. In saying this we do not mean that Christ is only symbolically there, although it is true that every sacrament is a sign, but we understand that Christ's body is there, as we have said, in a way that is proper to this sacrament.

4. This objection considers the presence of Christ's body as if it were present in the way that is natural for a body to be present, that is visibly in its normal appearance; it does not envisage a spiritual, non-visible presence, in the way of a spirit and by the power of the Spirit. For this reason Augustine says, *if you have understood in a spiritual way* the words of Christ about his flesh, *they are spirit and life for you; if you have understood them in a carnal manner, they are still spirit and life, but not for you.*[22]

article 2. does the substance of the bread and wine remain in this sacrament after the consecration?[a]

THE SECOND POINT:[1] 1. It seems that it does. We read in John Damascene, *because bread and wine is typical human nourishment, he joined his godhead to*

the doctrine of *companation* holds that the substance of the bread is united in some unspecified way to the body of Christ; the Catholic dogma defined at the Council of Trent teaches that the substance of the bread does not remain but is changed into the body of Christ—*transubstantiation.*

Quia consuetudo est hominibus comedere panem et vinum bibere, conjugavit eis Deus deitatem, et fecit ea corpus et sanguinem suum.[2] Et infra, *Panis communicationis non panis simplex est, sed unitus deitati.* Sed conjugatio est rerum actu existentium. Ergo panis et vinum simul sunt in hoc sacramento cum corpore et sanguine Christi.

2. Præterea, inter Ecclesiæ sacramenta debet esse conformitas. Sed in aliis sacramentis substantia materiæ manet: sicut in Baptismo substantia aquæ, et in Confirmatione substantia chrismatis. Ergo et in hoc sacramento substantia panis et vini manet.

3. Præterea, panis et vinum assumitur in hoc sacramento inquantum significant ecclesiasticam unitatem, prout *unus panis fit ex multis granis, et unum vinum ex multis racemis,*[3] ut Augustinus dicit, in libro de Symbolo. Sed hoc pertinet ad ipsam substantiam panis et vini. Ergo substantia panis et vini remanet in hoc sacramento.

SED CONTRA est quod Ambrosius dicit, in libro *de Sacramentis, Licet figura panis et vini videatur, nihil tamen aliud quam caro Christi et sanguis post consecrationem credenda sunt.*[4]

RESPONSIO: Dicendum quod quidam[5] posuerunt post consecrationem substantiam panis et vini in hoc sacramento remanere. Sed hæc positio stare non potest. Primo quidem, quia per hanc positionem tollitur veritas hujus sacramenti, ad quam pertinet ut verum corpus Christi in hoc sacramento existat. Quod quidem ibi non est ante consecrationem. Non autem aliquid potest esse alicubi ubi prius non erat, nisi per loci mutationem vel per alterius conversionem in ipsum: sicut in domo aliqua de novo incipit esse ignis aut quod illuc defertur aut quod ibi generatur. Manifestum est autem quod corpus Christi non incipit esse in hoc sacramento per motum localem. Primo quidem, quia sequeretur quod desineret esse in cælo: non enim quod localiter movetur pervenit de novo ad

---

[2]*De Fide Orthodoxa* IV, 13. PG 94, 1144, 1149

[3]*In Joan. Tract.* 26. PL 35, 1614

[4]*De Sacramentis* 4, 5. PL 16, 458. cf Gratian, *Decretum* 3, 2, 74 *Omnia quæcumque.* Richter-Friedberg I, 1344

[5]cf the Master of the Sentences, *Sententiarum* IV, 11, 2. Alger of Liège, *De Sacramento Corp. et Sanguinis Domini, prol., c.* 6. PL 180, 739, 754

[b]One wonders how convincing this *a priori* proof really is. Anyway, it has the value of a suggestion and it can support the second argument which is stronger. The principle *a thing cannot be where it was not before, except by being brought in locally or by something being changed into it* is universally valid where natural presence is

them and made them to be his body and his blood.[2] And further on, *the bread we receive in communion is not ordinary bread, but united to the godhead.* Now, we join together realities that actually exist. Therefore, the bread and the wine exist in this sacrament alongside the body and the blood of Christ.

2. Moreover, the Church's sacraments should resemble one another. In the other sacraments the substance of the material elements remains, as in Baptism the substance of the water and in Confirmation the substance of the chrism. Therefore the substance of the bread and wine remains in the Eucharist.

3. Furthermore, bread and wine are employed in this sacrament to bring out its significance of the unity of the Church. As Augustine says, *one loaf is made of many grains and one wine of many bunches of grapes.*[3] But the substance of the bread and wine is required for this significance. Therefore, the substance of the bread and wine remains in this sacrament.

ON THE OTHER HAND, Ambrose says, *although we see the appearance of bread and wine, we should believe that, after the consecration, there is nothing other than the flesh of Christ and his blood.*[4]

REPLY: Some[5] have held that after the consecration the substance of the bread and wine remains in this sacrament. But this position cannot be sustained. First of all, it would destroy the reality of this sacrament which demands that the very body of Christ exist in it. Now, his body is not there before the consecration. But a thing cannot be where it was not before, except by being brought in locally or by something already there being changed into it.[b] For example, a fire is started in a household because either it is brought into it from outside or is newly kindled there. Now it is clear that the body of Christ does not begin to exist in this sacrament by being brought in locally. First, because it would thereby cease to be in heaven,

---

concerned. But the Eucharistic presence is not a natural one, though it is a real one. Moreover, the second mode of beginning to be, viz. by something being generated out of a prior matter, as fire out of paper and sticks, does not really apply to the body of Christ which is not produced out of the bread. It existed before the bread did, and the bread is changed into what existed before it by a unique and miraculous change. That this change should result in the body of Christ being 'where' the substance of the bread was is a further and gratuitous disposition of divine wisdom and power. But the principle helps our analogous thinking and it is intellectually satisfying to think that it must have happened in this way. Actually, the Scotist school of theology, although it will use the word '*conversio*', will conceive of this *conversio* not as genuinely such at all, but as involving an annihilation of the bread and a *bringing in* of the body of Christ. The first limb of St Thomas's alternative will appeal more to them.

aliquem locum nisi deserat priorem. Secundo, quia omne corpus localiter motum pertransit omnia media, quod hic dici non potest. Tertio, quia impossibile est quod unus motus ejusdem corporis localiter moti terminetur simul ad diversa loca; cum tamen in pluribus locis corpus Christi sub hoc sacramento simul esse incipiat. Et propter hoc relinquitur quod non possit aliter corpus Christi incipere esse de novo in hoc sacramento nisi per conversionem substantiæ panis in ipsum. Quod autem convertitur in aliquid, facta conversione, non manet. Unde relinquitur quod, salva veritate hujus sacramenti, substantia panis post consecrationem remanere non possit.

Secundo, quia hæc positio contrariatur formæ hujus sacramenti, in qua dicitur, 'Hoc est corpus meum'. Quod non esset verum si substantia panis ibi remaneret: nunquam enim substantia est corpus Christi. Sed potius esset dicendum, 'Hic est corpus meum'.

Tertio, quia contrariaretur venerationi hujus sacramenti, si aliqua substantia esset ibi quæ non posset adorari adoratione latriæ.

Quarto, quia contrariaretur ritui Ecclesiæ, secundum quem post corporalem cibum non licet sumere corpus Christi: cum tamen post unam hostiam consecratam liceat sumere aliam.

Unde hæc positio vitanda est tanquam hæretica.

1. Ad primum dicendum quod Deus conjugavit *divinitatem suam*, id est divinam virtutem, pani et vino, non ut remaneant in hoc sacramento, sed ut faciat inde corpus et sanguinem suum.

2. Ad secundum dicendum quod in aliis sacramentis non est ipse Christus realiter, sicut in hoc sacramento. Et ideo in sacramentis aliis manet substantia materiæ, non autem in isto.

3. Ad tertium dicendum quod species quæ remanent in hoc sacramento, ut infra dicetur,[6] sufficiunt ad significationem hujus sacramenti: nam per accidentia cognoscitur ratio substantiæ.

articulus 3. *utrum substantia panis post consecrationem hujus sacramenti, annihiletur, aut in pristinam materiam resolvatur*

AD TERTIUM sic proceditur.[1] 1. Videtur quod substantia panis, post consecrationem hujus sacramenti, annihiletur, aut in pristinam materiam resolvatur. Quod enim est aliquid corporale oportet alicubi esse. Sed

---

[6] 3a. 75, 5

[1] cf IV *Sent.* 11, 1, 2. *CG* IV, 63. *Quodl.* V, 6, 1. *In Matt.* 26. *In* 1 *Cor.* 11, *lect.* 5

[c] In saying this, St Thomas is formulating a point of view and using its language. Actually, the body of Christ in the Eucharist is not locally there at all. See later, 76, 5.

since anything that is locally moved begins to be somewhere only by leaving where it was. Second, every bodily thing that is moved from place to place must pass through all the intermediate places, and there is no question of that in the present case. Third, it is impossible that the one movement of a bodily thing that is being locally moved should end up at the same time in different places; now the body of Christ in this sacrament begins simultaneously to be in different places.[c] For these reasons it remains that there is no other way in which the body of Christ can begin to be in this sacrament except through the substance of the bread being changed into it. Now, what is changed into something else is no longer there after the change. The reality of Christ's body in this sacrament demands, then, that the substance of the bread be no longer there after the consecration.

Secondly, this position contradicts the form of this sacrament which says, 'This is my body'.[d] This would not be true if the substance of the bread was still there, as the substance of bread is not Christ's body. One would rather have to say, 'Here is my body'.

Thirdly, it would go against the reverence which is accorded to this sacrament if there were another substance present there which ought not to be given the worship of *latria*.

Fourthly, it would not correspond to the rite of the Church which forbids us to receive the body of Christ after taking bodily food but allows us to take one consecrated host after another.

This position should, then, be avoided as being heretical.

Hence: 1. God joined *his godhead*, that is, the power of his godhead, to the bread and wine, not to leave them to remain, but to make from them his body and his blood.

2. In the other sacraments we have not got Christ himself really, as we have in this sacrament. Hence in the others the substance of the material element remains, but not in this one.

3. The appearances which remain in this sacrament, as we shall say later on,[6] are enough to bring out what the sacrament signifies; it is actually through the accidents that the nature of any substance is discerned.

article 3. *is the substance of the bread annihilated when this sacrament is consecrated, or is it perhaps reduced to a more elementary kind of matter*

THE THIRD POINT:[1] 1. It seems that when this sacrament is consecrated, the substance of the bread is annihilated, or at least reduced to a more elementary kind of matter. Whatever has a bodily nature must be somewhere.

---

[d] '*This*' means this thing, this reality, this substance, underlying the visible appearances, the accidental qualities which are the object of sight and of the other senses.

substantia panis, quæ est quiddam corporale, non manet in hoc sacramento, ut dictum est:[2] nec etiam est dare aliquem locum ubi sit.* Ergo non est aliquid post consecrationem. Igitur aut est annihilata, aut in præjacentem materiam resoluta.

2. Præterea, illud quod est terminus a quo in qualibet mutatione non remanet, nisi forte in potentia materiæ; sicut, quando ex aere fit ignis, forma aëris non manet nisi in potentia materiæ; et similiter quando ex albo fit nigrum. Sed in hoc sacramento substantia panis et vini se habet sicut terminus a quo, corpus autem vel sanguis Christi sicut terminus ad quem: dicit enim Ambrosius, *Ante benedictionem alia species nominatur, post benedictionem corpus significatur.*[3] Ergo, facta consecratione, substantia panis vel vini non manet, nisi forte resoluta in suam materiam.

3. Præterea, oportet alterum contradictoriorum esse verum. Sed hæc est falsa, 'Facta consecratione, substantia panis vel vini est aliquid'. Ergo hæc est vera, 'Substantia panis vel vini est nihil'.

SED CONTRA est quod Augustinus dicit, *Deus non est causa tendendi in non esse.*[4] Sed hoc sacramentum divina virtute perficitur. Ergo in hoc sacramento non annihilatur substantia panis aut vini.

RESPONSIO: Dicendum quod, quia substantia panis vel vini non manet in hoc sacramento, quidam, impossibile reputantes quod substantia panis vel vini in corpus vel sanguinem Christi convertatur, posuerunt quod per consecrationem substantia panis vel vini vel resolvitur in præjacentem materiam, vel quod annihiletur.

Præjacens autem materia in quam corpora mixta resolvi possunt, sunt quatuor elementa: non enim potest fieri resolutio in materiam primam ita quod sine forma existat, quia materia sine forma esse non potest. Cum autem post consecrationem nihil sub speciebus sacramenti remaneat nisi corpus et sanguis, oportebit dicere quod elementa in quæ resoluta est

---

*Piana: *fit*

[2] 3a. 75, 2

[3] *De Mysteriis* 9. PL 16, 424. Gratian, *Decretum* 3, 2, 74. *Omnia quæcumque*. Richter-Friedberg I, 1344

[4] *Eighty-three Questions* 21. PL 40, 16

[a] The point here is that bread is solid and bulky. If it is reduced to its basic and less bulky elements—the four elements of medieval physics—it will require less space. Also, the substance of the bread has lost its original accidents. It must have accidents, even if more *subtle* accidents than before.

[b] These are examples of what is called substantial and accidental changes. In the first case, the substance is changed in its depths, where primal matter (pure potentiality) is actuated by substantial form. This is the hylomorphic theory of the constitution of bodily substance. In the second case, the substance is changed only on its surface.

Now the substance of the bread is of a bodily nature, and it no longer remains in this sacrament, as we have just seen.[2] But there is no place for it to go. Therefore, it can no longer exist. It must then be reduced to nothing or at least to a more elementary kind of matter.[a]

2. Moreover, the *terminus a quo* of any change does not remain, except to the extent that it is now in the potentiality of the subject of the change: for example, when fire is made from air, the form of air does not remain, except in the potentiality of matter; and it is the same when something black is made from something white.[b] Now, in this sacrament the substance of the bread and wine is the *terminus a quo* and the body and blood of Christ is the *terminus ad quem*. As Ambrose in his *De Officiis* says, *before the consecration it is called by the name of another nature, after the consecration it is called the body.*[3] Hence, when the consecration has taken place, the substance of the bread and wine no longer remains. It may be that they are reduced into a more elementary kind of matter.

3. Again, one or other of two contradictories must be true. Now it is untrue to say, 'After the consecration the substance of the bread and wine is something'. Therefore, it must be true to say, 'The substance of the bread and wine is nothing'.

ON THE OTHER HAND, Augustine says in his *Eighty-three Questions*, *God is not the cause that anything should tend towards non-existence.*[4] But this sacrament is a work of divine power. Therefore, the substance of the bread and wine is not annihilated.

REPLY: The substance of the bread and wine does not remain in this sacrament. Some theologians thought it was impossible that they should be changed into the body and blood of Christ.[c] They held then that at the consecration the substance of the bread and wine is either reduced to its underlying material constituents or annihilated.

These underlying material constituents, into which mixed bodily natures can be resolved, are the four elements. There is no question of a resolution into primal matter, leaving it without any form at all, because primal matter cannot be without a form. Now, since after the consecration nothing remains under the sacramental appearances but the body and the blood, we shall have to say that the elements into which the substance of the

[c]The reference is to William of Paris (*De Sacramento Eucharistiæ*, 1) and Roland Bandinelli (see the Master of the Sentences, Book 4, 11, 2 *Quidam vero*). But the later theologians of the Scotist tradition, although they use the term '*conversio*', are really in agreement with William of Paris, and hold with him that the substance of the bread and wine is annihilated. Roland thought it was reduced to more elemental constituents.

substantia panis et vini, inde discedant per motum localem. Quod sensu perciperetur. Similiter etiam substantia panis vel vini manet usque ad ultimum instans consecrationis. In ultimo autem instanti consecrationis jam est ibi substantia vel corporis vel sanguinis Christi: sicut in ultimo instanti generationis jam inest forma. Unde non erit dare aliquod instans in quo sit ibi præjacens materia.

Non enim potest dici quod paulatim substantia panis vel vini resolvatur in præjacentem materiam, vel successive egrediatur de loco specierum. Quia, si hoc inciperet fieri in ultimo instanti suæ consecrationis, simul sub aliqua parte hostiæ esset corpus Christi cum substantia panis: quod est contra prædicta. Si vero incipiat fieri ante consecrationem, erit dare aliquod tempus in quo sub aliqua parte hostiæ neque erit substantia panis, neque erit corpus Christi: quod est inconveniens.

Et hoc ipsimet perpendisse videntur. Unde posuerunt aliud sub disjunctione, scilicet quod annihiletur. Sed nec hoc potest esse. Quia non erit dare aliquem modum quo corpus Christi verum incipiat esse in hoc sacramento nisi per conversionem substantiæ panis in ipsum: quæ quidem conversio tollitur, posita vel annihilatione panis vel resolutione in præjacentem materiam. Similiter etiam non est dare unde talis resolutio vel annihilatio in hoc sacramento causetur: cum effectus sacramenti significetur per formam; neutrum autem horum significatur per hæc verba formæ, 'Hoc est corpus meum'.

Unde patet prædictam positionem esse falsam.

1. Ad primum ergo dicendum quod substantia panis vel vini, facta consecratione, neque sub speciebus sacramenti manet, neque alibi. Non tamen sequitur quod annihiletur: convertitur enim in corpus Christi. Sicut non sequitur, si aër ex quo generatus est ignis, non sit ibi vel alibi, quod sit annihilatus.

2. Ad secundum dicendum quod forma quæ est terminus a quo non convertitur in aliam formam, sed una forma succedit alteri in subjecto: et ideo prima forma non remanet nisi in potentia materiæ. Sed hic substantia panis convertitur in corpus Christi, ut supra dictum est.[5] Unde ratio non sequitur.

---

[5]In the body of the article; 3a. 75, 2

[d]The idea that the substance of the bread could leave at the very instant the body of Christ is present is ruled out by the fact that bodily movement takes time and is not instantaneous.

[e]This is the key-principle of St Thomas. Scotist theologians do not agree. They think of the body of Christ as being brought in from without. This is called the adduction-theory. They think of annihilating the bread and of doing something to Christ's body, analogous to local motion. St Thomas thinks of doing something only to the bread—*changing* it into Christ's body.

[f]Note that St Thomas qualifies the annihilation theory (and implicitly the adduction theory) as false, not as heretical.

bread and wine has been resolved have departed, and this by local motion. But our senses would have perceived this. And, again, the substance of the bread or wine remain until the last instant of the consecration. In the last instant of the consecration we already have the substance of the body or of the blood of Christ, just as in the last instant of generation the new form is present. There could then be no instant in which the underlying material elements could be present.

Nor could we say that the substance of the bread and wine is gradually reduced to its underlying material elements or that it gradually[d] departs from the place occupied by the sacramental appearances. Because, if this were to begin to happen in the last instant of the consecration of the host, under a part of the host you would have the body of Christ along with the substance of bread. But this has been already ruled out. If this were to begin to happen before the instant of consecration, there would be some time during which under a part of the host you would have neither the substance of bread nor the body of Christ. This would be a most undesirable situation.

These theologians were aware of these difficulties. Accordingly they postulated an alternative, namely annihilation. But this also is impossible. There is absolutely no other way in which the real body of Christ can begin to exist in this sacrament, except by the changing of the substance of the bread into it.[e] But there is no room for this change, if you say that the bread is annihilated or that it is reduced to its underlying elementary kinds of matter. It is also impossible to find a cause for such a reduction or annihilation in this sacrament. In a sacrament the effect should be signified by the form of the sacrament. But neither reduction nor annihilation is signified by the words of the form, 'This is my body'.

The position, then, of these theologians is clearly false.[f]

Hence: 1. After the consecration the substance of the bread and wine is neither under the sacramental appearances nor anywhere else. But it does not follow that it is annihilated; for it is changed into the body of Christ. Likewise, if the air from which fire has been made is no longer here or there, it does not follow that it has been annihilated.

2. The form which is the *terminus a quo* is not changed into the other form, but one form succeeds to another in the same subject; hence the first form does not remain except in so far as it is in the potentiality of the matter. But here the very substance of the bread is changed into the body of Christ, as we have said.[5] Therefore, the objection does not conclude.[g]

---

[g]The Eucharistic change is miraculous and unique. It is a passing of complete substance, matter and form, into complete substance. The substantial change of the Aristotelean hylomorphic theory is the reduction of a first form into the potentiality

Footnote g continued on page 68

3. Ad tertium dicendum quod, licet post consecrationem hæc sit falsa, 'Substantia panis est aliquid'; id tamen in quod substantia panis conversa est, est aliquid. Et ideo substantia panis non est annihilata.

articulus 4. *utrum panis possit converti in corpus Christi*

AD QUARTUM sic proceditur:[1] 1. Videtur quod panis non possit converti in corpus Christi. Conversio enim quædam mutatio est. Sed in omni mutatione oportet esse aliquod subjectum, quod prius est in potentia et postea est in actu: ut enim dicitur *Physic.*, *motus est actus existentis in potentia.*[2] Non est autem dare aliquod subjectum substantiæ panis et corporis Christi: quia de ratione substantiæ est quod *non sit in subjecto*, ut dicitur in *Prædicamentis.*[3] Non ergo potest esse quod tota substantia panis convertatur in corpus Christi.

2. Præterea, forma illius in quod aliquid convertitur de novo incipit esse in materia ejus quod in ipsum convertitur; sicut cum aër convertitur in ignem prius non existentem forma ignis incipit de novo esse in materia aëris, et similiter cum cibus convertitur in hominem prius non existentem forma hominis incipit esse de novo in materia cibi. Si ergo panis convertitur in corpus Christi, necesse est quod forma corporis Christi de novo incipiat esse in materia panis: quod est falsum. Non ergo panis convertitur in substantiam corporis Christi.

3. Præterea, quæ sunt secundum se divisa,* nunquam unum eorum fit alterum: sicut albedo nunquam fit nigredo, sed subjectum albedinis fit subjectum nigredinis, ut dicitur in *Physic.*[4] Sed sicut duæ formæ contrariæ sunt secundum se divisæ, utpote principia formalis differentiæ existentes, ita duæ materiæ signatæ sunt secundum se divisæ, utpote principium†

---

of matter and the simultaneous eduction of a second form out of the potentiality of matter. The Eucharistic change of a substance into a (pre-existing) substance is only remotely analogous to the normal change of one substance into another that is thus generated or produced as a result of the succession of substantial forms. For this reason, one must be cautious in speaking of 'producing' the body of Christ. See Art. 8 below.

*Piana: *diversa*, diverse, for *divisa* throughout the argument
†Piana: *principia*

[1]cf IV *Sent.* 11, 1, 3, i. *CG* IV, 63. *Quodl.* V, 6, 1. *In* 1 *Cor.* 11, *lect.* 4, 5. *Contra Græcos et Armenos* 8
[2]*Physics* I, 6. 201a10 [3]*Categories* 3. 2a13 & 3a7
[4]*Physics* V, 3. 188a31

[a]In the hylomorphic theory, form *passes into* form—blackness, for example, into whiteness—by going down into the potentiality of the subject and allowing the new

3. Although it is untrue to say, after the consecration, 'The substance of the bread is something real', nevertheless that into which the substance of the bread has been changed is something real. Thus, the substance of the bread is not annihilated.

article 4. can the bread be turned into the body of Christ?

THE FOURTH POINT:[1] 1. It does not seem possible for the bread to be turned into the body of Christ. This conversion would have to obey the general law of change. But the general law of change is that there is a subject which is first of all in potentiality to, and then actuated by, the final actuation. As Aristotle puts it, *change is the actuation of that which is still in potentiality*[2] (to the final actuation). But there is no subject underlying the substance of the bread and the substance of the body of Christ, because it is of the nature of substance *not to be in a subject*, as Aristotle says.[3] The whole substance of the bread cannot then be turned into the body of Christ.[a]

2. Moreover, the form of that into which a thing is changed begins to exist in the matter[b] of that which is changed into it; thus when air is turned into fire, which did not previously exist, the form of the fire begins to be in the matter of the air; and likewise, when food is changed into a man who already exists,[c] the form of that man begins now to exist in the matter of the food. If then the bread is changed into the body of Christ, you will have to say that the form of Christ's body is now beginning to be in the primal matter of the bread.[d] But this is not true. We cannot then say that the bread is converted into the body of Christ.

3. Furthermore, when two realities are essentially opposed, one of them never becomes the other; thus whiteness never becomes blackness, although the subject of whiteness may become the subject of blackness, as Aristotle remarks.[4] Now just as two contrary forms are essentially opposed as being the very sources of formal difference, so also two individuated parts of matter are essentially opposed as being the very sources of

---

form simultaneously to emerge. In the Eucharistic conversion whole substance *passes into* whole substance. The point of the objection is that this cannot be, because there is no underlying subject into which the first substance descends and from which the second substance emerges. See note *g* on previous article.

[b]This is the primal matter, *materia prima*, pure potentiality, in the case of substantial change, as in the turning of air into fire. In the case of accidental or superficial change, the substance itself is the subject or matter in which the change takes place.

[c]The translation 'who did not previously exist' does not fit the sense.

[d]Actually, a proposition of the Venerable Antonio Rosmini, condemned by Leo XIII in 1888, conceived the Eucharistic change in just such a way.

materialis divisionis existentes. Ergo non potest esse quod hæc materia panis fiat hæc materia qua individuatur corpus Christi. Et ita non potest esse quod substantia hujus panis convertatur in substantiam corporis Christi.

SED CONTRA est quod Eusebius Emesenus dicit, *Novum tibi et impossibile esse non debet quod in Christi substantiam terrena et mortalia convertuntur.*[5]

RESPONSIO: Dicendum quod, sicut supra dictum est, cum in hoc sacramento sit verum corpus Christi, nec incipiat ibi esse de novo per motum localem; cum etiam nec corpus Christi sit ibi sicut in loco, ut ex dictis patet,[6] necesse est dicere quod ibi incipiat esse per conversionem substantiæ panis in ipsum.

Hæc tamen conversio non est similis conversionibus naturalibus, sed est omnino supernaturalis, sola Dei virtute effecta. Unde Ambrosius dicit, in libro *de Sacramentis*, *Liquet quod præter naturæ ordinem Virgo generavit. Et hoc quod conficimus, corpus ex Virgine est. Quid igitur quæris naturæ ordinem in Christi corpore: cum præter naturam sit ipse Dominus Jesus partus ex Virgine?*[7] Et super illud *Joan.* vi, *Verba quæ ego locutus sum vobis* scilicet de hoc sacramento, *spiritus et vita sunt*,[8] dicit Chrysostomus, *Id est: spiritualia sunt, nihil habentia carnale neque consequentiam naturalem, sed eruta sunt ab omni tali necessitate quæ in terra, et a legibus quæ hic positæ sunt.*[9]

Manifestum est enim quod omne agens agit inquantum est actu. Quodlibet autem agens creatum est determinatum in suo actu: cum sit determinati generis et speciei. Et ideo cujuslibet agentis creati actio fertur super aliquem determinatum actum. Determinatio autem cujuslibet rei in esse actuali est per ejus formam. Unde nullum agens naturale vel creatum potest agere nisi ad immutationem formæ. Et propter hoc omnis conversio quæ fit secundum leges naturæ, est formalis. Sed Deus est infinitus actus, ut in Prima Parte habitum est.[10] Unde ejus actio se extendit ad totam

---

[5]Pseudo-Isidore, *Sermones* 4. PL 83, 1225. cf Gratian, *Decretum* 3, 2, 35 *Quia corpus*. Richter-Friedberg 1, 1325

[6]3a. 75, 1 ad 3

[7]*De Mysteriis* 9. PL 16, 424. Gratian, *Decretum* 3, 2, 40 & 69. Richter-Friedberg 1, 1328 & 1340

[8]*John* 6, 64

[9]*In Joan.* Homily 47. PG 59, 265

[10]1a. 7, 1; 25, 2

[e]This is St Thomas's constant alternative—either local bringing in or changing what is already there.

[f]This is the metaphysical idea that the order of action is relative to the order of being. The higher a thing is in the order of being, the more actual it is, the greater is its power of action. To exist is to be able to cause and, where creatures are con-

individual distinction. Therefore, it cannot be that the individuated matter of this bread should become the matter which gives its individuation to the body of Christ. Thus it is impossible for the substance of this piece of bread to be changed into the substance of the body of Christ.

ON THE OTHER HAND, Eusebius of Emesa says, *do not think of it as surprising and impossible that earthly and corruptible elements should be changed into the substance of Christ.*[5]

REPLY: As we said earlier on, since in this sacrament we have the reality of Christ's body, and since it did not begin to be there by local motion (indeed, it is not there as in place, as we saw),[6] nothing remains but to say that it begins to be there because the substance of the bread and wine is turned into it.[e]

This conversion, however, is not like any natural change, but it is entirely beyond the powers of nature and is brought about purely by God's power. It is for this reason that Ambrose says, *it is clear that for the virgin to conceive was beyond the powers of nature. But what we consecrate is that body which was born of the virgin. Why then do you look for natural laws where the body of Christ is concerned, seeing that the Lord Jesus was born of the virgin in a way that transcends the natural order?*[7] And commenting on the text of *John*, *the words that I have spoken to you* concerning this sacrament *are spirit and life,*[8] Chrysostom says, *they are spiritual, not to be taken in a carnal sense or according to the laws of nature, but they have been lifted above all earthly necessity and natural laws.*[9]

Now it is clear that every agent is effective to the extent that it is in act.[f] But every created agent is limited in its actuality[g] since it is found within the limitations of a genus and of a species.[h] Hence, the action of every created agent has a definite and limited range. Now what limits everything in its actual existence is its form. Hence, no natural or created agent can act except to change a form. For this reason every change that takes place according to the laws of nature is a changing of form. But God is unlimited actuality as we saw in the first part of this work.[10] Hence, his

---

cerned, to exist demands the exercise of causality. *Agere sequitur esse,* action follows on existing.

[g]The limiting shadow of potentiality falls across every created thing. The lower a thing is in the order of being, the darker this shadow is. All created substances, no matter how high, are potential to their existence, and potential also to accidental perfections. And in bodily things the very substance is a composition of potentiality and act.

[h]To be limited, defined, in the logical order of intelligibility or essence corresponds to, and is a sign of being limited or contracted, in the order of realness or existence.

naturam entis. Non igitur solum potest perficere conversionem formalem, ut scilicet diversæ formæ sibi in eodem subjecto succedant: sed conversionem totius entis, ut scilicet tota substantia hujus convertatur in totam substantiam illius.

Et hoc agitur divina virtute in hoc sacramento. Nam tota substantia panis convertitur in totam substantiam corporis Christi, et tota substantia vini in totam substantiam sanguinis Christi. Unde hæc conversio non est formalis, sed substantialis. Nec continetur inter species motus naturalis, sed proprio nomine potest dici 'transubstantiatio'.

1. Ad primum igitur dicendum quod objectio illa procedit de mutatione formali; quia formæ proprium est in materia vel subjecto esse. Non autem habet locum in conversione totius substantiæ. Unde, cum hæc conversio substantialis importet quendam ordinem substantiarum quarum una convertitur in alteram, est sicut in subjecto in utraque substantia, sicut ordo et numerus.

2. Ad secundum dicendum quod etiam illa objectio procedit de conversione formali, seu mutatione; quia oportet, sicut dictum est, formam esse in materia vel subjecto. Non autem habet locum in conversione totius substantiæ, cujus non est accipere aliquod subjectum.

3. Ad tertium dicendum quod virtute agentis finiti non potest forma in formam mutari, nec materia in materiam. Sed virtute agentis infiniti, quod habet actionem in totum ens, potest talis conversio fieri: quia utrique formæ et utrique materiæ est communis natura entis; et id quod est entitatis in una, potest auctor* entis convertere ad id quod est entitatis in altera, sublato eo per quod ab illa distinguebatur.

articulus 5. utrum in hoc sacramento remaneant accidentia panis et vini

AD QUINTUM sic proceditur:[1] 1. Videtur quod in hoc sacramento non remaneant accidentia panis et vini. Remoto enim priori, removetur posterius. Sed substantia est naturaliter prior accidente, ut probatur *Meta.*[2] Cum ergo, facta consecratione, non remaneat substantia panis in hoc sacramento, videtur quod non possint remanere accidentia ejus.

2. Præterea, in sacramento veritatis non debet esse aliqua deceptio. Sed per accidentia judicamus de substantia. Videtur ergo quod decipiatur

---

*Piana: *actor*, the accomplisher

[1]cf IV *Sent.* 11, 1, 1, ii; 12, 1, 1, ii. *CG* IV, 62, 63, 65. *Contra Græcos et Armenos* 8. *In* 1 *Cor.* 11, *lect.* 5

[2]*Metaphysics* VI, 1. 1028a32

[3]Or transformation.

action reaches out to the whole extent of the being of a thing. He is then able to bring about not merely a changing of form, so that different forms follow after one another in the same subject, but the changing of the whole being of a thing, so that the complete substance of this is changed into the complete substance of that.

And this actually happens by divine power in this sacrament. The complete substance of the bread is converted into the complete substance of Christ's body, and the complete substance of the wine into the complete substance of Christ's blood. Hence this change is not a formal change, but a substantial one. It does not belong to the natural kinds of change, and it can be called by a name proper to itself—'transubstantiation'.

Hence: 1. This objection is concerned with formal change,[1] because it is a property of all forms to be in matter or in a subject. It does not apply here where it is a question of the complete substance. But since this substantial conversion involves a certain order of substances, one being converted into the other, you could say that the subject is to be found in both substances, in the same way as order and number are.

2. This objection also is thinking of a formal conversion or change, because as we have just said, form must have matter or a subject. But it is wide of the mark where it is a question of changing the complete substance and where there is consequently no subject.

3. Form cannot pass into form nor matter into matter by the power of a created agent. But the power of an infinite agent which bears on the whole being of a thing can bring about such a change. To the form of each thing and to the matter of each thing the nature *being* is common; and the author of being is able to change that which is *being* in the one into that which is *being* in the other, by taking away what kept this from being that.[j]

article 5. do the accidents of the bread and wine remain in this sacrament?

THE FIFTH POINT:[1] 1. It would seem that the accidents cannot remain in this sacrament. Take away that which is first and you remove that which follows on it. But substance naturally comes before accident, as Aristotle shows.[2] Since then, when the consecration is over, the substance of bread no longer remains in this sacrament, it seems that the accidents cannot possibly remain.

2. Moreover, in this sacrament of truth there should be no deception. Now it is through the accidents that we judge of the substance. It seems that

---

[j]M.-T. Penido, in *Le rôle de l'analogie en théologie dogmatique*, Paris, 1931, p. 437, says that the words of this reply are *the most profound words ever said on the possibility and nature of the Eucharistic conversion.*

humanum judicium si, remanentibus accidentibus, substantia panis non remaneat. Non ergo hoc est conveniens huic sacramento.

3. Præterea, quamvis fides non sit subjecta rationi, non tamen est contra rationem, sed supra ipsam: ut in principio hujus operis[3] dictum est. Sed ratio nostra habet ortum a sensu. Ergo fides nostra non debet esse contra sensum, dum sensus noster judicat esse panem, et fides nostra credit esse substantiam corporis Christi. Non ergo hoc est conveniens huic sacramento, quod accidentia panis subjecta sensibus maneant, et substantia panis non maneat.

4. Præterea, illud quod manet, conversione facta, videtur esse subjectum mutationis. Si ergo accidentia panis manent conversione facta, videtur quod ipsa accidentia sint conversionis subjectum. Quod est impossibile: nam accidentis non est accidens. Non ergo in hoc sacramento debent remanere accidentia panis et vini.

SED CONTRA est quod Augustinus dicit, in libro Sententiarum Prosperi, *Nos in specie panis et vini, quam videmus, res invisibiles, id est carnem et sanguinem honoramus.*[4]

RESPONSIO: Dicendum quod sensu apparet, facta consecratione, omnia accidentia panis et vini remanere. Quod quidem rationabiliter per divinam providentiam fit. Primo quidem, quia non est consuetum hominibus, sed horribile, carnem hominis comedere et sanguinem bibere, proponitur nobis caro et sanguis Christi sumenda sub speciebus illorum quæ frequentius in usum hominis veniunt, scilicet panis et vini.

Secundo, ne hoc sacramentum ab infidelibus irrideretur, si sub specie propria Dominum nostrum manducemus.

Tertio ut, dum invisibiliter corpus et sanguinem Domini nostri sumimus, hoc proficiat ad meritum fidei.

1. Ad primum ergo dicendum quod, sicut dicitur in libro *De Causis*,[5]

---

[3]1a. 1, 6 ad 2; 1, 8

[4]see Lanfranc, *De Corpore et Sanguine Domini* 13. PL 150, 423. Gratian, *Decretum* 3, 2, 41 *Nos autem*. Richter-Friedberg 1, 1328

[5]*De Causis*, prop. 1

[a]Accidents, i.e. quantity, quality and all the other extra-substantial forms that affect a substance and are real only because they inhere in a substance that exists, have the substance as the subject which they affect (essentially) and in which they inhere (existentially). Accidents cannot be the subject in which other accidents inhere, in the sense of deriving their *realness* from the subject of the inhering; they may be the immediate subject which is affected (essentially), as, for example, the mind is affected and enriched by an act of thought. But the subject in which this act of thinking ultimately *inheres* and from which it derives its realness is the existing

our human judgment is deceived if the substance of the bread departs but leaves its accidents behind. It is not right then that this should happen in this sacrament.

3. Again, although faith is not subject to reason, it is not opposed to it, but rather above it, as was said in the beginning of this work.[3] Now our reason starts off from sense-knowledge. Our faith, then, ought not to run counter to what our senses tell us. But to our senses that seems to be bread which our faith affirms to be the substances of Christ's body. It is not then desirable that in this sacrament the accidents of the bread, which are the object of our sense-knowledge, should still remain when the substance of the bread is no longer there.

4. Furthermore, that which still remains after the conversion has taken place would appear to be the subject of the change. If then the accidents of the bread remain after the conversion has taken place, they would seem to be the subject of the change. But this is impossible, because accident cannot be the subject of accident.[a] It is not then desirable in this sacrament that the accidents of the bread and wine should continue to endure.

ON THE OTHER HAND, Augustine says, in Prosper's *Book of Sentences, under the appearances of bread and wine which we see we honour the invisible realities of the flesh and blood.*[4]

REPLY: It is obvious to our senses that, after the consecration, all the accidents of the bread and wine remain. Divine providence very wisely arranged for this. First of all, men have not the custom of eating human flesh and drinking human blood; indeed, the thought revolts them. And so the flesh and blood of Christ are given to us to be taken under the appearances of things in common human use, namely bread and wine.

Secondly, lest this sacrament should be an object of contempt for unbelievers, if we were to eat our Lord under his human appearances.

Thirdly, in taking the body and blood of our Lord in their invisible presence, we increase the merit of our faith.

Hence: 1. As it is said in the *De Causis*,[5] every effect depends more on the

---

person (the substance) who thinks. All change is existential as well as essential; the existential subject is substance only, or in the case of change which affects the very depths of a bodily substance it is *materia prima*, which is something substantial (real substantial potentiality). In this sense, *accidentis non est accidens*, accident is not the subject of accident, and is not the subject of accidental change. The point of the objection is then that accident could not be the subject of this more than accidental, or trans-substantial, change.

effectus plus dependent a causa prima quam a causa secunda. Et ideo virtute Dei, qui est causa prima omnium, fieri potest ut remaneant posteriora, sublatis prioribus.

2. Ad secundum dicendum quod in hoc sacramento nulla est deceptio: sunt enim ibi secundum rei veritatem accidentia, quæ sensibus dijudicantur. Intellectus autem, cujus est proprium objectum substantia, ut dicitur in *De Anima*,[6] per fidem a deceptione præservatur.

3. Et sic patet responsio ad tertium. Nam fides non est contra sensum, sed est de eo ad quod sensus non attingit.

4. Ad quartum dicendum quod hæc conversio non proprie habet subjectum, ut dictum est.[7] Sed tamen accidentia, quæ remanent, habent aliquam similitudinem subjecti.

articulus 6. *utrum, facta consecratione, remaneat in hoc sacramento forma substantialis panis*

AD SEXTUM sic proceditur:[1] 1. Videtur quod, facta consecratione, remaneat in hoc sacramento forma substantialis panis. Dictum est[2] enim quod, facta consecratione, remanent accidentia. Sed, cum panis sit quoddam artificiale, etiam forma ejus est accidens. Ergo remanet, facta consecratione.

2. Præterea, forma corporis Christi est anima: dicitur enim in *De Anima*, quod anima est *actus corporis physici potentia vitam habentis*.[3] Sed non potest dici quod forma substantialis panis convertatur in animam. Ergo videtur quod remaneat, facta consecratione.

3. Præterea, propria operatio rei sequitur formam substantialem ejus. Sed illud quod remanet in hoc sacramento, nutrit, et omnem operationem facit quam faceret panis existens. Ergo forma substantialis panis remanet in hoc sacramento, facta consecratione.

SED CONTRA, forma substantialis panis est de substantia panis. Sed substantia panis convertitur in corpus Christi, sicut dictum est.[4] Ergo forma substantialis panis non manet.

---

[6]Aristotle, *De Anima* III, 6. 430b28
[7]3a. 75, 4 ad 1
[1]IV *Sent.* 11, 1, 1, iii. *In* 1 *Cor.* 11, *lect.* 4 [2]3a. 75, 5
[3]Aristotle, *De Anima*, 2, 1, 5. 412a27
[4]3a. 75, 2–4
[b]Existentially, accidents depend upon the substance *in* which they are. But the accidents—and the substance—depend upon God—*from* whom they are.
[a]The point of the objection is that the form of the bread, what makes it to be bread, its *breadness*, is not really a substantial form at all, but a quality or other accidental form affecting a more fundamental substance. The objector thinks that '*art*', or man's power of making, is only concerned with changes on the superficial level of

first cause than it does on secondary causes. Hence it is that by the power of God, who is the first cause of all things, it can come about that that which naturally follows on something else can still remain when that which is prior to it has been taken away.[b]

2. There is no deception in this sacrament; the accidents, which are the proper object for our senses to deal with, are genuinely there. Our intellect, which is properly concerned with the substance of a thing, as Aristotle says,[6] is kept by faith from being led into error.

3. And the reply to the third objection emerges from this. Our faith is not in opposition to what our senses tell us, but is concerned with something to which our senses do not reach.

4. Strictly speaking, there is no subject in this change, as we have said above.[7] All the same, the accidents which remain do bear a certain resemblance to a subject.

article 6. does the substantial form of the bread remain in this sacrament after the consecration?

THE SIXTH POINT:[1] 1. It seems that in this sacrament when the consecration is over the substantial form of the bread remains. We have just said[2] that the accidents remain after the consecration. Now, seeing that the bread is something produced by man's power of making, its form must be an accident.[a] It still remains then after the consecration.

2. Again, the form of Christ's body is his soul; as Aristotle says, the soul is *what makes a physical body to be such and also makes it fundamentally alive.*[3] But you could not say that the substantial form of the bread is converted into a soul. It follows then that it still remains after the consecration.

3. Moreover, a thing's characteristic operations derive from its substantial form. But whatever it is that remains in this sacrament nourishes and does everything that bread would do if it were there. Therefore, the substantial form of the bread still remains in this sacrament after the consecration.

ON THE OTHER HAND, the substantial form of the bread is part of the substance of the bread. But, as we have seen,[4] the substance of the bread is changed into the body of Christ. Therefore, the substantial form of the bread does not remain.

---

accidental form. Human art makes a house, for example, because it puts prior substantial elements, steel, cement, wood, etc., in a certain order or arrangement, the *houseness*, which makes the house to be such.

RESPONSIO: Dicendum quod quidam posuerunt quod, facta consecratione, non solum remanent accidentia panis, sed etiam forma substantialis ejus. Sed hoc esse non potest. Primo quidem quia, si forma substantialis remaneret, nihil de pane converteretur in corpus Christi nisi sola materia. Et ita sequeretur quod non converteretur in corpus Christi totum, sed in ejus materiam. Quod repugnat formæ sacramenti, qua dicitur, 'hoc est corpus meum'.

Secundo, quia, si forma substantialis panis remaneret, aut remaneret in materia aut a materia separata. Primum autem esse non potest. Quia, si remaneret in materia panis, tunc tota substantia panis remaneret: quod est contra prædicta.[5] In alia autem materia remanere non posset: quia propria forma non est nisi in propria materia. Si autem remaneret a materia separata, jam esset forma intelligibilis actu, et etiam intellectus:* nam omnes formæ a materia separatæ sunt tales.

Tertio, esset inconveniens huic sacramento. Nam accidentia panis in hoc sacramento remanent ut sub eis videatur corpus Christi, non autem sub propria specie, sicut supra dictum est.[6]

Et ideo dicendum est quod forma substantialis panis non manet.

1. Ad primum ergo dicendum quod nihil prohibet arte fieri aliquid cujus forma non est accidens, sed forma substantialis: sicut arte possunt produci ranæ et serpentes. Talem enim formam non producit ars virtute propria, sed virtute naturalium principiorum. Et hoc modo producit formam substantialem panis, virtute ignis decoquentis materiam ex farina et aqua confectam.

2. Ad secundum dicendum quod anima est forma corporis dans ei totum ordinem esse perfecti, scilicet esse, et esse corporeum, et esse animatum, et sic de aliis. Convertitur igitur forma panis in formam corporis Christi secundum quod dat esse corporeum: non autem secundum quod dat esse animatum tali anima.

3. Ad tertium dicendum quod operationum panis quædam consequuntur ipsum ratione accidentium, sicut immutare sensum. Et tales operationes inveniuntur in speciebus panis post consecrationem, propter ipsa accidentia, quæ remanent.

---

*Piana: *intelligens*, and actively understanding

[5]3a. 75, 2

[6]3a. 75, 5

[b]An allusion to what the magicians of Egypt did by their secret arts, see *Exodus* 7, 11 & 8, 7.

[c]The form of the body of Christ at the Last Supper was his soul. The form of the body of the glorious Christ in heaven is his soul. The form of the body of Christ in

REPLY: Some theologians have held that not merely do the accidents of the bread remain after the consecration, but also the substantial form. But this is an impossible position. First of all, if the substantial form were to remain, the only part of the bread that would be changed into Christ's body would be the primal matter. Consequently, this conversion would have for its term, not the complete body of Christ, but its matter. But that would go against the form of this sacrament which is, 'This is my body'.

Secondly, were the substantial form of the bread to remain, it would do so either as informing primal matter or as separate from it. Now the first alternative is ruled out. Because, were it to remain as informing primal matter, then the complete substance of the bread would remain; but we have already seen the opposite.[5] Nor could it remain in some other piece of matter, because each piece of matter is exclusively actuated by the form it has. Were it to remain as separate from matter, it would now be an intelligible form, indeed it would be an intelligence, because all forms separate from matter are such.

Thirdly, it would be out of keeping with the purpose of this sacrament. The appearances of bread remain in this sacrament in order that under them the body of Christ may be seen, and not under his natural appearances, as has been said.[6]

For those reasons we conclude that the substantial form of the bread no longer remains.

Hence: 1. There is no reason why human art should not produce something of which the form is not an accidental one, but a substantial one; for example, frogs and serpents were produced by art.[b] But art does not produce such a form by its own power, but by exploiting the powers of nature. In this way man's artistic powers can produce the substantial form of bread, by using fire which cooks the matter composed of flour and water.

2. The soul is the form of the body and gives it the complete range of its perfect being, namely its being, its being a body, its being alive and so on. The form of the bread is changed into the form of the body of Christ precisely in so far as it is the principle of its being a body, and not in so far as it is the principle of its being alive in the precise way that it is.[c]

3. Some of the things that bread does, it does because of its accidents, as, for example, the impression it makes on our senses. We can observe activities of this kind in the appearances of bread after the consecration; they derive from the accidents themselves, which are still there.

---

the tomb was not his soul. Had a consecration taken place then the form of the bread would have been changed, not into his soul, but into whatever was then the form of his body. See 76, 1 ad 1.

Quædam autem operationes consequuntur panem vel ratione materiæ, sicut quod convertitur in aliquid; vel ratione formæ substantialis, sicut est operatio consequens speciem ejus, puta quod *confirmat cor hominis.* Et tales operationes inveniuntur in hoc sacramento, non propter formam vel materiam quæ remaneat, sed quia miraculose conferuntur ipsis accidentibus, ut infra dicetur.[7]

articulus 7. utrum ista conversio fiat in instanti, vel fiat successive

AD SEPTIMUM sic proceditur:[1] 1. Videtur quod ista conversio non fiat in instanti, sed fiat successive. In hac enim conversione prius est substantia panis, et postea substantia corporis Christi. Non ergo utrumque est in eodem instanti, sed in duobus instantibus. Sed inter quælibet duo instantia est tempus medium. Ergo oportet quod hæc conversio fiat secundum successionem temporis quod est inter ultimum instans quo est ibi panis, et primum instans quo est ibi corpus Christi.

2. Præterea, in omni conversione est *fieri* et *factum esse.* Sed hæc duo non sunt simul: quia quod fit, non est; quod autem factum est, jam est. Ergo in hac conversione est prius et posterius. Et ita oportet quod non sit instantanea, sed successiva.

3. Præterea, Ambrosius dicit quod istud sacramentum Christi *sermone conficitur.*[2] Sed sermo Christi successive profertur. Ergo hæc conversio fit successive.

SED CONTRA est quod hæc conversio perficitur virtute infinita, cujus est subito operari.

RESPONSIO: Dicendum quod aliqua mutatio est instantanea triplici ratione. Uno quidem modo, ex parte formæ, quæ est terminus mutationis. Si enim sit aliqua forma quæ recipiat magis aut minus, successive acquiritur subjecto, sicut sanitas. Et ideo, quia forma substantialis non recipit magis et minus, inde est quod subito fit ejus introductio in materia. Alio modo, ex parte subjecti, quod quandoque successive præparatur ad susceptionem formæ: et ideo aqua successive calefit. Quando vero ipsum subjectum est in ultima dispositione ad formam, subito recipit ipsam: sicut diaphanum subito illuminatur. Tertio, ex parte agentis, quod est infinitæ virtutis: unde statim potest materiam ad formam disponere. Sicut dicitur *Marc.* vii, quod, cum Christus dixisset, *Ephphetha, quod est adaperire, statim apertæ sunt aures hominis, et solutum est vinculum linguæ ejus.*[3]

---

[7]3a. 77, 3 ad 2, 3; 5, 6
[1]cf IV *Sent.* 11, 1, 3, ii. *Quodl.* VII, 4, 2

But there are other things that bread does, either because of the primal matter, as when it changes into something else, or because of the substantial form, when it exercises its specific causality, as when *it strengthens the heart of man*. Such operations can be observed in this sacrament, not because of any still remaining form or matter, but because the accidents have been miraculously allowed to produce them, as we shall see later on.[7]

article 7. is this change an instantaneous one?

THE SEVENTH POINT:[1] 1. It would seem that this change does not take place instantaneously but that it is a successive one. In this change there is first the substance of the bread and then the substance of Christ's body. You have not got both in the same instant, but in two distinct instants. But between every two instants there is an intervening time. Therefore, this change must take place in the flow of time between the last instant when the bread is there and the first instant when the body of Christ is there.

2. Besides, in every change we can distinguish the *becoming* and the *having become*. These two do not coincide, because what is in the process of becoming does not yet exist, but what has actually become now exists. Therefore, there is a first and after in this change. It must then be successive and not instantaneous.

3. Moreover, Ambrose says that this sacrament is consecrated by *the utterance of Christ's words*.[2] But the words of Christ are uttered one after the other. Therefore this change takes place successively.

ON THE OTHER HAND, this change is wrought by an infinite power which produces its effects instantaneously.

REPLY: There are three reasons why a particular change should be an instantaneous one. First, the kind of form which is the term of the change, may demand this. If it is the kind of form which admits of degrees, as, for example, health, the subject can acquire it by degrees. But since substantial form *does not admit of degrees*, its being acquired by its subject is a sudden affair.

Again, it may be that a subject is gradually prepared to receive a form, as water is gradually heated. But when it is completely ready to receive the form, it does so instantaneously, as, for example, when a transparent body is suddenly filled with light. Finally, the agent may be one of infinite power, which in one instant can make the matter ready to receive the form. We read in *Mark* that when Christ had said *Ephphatha, that is, Be opened. And immediately his ears were opened, his tongue was released.*[3]

[2]*De Sacramentis* IV, 4. PL 16, 459

[3]*Mark* 7, 34, 35

Et his tribus rationibus hæc conversio est instantanea. Primo quidem, quia substantia corporis Christi, ad quam terminatur ista conversio, non suscipit magis neque minus. Secundo, quia in hac conversione non est aliquod subjectum, quod successive præparetur. Tertio, quia agitur Dei virtute infinita.

1. Ad primum ergo dicendum quod quidam[4] non simpliciter concedunt quod inter quælibet duo instantia sit tempus medium. Dicunt enim quod hoc habet locum in duobus instantibus quæ referuntur ad eundem motum, non autem in duobus instantibus quæ referuntur ad diversa. Unde inter instans quod mensurat finem quietis, et aliud instans quod mensurat principium motus, non est tempus medium. Sed in hoc decipiuntur. Quia unitas temporis et instantis, vel etiam pluralitas eorum, non accipitur secundum quoscumque motus, sed secundum primum motum cæli, qui est mensura omnis motus et quietis.

Et ideo alii hoc concedunt in tempore quod mensurat motum dependentem ex motu cæli. Sunt autem quidam motus ex motu cæli non dependentes, nec ab eo mensurati: sicut in *Prima Parte* dictum est de motibus angelorum.[5] Unde inter duo instantia illis motibus respondentia, non est tempus medium. Sed hoc non habet locum in proposito. Quia, quamvis ista conversio secundum se non habeat ordinem ad motum cæli, consequitur tamen prolationem verborum, quam necesse est motu cæli mensurari. Et ideo necesse est inter quælibet duo instantia circa istam conversionem signata esse tempus medium.

Quidam ergo dicunt quod instans in quo ultimo est panis, et instans in quo primo est corpus Christi, sunt quidem duo per comparationem ad mensurata, sed sunt unum per comparationem ad tempus mensurans: sicut, cum duæ lineæ se contingunt, sunt duo puncta ex parte duarum linearum, unum autem punctum ex parte loci continentis. Sed hoc non est simile. Quia instans et tempus particularibus motibus non est mensura intrinseca, sicut linea et punctus corporibus: sed solum extrinseca, sicut corporibus locus.

Unde alii dicunt quod est idem instans re, sed aliud ratione. Sed secundum hoc sequeretur quod realiter opposita essent simul. Nam diversitas rationis non variat aliquid ex parte rei.

Et ideo dicendum est quod hæc conversio, sicut dictum est,[6] perficitur per verba Christi, quæ a sacerdote proferuntur, ita quod ultimum instans prolationis verborum est primum instans in quo est in sacramento corpus Christi, in toto autem tempore præcedente est ibi substantia panis. Cujus

---

[4]cf Albert the Great, *In* IV *Sent.* 11, 3. Bonaventure, *In* IV *Sent.* 1, 1, 5
[5]1a. 53, 3
[6]3a. 75, 3

And for these three reasons this change is instantaneous. First, the substance of the body of Christ which is the term of this conversion does not allow of degrees. Second, in this change, there is no subject to allow of a gradual preparation. Third, the whole thing happens by the infinite power of God.

Hence: 1. Some[4] say that it is not absolutely true that between every two instants there is always an intervening time. They say that this is true enough when the two instants refer to the same change process, but not when they do not. For example, between the last instant of a thing's being at rest and the first instant of its being in movement they say there is no intervening time. But they are mistaken in this. Because the unity and plurality of times and instants does not follow on this or that particular change process, but on the first change process of the heavens which is the measure of all other change and rest.

For this reason, others concede (that between every two instants there is always an intervening time) in the time that measures all changes that depend on the movements of the heavens. But there are changes that do not depend on the movements of the heavens and that are not measured by them, as, for example, the changes that happen in the angels, of which we spoke in the *Prima Pars.*[5] Between two instants corresponding to such changes there is no intervening time. But all this is irrelevant here. Although the Eucharistic change in itself has no connection with the movements of the heavens, it is bound up with the uttering of the words, and they are necessarily measured by the heavenly movements. So we must conclude that between any two instants at all in connection with the Eucharistic change there is always an intervening time.

Some would then hold that the last instant in which you have the bread and the first instant in which you have the body of Christ are really the same instant in regard of the measuring time, although they are two in regard of the things being measured. They see an analogy in two lines passing through one another; the point of intersection is two when you think of the two lines, it is one when you think of the *place* containing the point. But there is really no analogy here. Instant and time are not a measure which is intrinsic to particular changes, as line and point are to bodies; they are extrinsic to it, in the way that place is to bodies.

Others would then say that it is the same instant really, but two instants mentally. But it would follow on this position that opposites would really coincide. A mental distinction does not imply any real one.

It remains then to say that this change (as already noted)[6] is brought about by the words of Christ, which are uttered by the priest; the change happens in such a way that the last instant of the utterance of the words is the first instant in which the body of Christ is in the sacrament; during

temporis non est accipere aliquod instans proxime præcedens ultimum: quia tempus non componitur ex instantibus consequenter se habentibus ut probatur in *Physic.*[7] Et ideo est quidem dare instans in quo est corpus Christi, non est autem dare ultimum instans in quo sit substantia panis, sed est dare ultimum tempus. Et idem est in mutationibus naturalibus, ut patet per Philosophum, in *Physic.*[8]

2. Ad secundum dicendum quod in mutationibus instantaneis simul est *fieri* et *factum esse*: sicut simul est illuminari et illuminatum esse. Dicitur enim in talibus 'factum' esse secundum quod jam est; 'fieri' autem, secundum quod ante non fuit.

3. Ad tertium dicendum quod ista conversio, sicut dictum est,[9] fit in ultimo instanti prolationis verborum: tunc enim completur verborum significatio, quæ est efficax in sacramentorum formis. Et ideo non sequitur quod ista conversio sit successiva.

articulus 8. *utrum hæc sit vera, 'Ex pane fit corpus Christi'*

AD OCTAVUM sic proceditur:[1] 1. Videtur quod hæc sit falsa, 'Ex pane fit corpus Christi'. Omne enim id ex quo fit aliquid, est id quod fit illud, sed non convertitur: dicimus enim quod 'ex albo fit nigrum', et quod 'album fit nigrum'; et licet dicamus quod 'homo fiat niger', non tamen dicimus quod 'ex homine fiat nigrum', ut patet in *Physic.*[2] Si ergo verum est quod ex pane fiat corpus Christi, verum erit dicere quod 'panis fiat corpus Christi'. Quod videtur esse falsum: quia panis non est subjectum factionis, sed magis est terminus. Ergo non vere dicitur quod ex pane fit corpus Christi.

2. Præterea, fieri terminatur ad esse, vel ad factum esse. Sed hæc nunquam est vera, 'Panis est corpus Christi', vel, 'Panis est factus corpus Christi', vel etiam, 'Panis erit corpus Christi'. Ergo videtur quod nec hæc sit vera, 'Ex pane fit corpus Christi'.

3. Præterea, omne id ex quo fit aliquid, convertitur in id quod fit ex eo. Sed hæc videtur esse falsa, 'Panis convertitur in corpus Christi': quia hæc conversio videtur esse miraculosior quam creatio; in qua tamen non dicitur quod non ens convertatur in ens. Ergo videtur quod etiam hæc sit falsa, 'Ex pane fit corpus Christi'.

4. Præterea, illud ex quo fit aliquid, potest esse illud. Sed hæc est falsa,

---

[7]*Physics* VII, 1. 231b9
[8]*Physics* VIII, 8. 263b9
[9]ad 1
[1]cf IV *Sent.* 11, 1, 4
[2]*Physics* I, 5. 188a35

all the preceding time, the substance of the bread is there. You are not to imagine that this time is ended by an instant immediately prior to the last instant (of the utterance of the words); time is not composed of instants one immediately after the other, as Aristotle proves.[7] Hence, you can point to an instant in which we now have the body of Christ, but you cannot point to an instant and say, *that is the last of the substance of the bread*, because the last of the bread is time. It is the same in natural changes, as Aristotle shows.[8]

2. In instantaneous changes the *becoming* and the *having become* coincide, as, for example, becoming and having become illuminated. In such changes, when we think of a thing as it actually is, we speak of its 'having become'; when we think of when it was not, we speak of its 'becoming'.

3. This change, as we have just said,[9] takes place in the last instant of the utterance of the words; it is only then the significance of the words is fully complete, and in sacramental forms that is what is effective. It does not follow then that this change must be a successive one.

article 8. is this proposition true, 'The body of Christ comes from the bread'?

THE EIGHTH POINT:[1] 1. It seems to be false to say, 'from the bread comes the body of Christ'. Everything from which something comes is that which becomes the other (something), but the opposite is not true. We say that 'something black comes from something white' and we say that 'a white thing becomes a black thing'. But although we say that 'a man becomes black', we do not say that 'from a man comes something black'. Aristotle makes all this clear.[2] If then it is true to say that 'from the bread comes the body of Christ', it will be true to say that 'the bread becomes the body of Christ'. But this is not true, because the bread is not the subject of any change, but is rather only one of the terms of a change. Therefore, it is not true to say that from the bread comes the body of Christ.

2. Furthermore, becoming terminates in being or in having been made. But it is never correct to say 'the bread is the body of Christ' or 'the bread has been made the body of Christ' or 'the bread will be the body of Christ'. Therefore, it would seem that we should also rule out 'from the bread comes the body of Christ'.

3. Besides, everything from which something comes is changed into that which has come from it. But it seems to be untrue to say 'the bread is changed into the body of Christ', because what happens here would seem to be more wonderful even than creation, in which we do not say that non-being is changed into being. It would appear then that this proposition also is false, 'from the bread comes the body of Christ'.

4. Moreover, that from which something comes is able to be that thing.

'Panis potest esse corpus Christi.' Ergo etiam hæc est falsa, 'Ex pane fit corpus Christi'.

SED CONTRA est quod Ambrosius dicit, *Ubi accedit consecratio, de pane fit corpus Christi.*[3]

RESPONSIO: Dicendum quod hæc conversio panis in corpus Christi, quantum ad aliquid convenit cum creatione et cum transmutatione naturali, et quantum ad aliquid differt ab utroque. Est enim commune his tribus ordo terminorum, scilicet ut post hoc sit hoc, in creatione enim est esse post non esse, in hoc sacramento corpus Christi post substantiam panis, in transmutatione naturali album post nigrum vel ignis post aerem; et quod prædicti termini non sint simul.

Convenit autem conversio de qua nunc loquimur cum creatione, quia in neutra earum est aliquod commune subjectum utrique extremorum. Cujus contrarium apparet in omni transmutatione naturali.

Convenit vero hæc conversio cum transmutatione naturali in duobus, licet non similiter. Primo quidem, quia in utraque unum extremorum transit in aliud, sicut panis in corpus Christi, et aër in ignem: non autem non ens convertitur in ens. Aliter tamen hoc accidit utrobique. Nam in hoc sacramento tota substantia panis transit in totum corpus Christi: sed in transmutatione naturali materia unius suscipit formam alterius, priori forma deposita. Secundo conveniunt in hoc, quod utrobique remanet aliquid idem: quod non accidit in creatione. Differenter tamen: nam in transmutatione naturali remanet eadem materia vel subjectum; in hoc autem sacramento remanent eadem accidentia.

Et ex his accipi potest qualiter differenter in talibus loqui debeamus. Quia enim in nullo prædictorum trium extrema sunt simul, ideo in nullo eorum potest unum extremum de alio prædicari per verbum substantivum præsentis temporis: non enim dicimus, 'Non ens est ens', vel 'Panis est corpus Christi', vel 'Aer est ignis' aut 'album est nigrum'.

Propter ordinem vero extremorum, possumus uti in omnibus hac præpositione 'ex', quæ ordinem designat. Possumus enim vere et proprie dicere quod 'ex non ente fit ens', et 'ex pane corpus Christi', et 'ex aere ignis' vel 'ex albo nigrum'.

Quia vero in creatione unum extremorum non transit in alterum, non possumus in creatione uti verbo 'conversionis', ut dicamus quod 'non

---

[3]*De Sacramentis* IV, 4. PL 16, 459

[a]The Latin word '*ex*', need suggest nothing more than order. If the English word 'from' necessarily implies more than order, it would be better here to translate '*ex*' as 'after'. The Latin preposition '*de*', could be rendered 'from', but to make sure that something much more than succession is involved, in the article it is translated 'out of'.

But it is not true to say, 'the bread is able to be the body of Christ'. Therefore, this also is false, 'from the bread comes the body of Christ'.

ON THE OTHER HAND, Ambrose says, *at the consecration from the bread comes the body of Christ.*[3]

REPLY: This conversion of the bread into Christ's body has certain resemblances, both to creation and to natural change, but in some respects it differs from each of them. All three have this in common—an order of terms, viz. after this we have this. In creation, we have being after non-being, in this sacrament the body of Christ after the substance of the bread, in physical changes white after black or fire after air. And these terms do not co-exist.

The conversion which is the object of our present study resembles creation in this, that in neither one nor the other is there any underlying subject present to each extreme term. But the contrary of this is observed in all natural changes.

This conversion, however, resembles natural change in two things, but does so in its own way. First of all, in each you have one of the extremes passing into the other, as bread into the body of Christ and air into fire. In creation non-being is not converted into being. But this happens in a different way in each case. In this sacrament the whole substance of the bread passes into the whole body of Christ, but in natural change the matter of the first thing takes on the form of the second one, having laid aside the first form. The second common feature of the Eucharistic change and natural change is this, that an identical element survives the change in both cases. This does not happen in creation. But the survival is different in each case. In natural change the same matter or subject remains; in this sacrament what survives is the same accidents.

From all these distinctions we can gather what is the correct choice of words for each case. Since in none of the three cases we have considered are the extremes together, in none of them can we predicate one extreme of the other, using a verb in the present tense. We do not say, 'non-being is being', or 'the bread is the body of Christ', or 'air is fire', or 'white is black'.

Because, however, of the order of the extremes, we can use the proposition 'from',[a] which can signify order. We can truly and rightly say that 'from non-being comes being', and 'from the bread comes the body of Christ', and 'from air comes fire', and 'from white comes black'.

But, because in creation one of the extremes does not pass into the other, the word conversion is ruled out in creation; we cannot say, 'non-being is converted into being'. But it is a word we can use of this sacrament, as also of all natural transformations. Since, however, in this sacrament

ens convertitur in ens'. Quo tamen verbo uti possumus in hoc sacramento, sicut et in transmutatione naturali. Sed quia in hoc sacramento tota substantia in totam mutatur, propter hoc hæc conversio proprie 'transubstantiatio' vocatur.

Rursus, quia hujus conversionis non est accipere aliquod subjectum, ea quæ verificantur in conversione naturali ratione subjecti, non sunt concedenda in hac conversione. Et primo quidem, manifestum est quod potentia ad oppositum consequitur subjectum: ratione cujus dicimus quod 'album potest esse nigrum', vel 'aër potest esse ignis'. Licet hæc non sit ita propria sicut prima: nam subjectum albi, in quo est potentia ad nigredinem, est tota substantia albi, non enim albedo est pars ejus; subjectum autem formæ aeris est pars ejus; unde, cum dicitur, 'aer potest esse ignis', verificatur ratione partis per synecdochen. Sed in hac conversione, et similiter in creatione, quia nullum est subjectum, non dicitur quod unum extremum possit esse aliud, sicut quod 'non ens possit esse ens', vel quod 'panis possit esse corpus Christi'. Et eadem ratione non potest proprie dici quod 'de non ente fiat ens', vel quod 'de pane fiat corpus Christi': quia hæc præpositio 'de' significat causam consubstantialem; quæ quidem consubstantialitas extremorum in transmutationibus naturalibus attenditur penes convenientiam in subjecto. Et simili ratione non conceditur quod 'panis erit corpus Christi', vel quod 'fiat corpus Christi', sicut neque conceditur in creatione quod 'non ens erit ens', vel quod 'non ens fiat ens': quia hic modus loquendi verificatur in transmutationibus naturalibus ratione subjecti, puta cum dicimus quod 'album fit nigrum', vel 'album erit nigrum'.

Quia tamen in hoc sacramento, facta conversione, aliquid idem manet, scilicet accidentia panis, ut supra dictum est,[4] secundum quandam similitudinem aliquæ harum locutionum possunt concedi: scilicet quod 'panis fit corpus Christi', vel, 'panis erit corpus Christi', vel, 'de pane fit corpus Christi'; ut nomine 'panis' non intelligatur substantia panis, sed in universali hoc quod sub speciebus panis continetur, sub quibus prius continetur substantia panis, et postea corpus Christi.

1. Ad primum ergo dicendum quod illud ex quo aliquid fit, quandoque quidem importat simul subjectum cum uno extremorum transmutationis: sicut cum dicitur, 'Ex albo fit nigrum'. Quandoque vero importat solum oppositum, vel extremum: sicut cum dicitur, 'Ex mane fit dies'. Et sic

---

[4]In this article and Art. 5

whole substance is changed into whole substance, this conversion has the name all to itself of 'transubstantiation'.

Furthermore, seeing that there is no subject of the change in this conversion, all those affirmations which would be true in a natural change, because of the subject, are here ruled out. First of all, it is clear that the ability of a thing to be the opposite to what it is, is something that follows on there being a subject. It is because of this that we say 'something white can be black', or 'air can be fire'. This last, however, is not quite as correct as the first, because the underlying subject of the white thing, in which there is the ability to receive the form of blackness, is the whole substance of the white thing and the whiteness is not part of this substance; but the subject which receives the form of air is only part of the substance, so that when we say 'the air can be fire', this is true because of part of the air, taking the part for the whole by synecdoche. But in this conversion, and also in creation, there is no underlying subject of change. Therefore, we do not speak of one of the extremes being able to be the other, and for instance say that 'non-being is able to be being', or that 'the bread is able to be the body of Christ'. This is the reason also why it is not correct to say that 'out of non-being comes being' or that 'out of the bread comes the body of Christ', because this proposition 'out of' signifies a material cause common to the substance of both extremes; and in natural changes this substantial element common to both extremes is the underlying subject which they share. For the same reason one cannot admit that 'the bread will be the body of Christ', or that 'it becomes the body of Christ', just as we cannot admit in creation that 'non-being will be being', or that 'non-being becomes being'. This manner of speaking is perfectly right where it is a question of natural changes, because there you have a subject, as when we say 'something white becomes black' or that 'it will be black'.

Since, however, in this sacrament after the change has taken place, something which is the same does still remain, namely, the accidents of the bread, as we saw above,[4] there is a certain sense in which some of these modes of expression may be allowed. It is allowable to say that 'the bread is the body of Christ', or that 'the bread will be the body of Christ' or that 'the body of Christ comes out of the bread', if by the word 'bread' we understand, not the substance of the bread, but in a vague sense that which is contained under the appearances of the bread, under which there is first the substance of the bread and afterwards the body of Christ.

Hence: 1. That from which something comes may mean sometimes the subject along with one of the extremes of the change, as when we say that 'something black comes from something white'. At other times it means merely the opposite or the other extreme, as when we say that 'the day comes from the morning'. In this case, we do not allow that this

non conceditur quod hoc fiat illud, id est quod 'mane fiat dies'. Et ita etiam in proposito, licet proprie dicatur quod 'ex pane fiat corpus Christi', non tamen proprie dicitur quod panis fiat corpus Christi, nisi secundum quandam similitudinem, ut dictum est.

2. Ad secundum dicendum quod illud ex quo fit aliquid, quandoque erit illud, propter subjectum quod importatur. Et ideo, cum hujus conversionis non sit aliquod subjectum, non est similis ratio.

3. Ad tertium dicendum quod in hac conversione sunt plura difficilia quam in creatione, in qua hoc solum difficile est, quod aliquid fit ex nihilo: quod tamen pertinet ad proprium modum productionis primæ causæ, quæ nihil aliud præsupponit. Sed in hac conversione non solum est difficile quod hoc totum convertitur in illud totum, ita quod nihil prioris remaneat, quod non pertinet ad communem modum productionis alicujus causæ: sed etiam habet hoc difficile, quod accidentia remanent corrupta substantia, et multa alia, de quibus in sequentibus agetur.[5] Tamen verbum 'conversionis' recipitur in hoc sacramento, non autem in creatione, sicut dictum est.

4. Ad quartum dicendum quod, sicut dictum est, potentia pertinet ad subjectum, quod non est accipere in hac conversione. Et ideo non conceditur quod panis possit esse corpus Christi: non enim hæc conversio fit per potentiam passivam creaturæ, sed per solam potentiam activam Creatoris.

---

[5]Question 77

becomes that, 'that the morning becomes the day'. It is the same in our present case; it is correct to say that 'the body of Christ comes from the bread', but it is not correct to say that 'the bread becomes the body of Christ', except, as we have seen, in a certain analogical sense.

2. That from which something else comes will at times be said to be that thing. This will occur when it is a change which has a subject. But in the Eucharistic change there is no subject and therefore the argument does not hold.

3. This change involves far more difficulties than does creation, in which there is just the one difficulty that something comes from nothing. And note that to bring something from nothing is the characteristic mode of operation of the first cause, which needs absolutely nothing to start with. In this conversion, however, it is only a first difficulty when this complete thing is changed into that complete thing, so that absolutely nothing of the first thing remains—a change that is outside the normal mode of action of any cause. There is then the difficulty that the accidents remain when their substance has disappeared, and there are many other difficulties which we shall treat of later on.[5] Notwithstanding all this, the word 'change' is acceptable in the Eucharistic context, but not in that of creation, for the reason given in the exposition.

4. As we also said there, the capacity to be this or that has to do with the subject of a change, and in the Eucharistic change there is no subject. Therefore, we do not admit that the bread is able to be the body of Christ. This change does not occur because of passive ability in the creature to be this or that, but solely through the active power of the Creator.

Quæstio 76. de modo quo Christus existit in hoc sacramento

Deinde considerandum est de modo quo Christus existit in hoc sacramento. Et circa hoc quæruntur octo:

1. utrum totus Chritus sit sub hoc sacramento;
2. utrum totus Christus sit sub utraque specie sacramenti;
3. utrum totus Christus sit sub qualibet parte specierum;
4. utrum dimensiones corporis Christi totæ sint in hoc sacramento;
5. utrum corpus Christi sit in hoc sacramento localiter;
6. utrum corpus Christi moveatur ad motum hostiæ vel calicis post consecrationem;
7. utrum corpus Christi sub hoc sacramento possit ab aliquo oculo* videri;
8. utrum verum corpus Christi remaneat quando miraculose apparet sub specie pueri vel carnis.

articulus 1. *utrum totus Christus contineatur sub hoc sacramento*

AD PRIMUM sic proceditur:[1] 1. Videtur quod non totus Christus contineatur sub hoc sacramento. Christus enim incipit esse in hoc sacramento per conversionem panis et vini. Sed manifestum est quod panis et vinum non possunt converti neque in divinitatem Christi, neque in ejus animam. Cum ergo Christus existat ex tribus substantiis, scilicet divinitate, anima et corpore, ut supra habitum est,[2] videtur quod Christus totus non sit in hoc sacramento.

2. Præterea, Christus est in hoc sacramento secundum quod competit refectioni fidelium, quæ in cibo et potu consistit, sicut supra dictum est.[3] Sed Dominus dicit, *Joan.* vi, *Caro mea vere est cibus, et sanguis meus vere est potus.*[4] Ergo solum caro et sanguis Christi continetur in hoc sacramento. Sunt autem multæ aliæ partes corporis Christi: puta nervi et ossa et alia hujusmodi. Non ergo totus Christus continetur sub hoc sacramento.

3. Præterea, corpus majoris quantitatis non potest totum contineri sub minoris quantitatis mensura. Sed mensura panis et vini consecrati est multo minor quam propria mensura corporis Christi. Non potest ergo esse quod totus Christus sit sub hoc sacramento.

---

*Piana adds *saltem glorificato,* at all events of a glorified body

[1]cf IV *Sent.* 10, 2, i, 2. *CG* IV, 64. *Quodl.* VII, 4, 1. *In Matt.* 26. *In Joan.* 6, *lect.* 6. *In* I *Cor.* 11, *lect.* 6

[2]3a. 2, 5; 5, 1–3

Question 76. how Christ exists in this sacrament

Let us pass on now to consider the way Christ exists in this sacrament. There are eight points of inquiry:

1. is the whole Christ under this sacrament?
2. is the whole Christ under each of the two species?[a]
3. is the whole Christ under each and every part of the species?
4. are the complete dimensions of Christ's body in this sacrament?
5. is the body of Christ in this sacrament as in place?
6. is the body of Christ moved when the host or the chalice is moved after the consecration?
7. could the body of Christ as it is under this sacrament be ever seen by the eye?
8. does the body of Christ really remain in this sacrament when there is a miraculous appearance of the likeness of a child or of flesh?

article 1. is the whole Christ under this sacrament?

THE FIRST POINT:[1] 1. The whole Christ does not seem to be contained under this sacrament. Christ begins to be present in this sacrament as the result of a change of the bread and wine. But it is clear that the bread and wine cannot be changed either into the divine nature of Christ or into his soul. Now Christ is made up of three substances, godhead, soul and body, as we saw earlier on.[2] It follows then that the whole Christ is not in this sacrament.

2. Moreover, in this sacrament he is present to be nourishment for the faithful, as we have already seen.[3] Now, nourishment consists of food and drink. And he says, *my flesh is food indeed and my blood is drink indeed.*[4] Hence, only the flesh and blood of Christ are contained in this sacrament. But Christ's body has many other parts, as nerves, bones, etc. Therefore, the whole Christ is not contained in this sacrament.

3. Again, a larger sized body cannot be completely contained under smaller dimensions. Yet the dimensions of the consecrated bread and wine are much less than the dimensions of Christ's body. Hence, it cannot be that the whole Christ is under this sacrament.

---

[3] 3a. 74, 1
[4] *John* 6, 56
[a] 'Species': the outward form or appearance of the consecrated elements.

SED CONTRA est quod Ambrosius dicit, in libro *de Offic.*, *In illo sacramento Christus est.*[5]

RESPONSIO: Dicendum quod omnino necesse est confiteri secundum fidem Catholicam quod totus Christus sit in hoc sacramento. Sciendum tamen quod aliquid Christi est in hoc sacramento dupliciter; uno modo, quasi ex vi sacramenti, alio modo, ex naturali concomitantia. Ex vi quidem sacramenti, est sub speciebus hujus sacramenti id in quod directe convertitur substantia panis et vini præexistens, prout significatur per verba formæ, quæ sunt effectiva in hoc sacramento sicut et in cæteris: puta cum dicitur, 'Hoc est corpus meum', 'Hic est sanguis meus'. Ex naturali autem concomitantia est in hoc sacramento illud quod realiter est conjunctum ei in quod prædicta conversio terminatur. Si enim aliqua duo sunt realiter conjuncta, ubicumque est unum realiter, oportet et aliud esse: sola enim operatione animæ discernuntur quæ realiter sunt conjuncta.

1. Ad primum ergo dicendum quod, quia conversio panis et vini non terminatur ad divinitatem vel animam Christi, consequens est quod divinitas vel anima Christi non sit in hoc sacramento ex vi sacramenti, sed ex reali concomitantia. Quia enim divinitas corpus assumptum nunquam deposuit, ubicumque est corpus Christi, necesse est et ejus divintatem esse. Et ideo in hoc sacramento necesse est esse divinitatem Christi concomitantem ejus corpus. Unde in Symbolo Ephesino legitur, *Participes, efficimur corporis et sanguinis Christi, non ut communem carnem percipientes, nec viri sanctificati et Verbo conjuncti secundum dignitatis unitatem, sed vere vivificatricem, et ipsius Verbi propriam factam.*[6]

Anima vero realiter separata fuit a copore, ut supra dictum est.[7] Et ideo, si in illo triduo mortis fuisset hoc sacramentum celebratum, non fuisset ibi anima, nec ex vi sacramenti nec ex reali concomitantia. Sed quia *Christus resurgens ex mortuis jam non moritur*, ut dicitur *Rom.* vi,[8] anima ejus semper est realiter corpori unita. Et ideo in hoc sacramento corpus quidem Christi est ex vi sacramenti, anima autem ex reali concomitantia.

2. Ad secundum dicendum quod ex vi sacramenti sub hoc sacramento continetur, quantum ad species panis, non solum caro, sed totum corpus Christi, id est ossa et nervi et alia hujusmodi. Et hoc apparet ex forma hujus sacramenti, in qua non dicitur, 'Hæc est caro mea', sed 'Hoc est corpus meum'. Et ideo, cum Dominus dixit, *Joan.* vi, *Caro mea vere est cibus*,[9]

---

[5] see Gratian, *Decretum* 3, 2, 40 *Ante benedictionem*. Richter-Friedberg I, 1328

[6] The words are from a letter of Cyril to Nestorius. *Ep.* 17. PG 77, 113

[7] 3a. 50, 5

[8] *Romans* 6, 9

[9] *John* 6, 55

ON THE OTHER HAND, we have Ambrose saying, *Christ is in this sacrament.*[5]

REPLY: Our Catholic Faith makes it absolutely necessary to profess that the whole Christ is in this sacrament. But note that there are two ways in which a part of Christ can be in it. The first way is as an immediate result of the sacramental sign; the second way is by a natural concomitance. As a result of the sacramental sign, you have under the sacramental appearances that into which the pre-existing substance of the bread and wine is directly changed. This change is signified by the words of the form, 'This is my body', 'This is my blood', which are here just as efficacious as the form of any sacrament is efficacious. And by a natural concomitance, you have here whatever is found to be actually joined to the term of the conversion. Because, wherever two things are actually joined together, wherever you have one, the other has to be. It is only by an act of our mind that we separate things that are thus really joined together.

Hence: 1. The change of the bread and wine does not have as its term either the godhead or the soul of Christ. Because of this, neither the godhead nor the soul of Christ is in this sacrament as a result of the sacramental sign; they are there by a natural concomitance. Since the godhead never laid aside the body which was taken up into hypostatic union, wherever the body of Christ may be, you must have the godhead with it. We read in the Creed of the Council of Ephesus, *we partake of the body and the blood of Christ; it is not ordinary flesh nor even the flesh of someone who is very holy and joined to the Word, sharing his dignity; but it is actually life-giving, it is the very flesh of the Word himself.*[6b]

There was a time when, as we saw earlier,[7] the soul was separated from the body. If this sacrament had been celebrated during those three days, the soul of Christ would not have been there, either as a result of the sacramental sign or by a natural concomitance. But since *Christ being raised from the dead will never die again*,[8] as we read in *Romans*, his soul is now always really united to his body. And so the body of Christ is in this sacrament as a result of the sacramental sign and his soul is there by a natural concomitance.

2. As a result of the sacramental sign, we have under this sacrament—under the appearances of the bread—not only the flesh, but the whole body of Christ, that is, the bones and nerves and all the rest. This is clear from the sacramental form which does not say, 'This is my flesh', but 'This is my body'. And so, when our Lord said in *John*, *my flesh is food indeed*,[9] the

[b]Cyril is arguing from Eucharistic belief to belief in the hypostatic union. The flesh of Jesus is life-giving; therefore, he is very God. Hypostatic union: the union of divine and human nature in one person or hypostasis.

caro ponitur ibi pro toto corpore, quia, secundum consuetudinem humanam, videtur esse magis manducationi accommodata: prout scilicet homines carnibus animalium vescuntur communiter, non ossibus vel aliis hujusmodi.

3. Ad tertium dicendum quod, sicut dictum est,[10] facta conversione panis in corpus Christi vel vini in sanguinem, accidentia utriusque remanent. Ex quo patet quod dimensiones panis vel vini non convertuntur in dimensiones corporis Christi, sed substantia in substantiam. Et sic substantia corporis Christi vel sanguinis est in hoc sacramento ex vi sacramenti, non autem dimensiones corporis vel sanguinis Christi. Unde patet quod corpus Christi est in hoc sacramento per modum substantiæ, et non per modum quantitatis. Propria autem totalitas substantiæ continetur indifferenter in parva vel magna quantitate: sicut tota natura aëris in magno vel parvo aëre, et tota natura hominis in magno vel parvo homine. Unde et tota substantia corporis Christi et sanguinis continetur in hoc sacramento post consecrationem, sicut ante consecrationem continebatur ibi substantia panis et vini.

articulus 2. utrum sub utraque specie hujus sacramenti totus Christus contineatur

AD SECUNDUM sic proceditur:[1] 1. Videtur quod non sub utraque specie hujus sacramenti totus Christus contineatur. Hoc enim sacramentum ad salutem fidelium ordinatur, non virtute specierum, sed virtute ejus quod sub speciebus continetur: quia species erant etiam ante consecrationem, ex qua est virtus hujus sacramenti. Si ergo nihil continetur sub una specie quod non contineatur sub alia, et totus Christus continetur sub utraque, videtur quod altera illarum superfluat in hoc sacramento.

2. Præterea, dictum est[2] quod sub nomine 'carnis' omnes aliæ partes corporis continetur, sicut ossa, nervi et alia hujusmodi. Sed sanguis est una partium humani corporis, sicut patet per Aristotelem, in libro *Animalium*.[3] Si ergo sanguis Christi continetur sub specie panis, sicut continentur

---

[10]3a. 75, 5
[1]3a. 78, 6 ad 1. IV *Sent.* 10, 2, i. *CG* IV, 64. *In Joan.* 6, *lect.* 6. *In* 1 *Cor.* 11, *lect.* 6
[2]3a. 76, 1 ad 1
[3]*Historia Animalium* I, 4. 489a30. *De Partibus Animalium* II, 2. 647b12

[c]The thought is here profound and compressed. *Per modum substantiæ* is the final clue to the nature of the real presence; and *per modum quantitatis* has to be paraphrased. Christ's body, i.e. the substance plus the accidents that affect it intrinsically, and as unrelated to the place which it naturally occupies, is now underneath the accidents of the bread in the same way as the substantial nature of the bread was underneath the accidents of bread. The whole '*quantified*' and individuated living body of Christ is now underneath the very quantity of the bread, which does not

word flesh stands there for the whole body, because it is more suitable in the context of eating, seeing that men normally eat the flesh of animals, not their bones or other such parts.

3. As we have already seen,[10] when the change of the bread into the body of Christ and of the wine into his blood has taken place, the accidents of the bread and wine remain. Since that is so, it is clear that the dimensions of the bread and wine are not changed into the dimensions of Christ's body; it is substance that is changed into substance. The substance of Christ's body or of his blood is in the sacrament as a result of the sacramental sign; not so the dimensions of his body or of his blood. It follows then that Christ's extended body is in the sacrament as if it was just substance and not in the way a substance already envisaged as affected by quantity is underneath its quantity or in a place.[c] But the whole specific nature of a substance is as truly contained by small as by large dimensions; for example, the complete specific nature of air is as truly found in a large as in a small amount, and human nature in its specific wholeness is equally present in a large and in a small man. It follows then that the whole substance of the body and the blood of Christ is contained in this sacrament after the consecration in the way that the complete specific nature of bread and wine was there before it.[d]

article 2. is the whole Christ under each of the two species?

THE SECOND POINT:[1] 1. It would seem that the whole Christ is not contained under each of the species.[a] This sacrament is productive of the spiritual good of the faithful, not through any power in the species, but through the power of that which is contained under them. The species were there before the consecration and it is from it that the sacrament has its power. If, then, there is nothing under one species which is not under the other, and if the whole Christ is contained equally under each, it would seem that either one or other of the two is superfluous.

1. Furthermore, we have already said[2] that by the word 'flesh' we are to understand all the other parts of the body as well, as the bones, the nerves, etc. But blood is one of the parts of the human body, as is clear from Aristotle.[3] If then, the blood of Christ is contained under the form of the

---

quantify or individuate it, but merely contains it, in the fundamental way that the quantity of the bread contained the bread before it *quantified* and individuated it.

[d]Cajetan, in a brilliant commentary on this reply, says that *totalitas substantiæ* means complete specific nature, *tota substantia corporis Christi* means the whole *quantified* and individuated nature of Christ's body.

[a]See note *a*, introduction to question.

etiam aliæ partes corporis, non deberet seorsum sanguis consecrari: sicut neque seorsum consecratur aliqua alia pars corporis.

3. Præterea, quod jam perfectum est, iterum fieri non potest. Sed corpus Christi jam incœpit esse in hoc sacramento per consecrationem panis. Ergo non potest esse quod de novo incipiat esse per consecrationem vini. Et ita sub specie vini non continebitur corpus Christi; et per consequens nec totus Christus. Non ergo sub utraque specie totus Christus continetur.

SED CONTRA est quod, 1 *Cor.* xi, super illud, *calicem*,[4] dicit glossa quod *sub utraque specie*, scilicet panis et vini, *idem sumitur*. Et ita videtur quod sub utraque specie totus Christus sit.

RESPONSIO: Dicendum certissime ex supra dictis[5] tenendum esse quod sub utraque specie sacramenti totus est Christus: aliter tamen et aliter. Nam sub speciebus panis est quidem corpus Christi ex vi sacramenti, sanguis autem ex reali concomitantia: sicut supra dictum est[6] de anima et divinitate Christi. Sub speciebus vero vini est quidem sanguis Christi ex vi sacramenti, corpus autem Christi ex reali concomitantia, sicut anima et deitas: eo quod nunc sanguis Christi non est ab ejus corpore separatus, sicut fuit tempore passionis et mortis. Unde, si tunc fuisset hoc sacramentum celebratum, sub speciebus panis fuisset corpus Christi sine sanguine, et sub specie vini sanguis sine corpore: sicut erat in rei veritate.

1. Ad primum ergo dicendum quod, quamvis totus Christus sit sub utraque specie, non tamen frustra. Nam primo quidem, hoc valet ad repræsentandum passionem Christi, in qua seorsum sanguis fuit a corpore. Unde et in forma consecrationis sanguinis fit mentio de ejus effusione.

Secundo, hoc est conveniens usui hujus sacramenti: ut seorsum exhibeatur fidelibus corpus Christi in cibum et sanguis in potum.

Tertio, quantum ad effectum: secundum quod supra dictum est[7] quod *corpus exhibetur pro salute corporis, et sanguis pro salute animæ.*

2. Ad secundum dicendum quod in passione Christi, cujus hoc sacramentum est memoriale, non fuerunt aliæ partes corporis ab invicem separatæ, sicut sanguis, sed corpus indissolutum permansit: secundum quod legitur *Exod.* xii, *Os non comminuetis ex eo.*[8] Et ideo in hoc sacramento seorsum consecratur sanguis a corpore, non autem aliqua alia pars ab alia.

[4] 1 *Corinthans* 11, 25. *Glossa Lombardi.* PL 191, 1645

[5] 3a. 76, 1

[6] 3a. 76, 1 ad 1

[7] 3a. 74, 1

[8] *Exodus* 12, 46

bread, as the other parts of the body are contained, the blood should not be consecrated separately. No other part of the body is consecrated separately.

3. Again, what has already come into being cannot again go through the process of coming into being. But by the consecration of the bread the body of Christ has come into being sacramentally. Therefore, that it should again come into being sacramentally by the consecration of the wine is impossible. It follows then that the body of Christ is not contained under the appearances of the wine; consequently, the whole Christ is not there. Hence, the whole Christ is not contained under each species.

ON THE OTHER HAND, a gloss on 'this cup' of 1 *Corinthians*[4] says, *the same thing is received under each species*, i.e. of the bread and of the wine. Thus it seems that the whole Christ is under each species.

REPLY: We must hold with complete certainty, because of what has already been seen,[5] that the whole Christ is under each of the sacramental species, but in different ways. Under the form of bread the body of Christ is present by means of the sacramental sign, and the blood is there by a natural concomitance, in the way we have already affirmed[6] of the soul and of the godhead. Under the form of wine the blood of Christ is present by reason of the sacramental sign, and the body of Christ by a natural concomitance, just as is the soul and the godhead, because the blood of Christ is not now separated from his body as it was at the time of his passion and death. If this sacrament had been celebrated then, the body of Christ without the blood would have been under the accidents of the bread and his blood without his body under the accidents of the wine, in correspondence to what was their actual situation.

Hence: 1. Although the whole Christ is under each of the species, there is a point in having the two species. First of all, this serves to represent Christ's passion, in which his blood was separated from his body. Hence, in the form of the consecration of the blood mention is made of its being poured out.

Then again, it is in keeping with sacramental usage; it enables the body of Christ to be given to the faithful as food and his blood as drink.

Finally, with regard to the effect; it has already been said[7] that the body is given for the well-being of our body and the blood is given for the well-being of our soul.

2. In Christ's passion, of which this sacrament is the memorial, the other parts of his body were not separated from one another in the way the blood was; the body remained unbroken, as in *Exodus* we read, *you shall not break a bone of it*.[8] It is for this reason that in this sacrament the blood is consecrated separately from the body, but not the other parts.

3. Ad tertium dicendum quod, sicut dictum est,[9] corpus Christi non est sub specie vini ex vi sacramenti, sed ex reali concomitantia. Et ideo per consecrationem vini non fit ibi corpus Christi per se, sed concomitanter.

articulus 3. utrum sit totus Christus sub qualibet parte specierum panis vel vini

AD TERTIUM sic proceditur:[1] 1. Videtur quod non sit totus Christus sub qualibet parte specierum panis vel vini. Species enim illæ dividi possunt in infinitum. Si ergo Christus totus est sub qualibet parte specierum prædictarum, sequeretur quod infinities esset in hoc sacramento. Quod est incoveniens: nam infinitum non solum repugnat naturæ, sed etiam gratiæ.

2. Præterea, corpus Christi, cum sit organicum, habet partes determinate distantes: est enim de ratione organici corporis determinata distantia singularum partium ad invicem, sicut oculi ab oculo et oculi ab aure. Sed hoc non posset esse si sub qualibet parte specierum esset totus Christus: oporteret enim quod sub qualibet parte esset quælibet pars; et ita, ubi esset una pars, esset et alia. Non ergo potest esse quod totus Christus sit sub qualibet parte hostiæ vel vini contenti in calice.

3. Præterea, corpus Christi semper veram retinet corporis naturam, nec unquam mutatur in spiritum. Sed de ratione corporis est ut sit *quantitas positionem habens*, ut patet in *Prædicamentis*.[2] Sed ad rationem hujus quantitatis pertinet quod diversæ partes in diversis partibus loci existant. Non ergo potest esse, ut videtur, quod totus Christus sit sub qualibet parte specierum.

SED CONTRA est quod Augustinus dicit in quodam sermone, *Singuli accipiunt Christum Dominum: et in singulis portionibus totus est, nec per singulas minuitur, sed integrum se præbet in singulis.*[3]

RESPONSIO: Dicendum quod, sicut ex supradictis patet,[4] quia in hoc sacramento substantia corporis Christi est ex vi sacramenti, quantitas autem dimensiva ex vi realis concomitantiæ, corpus Christi est in hoc sacramento per modum substantiæ, id est per modum quo substantia est sub dimensionibus: non autem per modum dimensionum, id est non per

---

[9] In the body of the article

[1] cf IV *Sent.* 10, 3, iii. *CG* IV, 67. *Quodl.* 7, 4, 1. *In Matt.* 26. *In* 1 *Cor.* 11, *lect.* 5

[2] *Categories* 4, 8. 5a23

[3] See Gratian, *Decretum* 3, 2, 77 *Singuli.* Richter-Friedberg 1, 1345. cf Gregory the Great, *Sacramentarium*, Preface for 5th Sunday after Epiphany. PL 78, 48

[4] 3a. 76, 1 ad 3

[a] Not in the sense that the integral parts of an extended substance are under the parts of the quantity that extends it, but in a more basic sense in which the whole ♦

3. As we have just seen,[9] the body of Christ is not under the appearances of the wine through the efficacy of the sacramental sign, but by reason of a natural concomitance. Hence, the consecration of the wine does not directly bring about the presence of Christ's body; it is a concomitant of the direct effect.

article 3. is the whole Christ under each and every part of the species?

THE THIRD POINT:[1] 1. There are reasons for thinking that the whole Christ is not under each and every part of the appearances of the bread or of the wine. These species can be divided to infinity. If then the whole Christ is under each part of these species, it follows that he is an infinite number of times in this sacrament. But we cannot say that, since just as in the natural order, so also in the order of grace, infinity is ruled out.

2. Moreover, the body of Christ is an organic whole and it has parts which are a definite distance from each other. This determinate distance of part from part, as of one eye from the other, or of eye from ear, is of the very nature of an organic body. But this could not be if the whole Christ were under each and every part of the species, because every part of Christ would then be under each and every part of the species and thus any one part of Christ would be where any other part of Christ is. It cannot then be that the whole Christ is under each and every part of the host or of the wine contained in the chalice.

3. Besides, the body of Christ always retains the true nature of a body, and is never turned into a spirit. But it is the nature of a body to be quantity having position, as Aristotle teaches.[2] Now it is part of the nature of quantity that its different parts are in different parts of place. It would seem, then, that the whole Christ cannot be under each and every part of the species.

ON THE OTHER HAND, Augustine says, *Everyone receives Christ our Lord; in each one's portion he is whole and entire; he is not lessened in being given to many; he gives himself entire to each.*[3]

REPLY: As is clear from what was said above,[4] since the body of Christ is in this sacrament because of the effectiveness of the sacramental sign and its quantitative dimensions as the result only of a natural concomitance, the body of Christ is here as if it were just substance, that is, in the way that substance is under its dimensions,[a] and not in any dimensive way, i.e. not

specific nature is *contained* by quantity, and is equally *under* any part of it. That quantity *contains* before extending is a theological insight. See also note *c* to Art. 1, and Appendix 3.

illum modum quo quantitas dimensiva alicujus corporis est sub quantitate dimensiva loci. Manifestum est autem quod natura substantiæ tota est sub qualibet parte dimensionum sub quibus continetur, sicut sub qualibet parte aëris est tota natura aëris et sub qualibet parte panis est tota natura panis. Et hoc indifferenter sive dimensiones sint actu divisæ, sicut cum aër dividitur vel panis secatur, vel etiam sint actu indivisæ, divisibiles vero potentia. Et ideo manifestum est quod Christus totus est sub qualibet parte specierum panis, etiam hostia integra manente: et non solum cum frangitur, sicut quidam dicunt, ponentes exemplum de imagine quæ apparet in speculo, quæ una apparet in speculo integro, speculo autem fracto apparent singulæ in singulis partibus. Quod quidem non est omnino simile. Quia multiplicatio hujusmodi imaginum accidit in speculo fracto propter diversas reflexiones ad diversas partes speculi; hic autem non est nisi una consecratio, propter quam corpus Christi est in sacramento.

1. Ad primum ergo dicendum quod numerus sequitur divisionem. Et ideo, quandiu quantitas manet indivisa actu, neque substantia alicujus rei est pluries sub dimensionibus propriis, neque corpus Christi sub dimensionibus panis. Et per consequens neque infinities: sed toties in quot partes dividitur.

2. Ad secundum dicendum quod illa determinata distantia partium in corpore organico fundatur supra quantitatem dimensivam ipsius: ipsa autem natura substantiæ præcedit etiam quantitatem dimensivam. Et quia conversio substantiæ panis directe terminatur ad substantiam corporis Christi, secundum cujus modum proprie et directe est in hoc sacramento corpus Christi, talis distantia partium est quidem in ipso corpore Christi vero, sed non secundum hanc distantiam comparatur ad hoc sacramentum, sed secundum modum suæ substantiæ, ut dictum est.[5]

3. Ad tertium dicendum quod ratio illa procedit de natura corporis quam habet secundum quantitatem dimensivam. Dictum est autem quod corpus Christi non comparatur ad hoc sacramentum ratione quantitatis dimensivæ, sed ratione substantiæ, ut dictum est.[6]

---

[5]In the body of the article and 3a. 76, 1 ad 3

[6]In the body of the article and ad 2

[b]For St Thomas this is the sequence. Where we could first say, 'this is bread', we now say, 'this is Christ's body'. The whole specific nature of bread was *contained* by the quantity of the host and was equally *under* each and every part of it, even before the division of the host. The body of Christ is now *contained* by and *under* each part of the quantity of the host in the same way.

in the way that the dimensive quantity of a body is under the dimensive quantity of the place that contains that body. Now it is clear that the whole nature of any substance is under any part of the dimensions that contain it; for example, under any part of air you have the whole nature of air and under any part of a loaf you have the whole nature of bread; and this is equally true whether the quantity is actually divided into parts (as when the air is divided or the loaf is cut into pieces), or it is not actually divided, but only potentially so. You are to think then of the whole Christ as being under each and every part of the appearances of the bread, even when the host remains unbroken.[b] Some people say that this is true only when the host is broken into pieces and they give the example of the image that appears in a mirror; when the mirror is unbroken, there is only one image, but when the mirror is broken, you have a separate image in each of the parts. But really, this analogy is not a valid one. The multiplication of these images occurs in the broken mirror as the result of many different reflections in the different pieces, but here it is one consecration that is the sole cause of Christ's body being in the sacrament.

Hence: 1. Number follows on division. Consequently, as long as the quantity of a thing remains undivided, the substance is not underlying the quantity a number of times; just so, the body of Christ is not under the dimensions of the bread a number of times. It follows then that it is not there an infinite number of times; a number of times follows on the number of parts into which the bread is broken.

2. The definite distance of the parts from one another in an organic body is something that follows on its being extended, but you must remember that the specific nature of any substance is prior to its being extended. And since the change of the substance of the bread has for its direct term the substance of Christ's body, which is properly and directly in this sacrament as if it were just substance, the aforementioned distance of part from part is actually in Christ's body, but it does not control the manner of the presence of that body in the sacrament; the manner of the presence is controlled solely by considerations of what it means to be there just as substance,[c] as we have said.[5]

3. This argument is concerned with the nature of a body precisely as it is affected by its extension. Now we have just seen[6] that the presence of the body of Christ in this sacrament is not controlled by factors deriving from its being extended; it is there purely and simple as it is substance.

---

[c]The next article will make clearer in what sense the extended body of Christ is in the sacrament.

articulus 4. utrum tota quantitas dimensiva corporis Christi sit in hoc sacramento

AD QUARTUM sic proceditur:[1] 1. Videtur quod non tota quantitas dimensiva corporis Christi sit in hoc sacramento. Dictum est[2] enim quod totum corpus Christi continetur sub qualibet parte hostiæ consecratæ. Sed nulla quantitas dimensiva tota continetur in aliquo toto et in qualibet parte ejus. Est ergo impossibile quod tota quantitas dimensiva corporis Christi contineatur in hoc sacramento.

2. Præterea, impossibile est duas quantitates dimensivas esse simul, etiam si una sit separata et alia in corpore naturali: ut patet per Philosophum, in *Meta.*[3] Sed in hoc sacramento remanet quantitas dimensiva panis, ut sensu apparet. Non ergo est ibi quantitas dimensiva corporis Christi.

3. Præterea, si duæ quantitates dimensivæ inæquales juxta se ponantur, major extenditur ultra minorem. Sed quantitas dimensiva corporis Christi est multo major quam quantitas dimensiva hostiæ ejus consecratæ, secundum omnem dimensionem. Si ergo in hoc sacramento sit quantitas dimensiva corporis Christi cum quantitate dimensiva hostiæ, quantitas dimensiva corporis Christi extendetur ultra quantitatem hostiæ. Quæ tamen non est sine substantia corporis Christi. Ergo substantia corporis Christi erit in hoc sacramento etiam præter species panis. Quod est inconveniens: cum substantia corporis Christi non sit in hoc sacramento nisi per consecrationem panis, ut dictum est.[4] Impossibile est ergo quod tota quantitas* corporis Christi sit in hoc sacramento.

SED CONTRA est quod quantitas dimensiva corporis alicujus non separatur secundum esse a substantia ejus. Sed in hoc sacramento est tota substantia corporis Christi, ut supra[5] habitum est. Ergo tota quantitas dimensiva corporis Christi est in hoc sacramento.

RESPONSIO: Dicendum quod, sicut supra dictum est,[6] dupliciter aliquid Christi est in hoc sacramento; uno modo, ex vi sacramenti, alio modo, ex naturali† concomitantia. Ex vi quidem sacramenti quantitas dimensiva corporis Christi non est in hoc sacramento. Ex vi enim sacramenti est in hoc sacramento illud in quod directe conversio terminatur. Conversio autem quæ fit in hoc sacramento terminatur directe ad substantiam corporis Christi, non autem ad dimensiones ejus. Quod patet ex hoc quod quantitas dimensiva remanet facta consecratione, sola autem substantia panis transeunte. Quia tamen substantia corporis Christi realiter non denudatur a

---

*Piana adds *dimensiva* †Piana for *naturali* reads *reali*

[1]cf IV *Sent.* 10, 2, iii, 4. *CG* IV, 63, 64, 67. *Quodl.* VII, 4, 1
[2]3a. 76, 3 [3]*Metaphysics* II, 2. 998a7 [4]3a. 76, 2
[5]3a. 76, 1, 3 [6]3a. 76, 1

article 4. are all the dimensions of the body of Christ in this sacrament?

THE FOURTH POINT:[1] 1. It would seem that all the quantitative dimensions of Christ's body are not in this sacrament. We have just said[2] that the whole body of Christ is contained under each and every part of the consecrated host. But the complete quantitative dimensions of anything could not possibly be contained in any whole and in each and every part of it. It is then quite impossible that the complete quantitative dimensions of Christ's body should be contained in this sacrament.

2. Again, you cannot have two sets of dimensions together, even though one be thought of as abstract and the other as affecting a natural body; Aristotle shows that this is so.[3] But in this sacrament, the dimensions of the bread remain, as is obvious to our senses. Therefore, the dimensions of Christ's body are not there.

3. Moreover, if two unequal sets of dimensions are placed together, the greater overlaps the lesser. But the dimensions of Christ's body are much greater than the dimensions of the consecrated host, no matter what dimension you consider. If then you have the dimensions of Christ's body in this sacrament they will pass out beyond the dimensions of the host. But they will not be without the substance of the body of Christ. Therefore, the substance of Christ's body will be in this sacrament even outside the appearances of the bread. But this cannot be, because the only way in which the substance of Christ's body is in this sacrament is by means of the consecration of the bread, as we saw earlier.[4] It is quite impossible then that the complete dimensions of Christ's body should be in this sacrament.

ON THE OTHER HAND, you cannot have a substance and separate its dimensions from it. But in this sacrament we have the complete substance of Christ's body, as we saw above.[5] Therefore, the complete dimensions of Christ's body are here also.

REPLY: As we said above,[6] there are two ways in which any part of the whole Christ may be made present in this sacrament; the first is as a result of the effectiveness of the sacramental sign, the second as a result of natural concomitance. Now, the dimensions of Christ's body are not in this sacrament as a result of the effectiveness of the sacramental sign. As a result of the sacramental effectiveness you have in the sacrament that precisely which is the direct term of the change. And the direct term of this sacramental change is the substance of Christ's body only, not with its dimensions. This is clear from the fact that it is only the substance of the bread which passes away at the consecration, but the dimensions of the bread remain. But since the substance of Christ's body is not despoiled of

sua quantitate dimensiva et ab aliis accidentibus, inde est quod, ex vi realis concomitantiæ, est in hoc sacramento tota quantitas dimensiva corporis Christi, et omnia alia accidentia ejus.

1. Ad primum ergo dicendum quod modus existendi* cujuslibet rei determinatur secundum illud quod est ei per se, non autem secundum illud quod est ei per accidens; sicut corpus est in visu secundum quod est album, non autem secundum quod est dulce, licet idem corpus sit album et dulce. Unde et dulcedo est in visu secundum modum albedinis, et non secundum modum dulcedinis. Quia agitur ex vi sacramenti hujus est in altari substantia corporis Christi, quantitas autem dimensiva ejus est ibi concomitanter et quasi per accidens, ideo quantitas dimensiva corporis Christi est in hoc sacramento, non secundum proprium modum, ut scilicet sit totum in toto et singulæ partes in singulis partibus, sed per modum substantiæ, cujus natura est tota in toto et tota in qualibet parte.

2. AD SECUNDUM dicendum quod duæ quantitates dimensivæ non possunt naturaliter simul esse in eodem ita quod utraque sit secundum proprium modum quantitatis dimensivæ. In hoc autem sacramento quantitas dimensiva panis est secundum proprium modum, scilicet secundum commensurationem quandam; non autem quantitas dimensiva corporis Christi, sed est ibi per modum substantiæ, ut dictum est.[7]

3. AD TERTIUM dicendum quod quantitas dimensiva corporis Christi non est in hoc sacramento secundum modum commensurationis, qui est proprius quantitati, ad quem pertinet quod major quantitas extendatur ultra minorem, sed est ibi per modum jam dictum.[8]

articulus 5. utrum corpus Christi sit in hoc sacramento sicut in loco

AD QUINTUM sic proceditur:[1] 1. Videtur quod corpus Christi sit in hoc sacramento sicut in loco. Esse enim in aliquo definitive vel circumscriptive est pars ejus quod est esse in loco. Sed corpus Christi videtur esse definitive in hoc sacramento, quia ita est ubi sunt species panis vel vini, quod non est in alio loco altaris. Videtur etiam ibi esse circumscriptiva, quia ita

---

*Piana: *essendi*

[7]ad 1

[8]ad 1 & 2

[1]cf 3a. 75, 1 ad 3. IV *Sent.* 10, 1 ad 5 & 6; 2, iii ad 4; 3, i & ii. *CG* IV, 62, 64, 67. *Opus.* XI, *de* 36 *Artic.* 33

[a]It is not deprived of its intrinsic accidents. See next article, ad 3.

[b]It is normal for the dimensions of a body to be locally in that which contains them. The dimensions of Christ's body are in the host, not as in a *containing* place, but as in accidents which are *containing* substance.

its dimensions or of its other accidents,[a] it follows that the dimensions of Christ's body and all its other accidents are in this sacrament by reason of natural concomitance.

Hence: 1. The way in which a thing properly exists follows on its essential nature and not on some non-essential factor. For example, it is precisely as white that a bodily thing exists in our vision of it; it may be that it is sweet as well as white, but it is not seen as sweet. Hence the sweetness is seen only as whiteness, and not properly as sweetness. Now, in virtue of the sacramental sign it is only the substance of Christ's body which is on the altar and his dimensions are there only because of a natural concomitance and, as it were, outside the essential demands of the situation. It follows then that the dimensions of Christ's body are in this sacrament, not in a way that it is normal for dimensions to be, i.e. the whole Christ in the whole sacrament and the parts of Christ in parts of the sacrament, but in a way that is natural for substance to be, i.e. the whole in the whole and the whole in every part also.[b]

2. Two sets of dimensions cannot naturally be found together, in the sense that each set is there in the way that it is normal for dimensions to be. In this sacrament, the dimensions of the bread are there in the normal way, i.e. as harmonizing with the dimensions of a containing place; but the dimensions of Christ's body are not there in the normal way, but in the way that it is normal for substance to be, as we have just said.[7]

3. The dimensions of Christ's body are not in this sacrament as harmonizing with the dimensions of a place that contains them. That would be the normal way for them to exist; and in that normal way, the greater overlaps the lesser. They are here in the way we have just explained.[8]

article 5. is the body of Christ in this sacrament locally?

THE FIFTH POINT:[1] 1. It would seem that Christ's body is in this sacrament as in a place. To be in something in the sense of being limited to it[a] or of being surrounded by it means being in place. Now, the body of Christ seems to be in this sacrament in a way that limits it to the sacrament, because it is wherever the appearances of the bread and wine are and not in any other part of the altar. It also seems to be there in the sense of being surrounded by something, because it is contained within the surface of the

[a]An angel is said to be in whatever place he is causing corporeal effects. Being a creature whose power is limited, the field of his activity at any one moment is limited. He is said, therefore, to be in a place '*definitive*', in a way that limits him to it.

continetur superficie hostiæ consecratæ quod nec excedit nec exceditur. Ergo corpus Christi est in hoc sacramento sicut in loco.

2. Præterea, locus specierum panis non est vacuus: natura enim non patitur vacuum. Nec est ibi substantia panis, ut supra habitum est,[2] sed est ibi solum corpus Christi. Ergo corpus Christi replet locum illum. Sed omne quod replet locum aliquem, est in eo localiter. Ergo corpus Christi est in hoc sacramento localiter.

3. Præterea, in hoc sacramento, sicut dictum est,[3] corpus Christi est cum sua quantitate dimensiva et cum omnibus suis accidentibus. Sed esse in loco est accidens corporis, unde et *ubi* connumeratur inter novem genera accidentium. Ergo corpus Christi est in hoc sacramento localiter.

SED CONTRA est quod oportet locum et locatum esse æqualia: ut patet per Philosophum, in *Physic.*[4] Sed locus ubi est hoc sacramentum est multo minor quam corpus Christi. Ergo corpus Christi non est in hoc sacramento sicut in loco.

RESPONSIO: Dicendum quod, sicut jam dictum est,[5] corpus Christi non est in hoc sacramento secundum proprium modum quantitatis dimensivæ, sed magis secundum modum substantiæ. Omne autem corpus locatum est in loco secundum modum quantitatis dimensivæ, inquantum scilicet commensuratur loco secundum suam quantitatem dimensivam. Unde relinquitur quod corpus Christi non est in hoc sacramento sicut in loco, sed per modum substantiæ, eo scilicet modo quo substantia continetur a dimensionibus. Succedit enim substantia corporis Christi in hoc sacramento substantiæ panis. Unde, sicut substantia panis non erat sub suis dimensionibus localiter, sed per modum substantiæ, ita nec substantia corporis Christi.

Non tamen substantia corporis Christi est subjectum illarum dimensionum, sicut erat substantia panis. Et ideo panis ratione suarum dimensionum localiter erat ibi, quia comparabatur ad locum mediantibus propriis dimensionibus. Substantia autem corporis Christi comparatur ad locum illum mediantibus dimensionibus alienis, ita quod e converso dimensiones propriæ corporis Christi comparantur ad locum illum mediante substantia. Quod est contra rationem corporis locati. Unde nullo modo corpus Christi est in hoc sacramento localiter.

---

[2] 3a. 75, 2
[3] 3a. 76, 4
[4] *Physics* IV, 4. 211a2
[5] 3a. 76, 1 ad 3; 76, 3

[b] The substance is envisaged as *contained* by the dimensions or the quantity. This '*being contained*' is understood as prior to '*being the subject*' which the quantity

consecrated host and neither goes beyond it nor falls short of it. It follows that Christ's body is in this sacrament as in a place.

2. Moreover, the place that surrounds the appearances of the bread is not empty, because nature abhors a vacuum. Now, the substance of the bread is not there, as we have already seen,[2] but only the body of Christ. Therefore, the body of Christ fills the place. Now, whatever fills a place is in it locally. Hence, the body of Christ is locally in this sacrament.

3. Again, the body of Christ is in this sacrament with his dimensions and with all his accidents, as we said earlier.[3] Now to be in place is an accident which all bodies have; hence, *where* corresponds to one of the nine types of accident. Therefore, the body of Christ is locally in this sacrament.

ON THE OTHER HAND, if a thing is in place, it must correspond exactly with the place in which it is, as Aristotle shows.[4] But the place this sacrament occupies is much smaller than the body of Christ. Therefore, Christ's body is not in this sacrament as in place.

REPLY: As we have already said,[5] Christ's body is not in this sacrament in the normal way an extended body exists, but rather just as if it were purely and simply substance. Now every body that is in a place is in place precisely as it is an extended body, that is, it corresponds to the place that contains it according to its dimensions. It follows then that Christ's body is in this sacrament not as in a place, but purely in the way that substance is, in the way that substance is contained by the dimensions.[b] It is to the substance of the bread that the substance of Christ's body succeeds in this sacrament. Hence, as the substance of the bread was not under its dimensions in the way an extended body is in a place, but in the way which is proper to substance to be under dimensions, so likewise the body of Christ is not under the dimensions of the bread locally.

Note also that the substance of Christ's body is not the subject of the dimensions of the bread as the substance of the bread was. The bread by reason of the dimensions was localized in a place, because it was related to a place by dimensions that were its own. But the substance of Christ's body is related to that place by dimensions that are not its own; and, contrariwise, the dimensions of Christ's own body are related to that place only in so far as the substance of his body is. But that is not the way in which a body is localized. Hence, Christ's body in this sacrament is in no way localized.

---

affects by dividing it into integral parts. This metaphysical distinction is solely an insight of Eucharistic theology; it is the key to an understanding of the Real Presence.

1. Ad primum ergo dicendum quod corpus Christi non est in hoc sacramento definitive, quia sic non esset alibi quam in hoc altari ubi conficitur hoc sacramentum; cum tamen sit et in cælo in propria specie, et in multis aliis altaribus sub specie sacramenti. Similiter etiam patet quod non est in hoc sacramento circumscriptive: quia non est ibi secundum commensurationem propriæ quantitatis, ut dictum est.[6] Quod autem non est extra superficiem sacramenti, nec est in alia parte altaris, non pertinet ad hoc quod sit ibi definitive vel circumscriptive: sed ad hoc quod incœpit ibi esse per consecrationem et conversionem panis et vini, ut supra dictum est.[7]

2. Ad secundum dicendum quod locus ille in quo est corpus Christi, non est vacuus. Neque tamen proprie est repletus substantia corporis Christi, quæ non est ibi localiter, sicut dictum est.[8] Sed est repletus speciebus sacramentorum, quæ habent replere locum vel propter naturam dimensionum; vel saltem miraculose, sicut et miraculose subsistunt per modum substantiæ.

3. Ad tertium dicendum quod accidentia corporis Christi sunt in hoc sacramento, sicut supra dictum est,[9] secundum realem concomitantiam. Et ideo illa accidentia corporis Christi sunt in hoc sacramento quæ sunt ei intrinseca. Esse autem in loco est accidens per comparationem ad extrinsecum continens. Et ideo non oportet quod Christus sit in hoc sacramento sicut in loco.

articulus 6. utrum corpus Christi sit mobiliter in hoc sacramento

AD SEXTUM sic proceditur:[1] 1. Videtur quod corpus Christi sit mobiliter in hoc sacramento. Dicit enim Philosophus, in *Topic.*, quod, *moventibus* nobis, moventur ea quæ in nobis sunt.*[2] Quod quidem verum est etiam de spirituali substantia animæ. Sed Christus est in hoc sacramento, ut supra habitum est.[3] Ergo movetur ad motum ipsius.

2. Præterea, veritas debet respondere figuræ. Sed de agno paschali, qui erat figura hujus sacramenti, *non remanebat quidquam usque mane*[4] sicut

---

*Piana: *motis*

[6]In the exposition
[7]3a. 76, 1; 75, 2–6
[8]In the exposition
[9]3a. 76, 4
[1]cf IV *Sent.* 10, 3, iv. *Resp. de XXXVI Artic.* (to the Venetian lecturer), 34
[2]*Topics* 7, 113a29
[3]3a. 74, 1
[4]*Exodus* 12, 10

[c]Christ's body as localized is in one place only, namely in heaven. The same body which is localized in heaven is really present in the Eucharist in a non-local way. Christ's body with its dimensions, with part distinct from part, is present to the

Hence: 1. Christ's body is not in this sacrament in the sense of being restricted to it. If that were so, it could only be on that altar where the sacrament is actually being consecrated. But it is always in heaven in its proper appearance and it is on many other altars under its sacramental appearance. It is also clear that it is not in this sacrament in the sense of being surrounded by it, because it is not there with its dimensions running in conformity with the dimensions of the bread, as we have just seen.[6] The fact that it is not outside the containing dimensions of the bread or that it is not in any other part of the altar does not prove that it is limited to the sacrament or circumscribed by it; all that that shows is that it began to be in the sacrament as a result of the consecration and of the changes of the bread and wine, as was said above.[7]

2. The place is not empty where the body of Christ is. But properly speaking it is not filled by the substance of the body of Christ, which is not locally present, as we have just seen.[8] It is filled by the sacramental appearances which are able to fill a place either because the dimensions themselves naturally do this or are enabled to do so by a miracle, just as they miraculously subsist as if they were substance.

3. The accidents of Christ's body are in this sacrament, as we saw earlier,[9] as the result of a natural concomitance. Hence, it is those accidents of Christ's body which are intrinsic to it which are in this sacrament. But to be in place is an accident which has to do with something extrinsic which contains a thing. So it does not follow that the body of Christ is in this sacrament as localized.[c]

article 6. *is the body of Christ in this sacrament in a mobile way?*

THE SIXTH POINT:[1] 1. It seems that Christ's body is in this sacrament in such a way that it can be moved around. According to Aristotle, *when we are in movement, the things that are in us are in movement too.*[2] And that is true even of the spiritual substance of our soul. Now Christ is in this sacrament, as has already been established.[3] Therefore, he is moved when it is moved.

2. Besides, the reality should correspond to that which is its figure or type. Now the paschal lamb was the figure of this sacrament, and *none of it remained until the morning*;[4] there was a precept on this matter. Hence,

---

dimensions of the bread not as to a containing place, but as substance is '*spiritually*' equally present to all the parts of the dimensions that contain it. Substance is '*spiritually*' contained by its dimensions, before they are considered as extending it. It is only as '*spiritually*' contained that the extended body of Christ is related to the dimensions of the bread.

præcipitur *Exod.* xii. Ergo neque etiam, si hoc sacramentum reservetur in crastinum, erit ibi corpus Christi. Et ita non est immobiliter in hoc sacramento.

3. Præterea, si corpus Christi remaneat sub hoc sacramento etiam in crastino, pari ratione remanebit et per totum sequens tempus: non enim potest dici quod desinat ibi esse cessantibus speciebus, quia esse corporis Christi non dependet a speciebus illis. Non autem remanet sub hoc sacramento Christus per totum tempus futurum. Videtur ergo quod statim in crastino, vel post modicum tempus, desinat esse sub hoc sacramento. Et ita videtur quod Christus mobiliter sit in hoc sacramento.

SED CONTRA, impossibile est idem esse motum et quietum: quia sic contraria verificarentur de eodem. Sed corpus Christi in cælo quietum residet. Non ergo est mobiliter in hoc sacramento.

RESPONSIO: Dicendum quod, cum aliquid est unum subjecto et multiplex secundum esse, nihil prohibet secundum aliquid moveri, et secundum aliud immobile permanere: sicut corpori aliud est esse album, et aliud est esse magnum, unde potest moveri secundum albedinem, et permanere immobile secundum magnitudinem. Christo autem non est idem esse secundum se, et esse sub sacramento: quia per hoc ipsum quod dicimus ipsum esse sub sacramento, significatur quædam habitudo ejus ad hoc sacramentum. Secundum igitur hoc esse non movetur Christus per se secundum locum, sed solum per accidens. Quia Christus non est in hoc sacramento sicut in loco, sicut prædictum est:[5] quod autem non est in loco, non movetur per se in loco, sed solum ad motum ejus in quo est.

Similiter autem neque per se movetur, secundum esse quod habet in hoc sacramento, quacumque alia mutatione: puta quantum ad hoc quod desinat esse sub hoc sacramento. Quia illud quod de se habet esse indeficiens non potest esse deficiendi principium: sed, alio deficiente, hoc desinit esse in eo; sicut Deus, cujus esse est indeficiens et immortale, desinit esse in aliqua creatura corruptibili per hoc quod creatura corruptibilis desinit esse. Et hoc modo, cum Christus habeat esse indeficiens et incorruptibile, non desinit esse sub sacramento neque per hoc quod ipsum

---

[5] 3a. 76, 5

[a] You will not go further in a metaphysical understanding of the Real Presence. It is a relationship of the body of Christ to the species of the bread and a corresponding relationship of the species to the body of Christ. In the body of Christ it is a relationship of being contained by the species; in the species it is a relationship of containing the body. In the body of Christ the relationship is probably merely something that exists in our minds when we observe the situation; in the species the relationship is real. See the ad 3.

also, if this sacrament be reserved till the morrow, the body of Christ will not be there. Therefore, in this sacrament the body of Christ is not exempt from movement.

3. Again, if the body of Christ did remain in this sacrament till the morrow, there is no reason why it should not remain for all time; you cannot say that it ceases to be there when the appearances of the bread cease to be, because Christ's body does not depend for its existence on those appearances. But Christ does not remain for all time in this sacrament. It would seem, therefore, that he ceases to be in this sacrament either immediately on the morrow or after a short time. It seems then that Christ is in this sacrament in a mobile way.

ON THE OTHER HAND, you cannot have something in movement and at rest at the same time; that would be to affirm contraries of the same thing. Now the body of Christ in heaven is at rest. Therefore, it is not in movement in this sacrament.

REPLY: A thing can be fundamentally one, but manifold in the modes of its being. So, there is nothing against its being in movement on one level of its being while it remains unchanged on another. There is a difference between a body's being white and its being large; it can then be involved in a process of change from the point of view of whiteness yet simultaneously remain unchanged from the point of view of size. Now it is not the same thing for Christ to be, simply, and for him to be under the sacrament; because when we say that he is under the sacrament we mean that he has a relationship to the sacrament.[a] Now, according to this mode of his being under the sacrament, Christ is not moved locally in any strict sense, but only after a fashion. Christ is not in this sacrament as if he were in a place, as we have already said;[5] and what is not in a place is not moved locally, but is only said to be moved when that in which it is is moved.

Neither is he directly subject to any other kind of change, precisely as he exists in this sacrament; for example, he is not the subject of a change leading up to his ceasing to be under the sacrament. That which of itself has unfailing being cannot be a principle of ceasing to be; it ceases to be in something because that thing has ceased to be. Thus God, whose being is unfailing and immortal, ceases to be in a corruptible creature by the fact that the corruptible creature has ceased to be. In the same way, since Christ has unfailing and immortal being, he does not cease to be under the sacrament because of any ceasing-to-be on his part. Nor does he cease to be under the sacrament because of any local movement, as is clear from

desinat esse, neque etiam per motum localem sui, ut ex dictis patet: sed solum per hoc quod species hujus sacramenti desinunt esse.

Unde patet quod Christus, per se loquendo, immobiliter est in hoc sacramento.

1. Ad primum ergo dicendum quod ratio illa procedit de motu per accidens, quo ad motum nostri moventur ea quæ in nobis sunt. Aliter tamen ea quæ per se possunt esse in loco, sicut corpora: et aliter ea quæ per se non possunt esse in loco, sicut formæ et spirituales substantiæ. Ad quem modum potest reduci quod dicimus Christum moveri per accidens secundum esse quod habet in hoc sacramento, in quo non est sicut in loco.

2. Ad secundum dicendum quod hac ratione moti videntur fuisse quidam ponentes quod corpus Christi non remanet sub hoc sacramento si in crastinum reservetur. Contra quod Cyrillus dicit, *Insaniunt quidam habentes mysticam benedictionem a sanctificatione cessare si quæ reliquiæ remanserint ejus in diem subsequentem. Non enim mutabitur sacrosanctum corpus Christi, sed virtus benedictionis et vivificativa gratia jugis in eo est.*[6] Sicut et omnes aliæ consecrationes immobiliter manent, permanentibus rebus consecratis; propter quod non iterantur. Veritas autem licet figuræ respondeat, tamen figura non potest eam adæquare.

3. Ad tertium dicendum quod corpus Christi remanet in hoc sacramento non solum in crastinum, sed etiam in futurum, quousque species sacramentales manent. Quibus cessantibus, desinit esse corpus Christi sub eis, non quia ab eis dependeat, sed quia tollitur habitudo corporis Christi ad illas species. Per quem modum Deus desinit esse Dominus creaturæ desinentis.

articulus 7. utrum corpus Christi prout est in hoc sacramento, possit videri ab aliquo oculo, saltem glorificato

AD SEPTIMUM sic proceditur:[1] 1. Videtur quod corpus Christi prout est in hoc sacramento, possit videri ab aliquo oculo, saltem glorificato. Oculus enim noster impeditur a visione corporis Christi in hoc sacramento existentis, propter species sacramentales ipsum circumvelantes. Sed oculut glorificatus non potest ab aliquo impediri, quin corpora quælibet videas prout sunt. Ergo oculus glorificatus potest videre corpus Christi prout est in hoc sacramento.

2. Præterea, corpora gloriosa sanctorum erunt *configurata corpori claritatis Christi*,[2] ut dicitur *Philipp*. iii. Sed oculus Christi videt seipsum prout est in hoc sacramento. Ergo pari ratione quilibet alius oculus glorificatus potest ipsum videre.

3. Præterea, sancti in resurrectione erunt *æquales angelis*,[3] ut dicitur

what has already been said, but simply because the sacramental species have ceased to be.

From all this, we conclude that Christ, as he is in this sacrament, is, strictly speaking, not subject to any kind of change.

Hence: 1. This argument is valid in regard to indirect movement, as when we are in movement the things that are in us are in movement too. This movement is different when it is a question of things that can be in place, as bodies, and when it is a question of things that cannot be in place, as forms and spiritual substances. Something after this fashion we say that Christ is moved indirectly, according to the mode of existence which is his in this sacrament, in which he does not exist as in place.

2. This was the reason why some people thought that the body of Christ does not remain under the sacrament if it is reserved till the next day. Cyril wrote against them, *certain persons quite wrongly think that the sacramental consecration loses its power if any fragments remain until the next day. For Christ's sacred body undergoes no change, but the power of consecration and its life-giving grace abide.*[6] Just so all other consecrations endure as long as the things that have been consecrated last; for this reason they are not repeated. Though the reality may answer to its figure or type, yet the figure can never be its equivalent.

3. The body of Christ remains in this sacrament not merely till the morrow, but as long in the future as the sacramental species endure. When they cease to exist, the body of Christ ceases to be under them, not because it depends on them, but because the relationship between the body of Christ and the species has ceased to be. It is in the same way that God ceases to be the Lord of a created thing when that has ceased to exist.

article 7. could the body of Christ as it is under this sacrament be ever seen by the eye?

THE SEVENTH POINT:[1] 1. It would seem that the body of Christ, as it is in this sacrament, could be seen by the eye, at least of somebody in heaven. Our eye is kept from seeing the body of Christ as it is in this sacrament by the sacramental species which veil him round about. But nothing can prevent the eyes of those in heaven from seeing all bodies just as they are. Hence, the heavenly eye can see the body of Christ as it is in this sacrament.

2. Again, the glorified bodies of the saints will be *like his glorious body.*[2] But Christ's eye beholds himself as he is in this sacrament. For the same reason the eyes of those in glory should be able to see him.

3. Moreover, the saints in the resurrection will be *equal to angels,*[3] as we

---

[6]*Epist.* 83 *Ad Calosyrium.* PG 76, 1076

[1]cf 3a. 76, 8. IV *Sent.* 10, 4, i, 4, 5

[2]*Philippians* 3, 21

[3]*Luke* 20, 36

Luc. xx. Sed angeli vident corpus Christi prout est in hoc sacramento: quia etiam dæmones inveniuntur huic sacramento reverentiam exhibere, et ipsum timere. Ergo pari ratione oculus glorificatus potest ipsum videre prout est in hoc sacramento.

SED CONTRA, nihil idem existens potest simul ab eodem videri in diversis speciebus. Sed oculus glorificatus semper videt Christum prout est in sua specie: secundum illud *Isaiæ* xxxiii: *Regem in decore suo videbunt.*[4] Ergo videtur quod non videat Christum prout est sub specie hujus sacramenti.

RESPONSIO: Dicendum quod duplex est oculus scilicet corporalis, proprie dictus et intellectualis, qui per similitudinem dicitur. A nullo autem oculo corporali corpus Christi potest videri prout est in hoc sacramento. Primo quidem, quia corpus visibile per sua accidentia immutat medium. Accidentia autem corporis Christi sunt in hoc sacramento mediante substantia; ita scilicet quod accidentia corporis Christi non habent immediatam habitudinem neque ad hoc sacramentum, neque ad corpora quæ ipsum circumstant. Et ideo non possunt immutare medium, ut sic ab aliquo corporali oculo videri possint.

Secundo quia, sicut supra dictum est,[5] corpus Christi est in hoc sacramento per modum substantiæ. Substantia autem, inquantum hujusmodi, non est visibilis oculo corporali, neque subjacet alicui sensui, neque imaginationi, sed soli intellectui, *cujus objectum est quod quid est*, ut dicitur in *De Anima.*[6] Et ideo, proprie loquendo, corpus Christi, secundum modum essendi quem habet in hoc sacramento, neque sensu neque imaginatione perceptibile est: sed solo intellectu, qui dicitur oculus spiritualis.

Percipitur autem diversimode a diversis intellectibus. Quia enim modus essendi quo Christus est in hoc sacramento est penitus supernaturalis, a supernaturali intellectu, scilicet divino, secundum se visibilis est: et per consequens ab intellectu beato vel angeli vel hominis, qui secundum participatam claritatem divini intellectus videt ea quæ supernaturalia sunt, per visionem divinæ essentiæ. Ab intellectu autem hominis viatoris non potest conspici nisi per fidem: sicut et cætera supernaturalia. Sed nec etiam intellectus angelicus, secundum sua naturalia, sufficit ad hoc intuendum. Unde dæmones non possunt videre per intellectum Christum in

---

[4] *Isaiah* 33, 17
[5] 3a. 76, 1 ad 3
[6] *De Anima* III, 6. 430b27

[a] The *supernatural* in the thought of St Thomas is that which lies beyond the natural power of any created substance, to know and/or to do. When the *supernatural* is beyond the creature's natural power of knowing it is intrinsically supernatural; examples of this are the mystery of the Blessed Trinity, the quality called sanctifying

read in *Luke*. But the angels see the body of Christ as it is in this sacrament; because even the devils are found to show reverence to this sacrament and to fear it. For the same reason heavenly eyesight is able to perceive him as he is in this sacrament.

ON THE OTHER HAND, a thing that remains unchanged cannot simultaneously be seen by the same observer under different aspects. Now the glorified sense of sight perceives Christ always as he is in his natural appearance, according to the text of *Isaiah*, *Your eyes will see the king in his beauty*.[4] It would appear then that it does not see Christ as he is under the form of this sacrament.

REPLY: There are two kinds of eyes, the eye of the body, properly so called, and the eye of the intelligence, called so by analogy. The body of Christ, as it is under this sacrament, cannot be seen by any bodily eye. First of all, because a body becomes visible in modifying the intermediary air by its accidents. Now the accidents of the body of Christ are in this sacrament only because of the substance; to this effect that they have no immediate reference either to the sacramental species or to the bodies that surround them. Hence they cannot modify the intermediary air so as to be seen by any bodily eye.

Again, because, as we saw earlier,[5] the body of Christ is in this sacrament as if it were just substance. But substance as such cannot be seen by the bodily eye, nor is it the object of any sense, nor can it be imagined; it is only open to the intellect, *the object of which is the essence of things*, as Aristotle says.[6] Hence, properly speaking, the body of Christ, according to the mode of existence which it has in this sacrament, can be reached neither by sense nor by imagination; it is open only to the intellect which may be called a spiritual eye.

But it is reached by different kinds of intellect in different ways. Now, because the way in which Christ exists in this sacrament is something that cannot be reached by the natural powers[a] of any created mind, it lies open only before the uncreated mind of God; but because of this it can be seen by the glorified intellect of angels or of men which, sharing in the brightness of the divine intellect and gazing into the essence of God, is able to see supernatural realities. As long, however, as man is still on the way to heaven, he can only know it by faith, in the same way as other supernatural realities are known. Not even angelic intelligence by its natural powers is able to see it. Hence, the devils are not able to see Christ in this sacrament

---

grace, the theological virtues, the real relationship of the consecrated species to the body of Christ.

hoc sacramento, nisi per fidem: cui non voluntate assentiunt, sed ad eam signorum evidentia convincuntur, prout dicitur, *Jac.* ii, quod *dæmones credunt et contremiscunt.*[7]

1. Ad primum ergo dicendum quod oculus noster corporeus per species sacramentales impeditur a visione corporis Christi sub eis existentis, non solum per modum tegumenti, sicut impedimur videre id quod est velatum quocumque corporali velamine; sed quia corpus Christi non habet habitudinem ad medium quod circumstat hoc sacramentum mediantibus propriis accidentibus, sed mediantibus speciebus sacramentalibus.

2. Ad secundum dicendum quod oculus corporalis Christi videt seipsum sub sacramento existentem; non tamen protest videre ipsum modum essendi quo est sub sacramento, quod pertinet ad intellectum. Nec tamen est simile de alio oculo glorioso; quia et ipse oculus Christi est sub hoc sacramento; in quo non conformatur ei alius oculus gloriosus.

3. Ad tertium dicendum quod angelus bonus vel malus non potest aliquid videre oculo corporeo, sed solum oculo intellectuali. Unde non est similis ratio, ut ex dictis patet.[8]

articulus 8. utrum, quando in hoc sacramento miraculose apparet vel caro vel puer, sit ibi vere corpus Christi

AD OCTAVUM sic proceditur:[1] 1. Videtur quod, quando in hoc sacramento miraculose apparet vel caro vel puer quod non sit ibi vere corpus Christi. Corpus enim Christi desinit esse sub hoc sacramento quando desinunt esse species sacramentales, ut dictum est.[2] Sed quando apparet caro vel puer desinunt esse species sacramentales. Ergo non est ibi vere corpus Christi.

2. Præterea, ubicumque est corpus Christi, vel est ibi sub specie propria, vel sub specie sacramenti. Sed quando tales apparitiones fiunt, manifestum est quod non est ibi Christus sub specie propria: quia in hoc sacramento totus Christus continetur, qui permanet integer in forma qua ascendit in cælum; cum tamen id quod miraculose apparet in hoc sacramento, quandoque videatur ut quædam parva caro, quandoque autem ut parvus puer. Manifestum est etiam quod non est ibi sub specie sacramenti, quæ est species panis vel vini. Ergo videtur quod corpus Christi nullo modo sit ibi.

3. Præterea, corpus Christi incipit esse in hoc sacramento per consecrationem et conversionem, ut supra dictum est.[3] Sed caro aut sanguis miraculose apparens non sunt consecrata, nec conversa in verum corpus et

---

[7]*James* 2, 19
[8]In the body of the article

by their natural intellect, but only by faith. The assent of their faith is not a free one, but they are forced to believe by the evidence of the signs; as St James put it, *the demons believe and tremble.*[7]

Hence: 1. Our bodily eye is unable, because of the sacramental species, to see the body of Christ which is underneath them; it is not just that they are a sort of covering, preventing us from seeing him in the way a bodily veil hides what it veils; it is rather because Christ's body has no connection with the ambient of this sacrament through its own proper accidents, but only by means of the sacramental species.

2. Christ's own bodily eye sees himself existing under the sacrament, but it cannot see the way in which he is under the sacrament; that is something only for an intellect. No other glorified eye, however, is in the same case as is Christ's, because his eye is actually under the sacrament, and no other glorified eye is like his in this.

3. No angel, be he good or bad, sees anything with a bodily eye, but only with the eye of the intellect. Hence the argument does not apply to our bodily eye, as is clear from what we have said.[8]

article 8. does the body of Christ really remain in this sacrament when there is a miraculous appearance of the likeness of a child or of flesh?

THE EIGHTH POINT:[1] 1. It would seem that whenever there is a miraculous appearance of flesh or of a child in this sacrament the body of Christ is no longer there. We have already seen[2] that the body of Christ ceases to exist in this sacrament when the sacramental species cease to exist. But the sacramental species cease to exist when there is an appearance of flesh or of a child. Therefore, the body of Christ is no longer really there.

2. Furthermore, wherever Christ's body is, it is under either its natural appearance or its sacramental appearance. Now, when such apparitions take place, it is obvious that Christ is not there under his natural appearance, because the whole Christ contained in this sacrament retains the complete form in which he ascended into heaven, and what appears miraculously in this sacrament is seen sometimes as just a small amount of flesh and at other times as a small infant. It is also obvious that he is not there under his sacramental appearance, viz. the species of bread and wine. It seems, therefore, that Christ's body is not there in any way at all.

3. Moreover, the body of Christ begins to exist in this sacrament as the result of consecration and change, as we said above.[3] But the flesh and the blood which appear miraculously are not consecrated, nor are they changed

[1] IV *Sent.* 10, 3, ii
[2] 3a. 76, 6
[3] 3a. 76, 1

sanguinem Christi. Non ergo sub his speciebus est corpus vel sanguis Christi.

SED CONTRA est quod, tali apparitione facta, eadem reverentia exhibetur ei quod apparet, quæ et prius exhibebatur. Quod quidem non fieret si non vere esset ibi Christi, cui reverentiam latriæ exhibemus. Ergo, etiam tali apparitione facta, Christus est sub hoc sacramento.

RESPONSIO: Dicendum quod dupliciter contingit talis apparitio, qua quandoque in hoc sacramento miraculose videtur caro aut sanguis, aut etiam aliquis puer. Quandoque enim hoc contingit ex parte videntium, quorum oculi immutantur tali immutatione ac si expresse viderent exterius carnem aut sanguinem vel puerum, nulla tamen immutatione facta ex parte sacramenti. Et hoc quidem videtur contingere quando uni videtur sub specie carnis vel pueri, aliis tamen videtur, sicut et prius, sub specie panis; vel quando idem ad horam videtur sub specie carnis vel pueri, et postmodum sub specie panis. Nec tamen hoc pertinet ad aliquam deceptionem, sicut accidit in magorum præstigiis: quia talis species divinitus formatur in oculo ad aliquam veritatem figurandam, ad hoc scilicet quod manifestetur vere corpus Christi esse sub hoc sacramento; sicut etiam Christus absque deceptione apparuit discipulis euntibus in Emmaus. Dicit enim Augustinus, quod *cum fictio nostra refertur ad aliquam significationem, non est mendacium, sed aliqua figura veritatis.*[4] Et quia per hunc modum nulla immutatio fit ex parte sacramenti, manifestum est quod non desinit esse Christus sub hoc sacramento, tali apparitione facta.

Quandoque vero contingit talis apparitio non per solam immutationem videntium, sed specie quæ videtur realiter exterius existente. Et hoc quidem videtur esse quando sub tali specie ab omnibus videtur; et non ad horam, sed per longum tempus ita permanet. Et in hoc casu quidam dicunt quod est propria species corporis Christi. Nec obstat quod quandoque non videtur ibi totus Christus, sed aliqua pars carnis; vel etiam videtur non in specie juvenili, sed in effigie puerili: quia in potestate est corporis gloriosi, ut infra dicetur, quod videatur ab oculo non glorificato vel secundum totum vel secundum partem, et in effigie vel propria vel aliena, ut infra dicetur.

Sed hoc videtur esse inconveniens. Primo quidem, quia corpus Christi non potest in propria specie videri nisi in uno loco, in quo definitive continetur. Unde, cum videatur in propria specie et adoretur in cælo, sub propria specie non videtur in hoc sacramento. Secundo, quia corpus

---

[4]*de Quæstionibus Evangelii* II, 51. PL 35, 1362

[a]*Their eyes were kept from recognizing him, Luke* 24, 16. See the homily of St Gregory in the Roman Breviary for Easter Monday.

into the real body and blood of Christ. Therefore, neither the body nor the blood of Christ is under these appearances.

ON THE OTHER HAND, when such an apparition takes place, the same respect is accorded to what now appears as was given earlier. This would not be if Christ were not still really present; it is to him that we offer the homage of supreme worship. Hence, even when such an apparition occurs, Christ is still under the sacrament.

REPLY: This kind of miraculous apparition, in which at times flesh or blood is seen, at times a child, can take place in two ways. Sometimes it happens as a subjective vision on the part of beholders. Their eyes are acted upon in such a way as if they were looking at flesh or blood or a child objectively there, although actually there is no change at all produced in the sacrament. This would seem to be the case when this appearance of flesh or of a child is seen by one person, but everybody else continues to see the appearance of bread, as before, or when the same person sees it for a while under the appearance of flesh or of a child and later on under the appearance of bread. In all this, however, there is no deception such as there is in a magician's tricks, because this kind of image is formed by God in the eye of the beholder in order to signify a certain truth, namely, that the body of Christ is really present in the sacrament; it was after this fashion too, without any deception,[a] that Christ appeared to the disciples on the way to Emmaus. On this point Augustine says, *when the image that we form genuinely signifies something, you cannot say it is a lie; it is a representation of the truth.*[4] Since in this way there is no objective change in the sacrament, it follows that Christ does not cease to be really there, when such an apparition takes place.

Sometimes, however, it happens that an apparition of this kind is not a merely subjective one but has an objective basis. This would seem to be the case when everybody sees the sacrament under this form, and when it remains thus not just for a short while but for a considerable time. In this case, some people think that it is Christ's own natural form that is seen. To the objection that sometimes the whole Christ is not seen, but only part of his flesh, or that he is not seen in the fulness of his manhood, but as a child, they reply that a glorified body has the powers of showing itself in whole or in part to a non-glorified eye and also of showing itself either in its proper likeness or in a borrowed one, as will be seen later on.

But this opinion does not seem to fit all the facts. First of all, the body of Christ cannot be seen in its natural form except in one place, to which, while it is there, it is restricted. So, since he is seen and adored in heaven in his natural form, he is not seen in this sacrament in his natural form.

gloriosum, quod apparet ut vult, post apparitionem cum voluerit disparet: sicut dicitur, *Luc.* ult., quod Dominus *ab oculis discipulorum evanuit.*[5] Hoc autem quod sub specie carnis in hoc sacramento, apparet, diu permanet: quinimmo quandoque legitur esse inclusum, et multorum episcoporum consilio in pixide reservatum;[6] quod nefas est de Christo sentire secundum propriam speciem.

Et ideo dicendum quod, manentibus dimensionibus quæ prius fuerant, fit miraculose quædam immutatio circa alia accidentia, puta figuram et colorem et alia hujusmodi, ut videatur caro vel sanguis, aut etiam puer. Et, sicut prius dictum est, hoc non est deceptio: quia fit in figuram cujusdam veritatis, scilicet ad ostendendum per hanc miraculosam apparitionem quod in hoc sacramento est vere corpus Christi et sanguis. Et sic patet quod, remanentibus dimensionibus, quæ sunt fundamenta aliorum accidentium, ut infra dicetur,[7] remanet vere corpus Christi in hoc sacramento.

1. Ad primum ergo dicendum quod, facta tali apparitione, species sacramentales quandoque quidem totaliter manent in seipsis, quandoque autem secundum illud quod est principale in eis, ut dictum est.[8]

2. Ad secundum dicendum quod in hujusmodi apparitionibus, sicut dictum est,[9] non videtur propria species Christi: sed species miraculosa formata vel in oculis intuentium, vel etiam in ipsis sacramentalibus dimensionibus, ut dictum est.[10]

3. Ad tertium dicendum quod dimensiones panis et vini consecrati manent, immutatione circa eas miraculose facta quantum ad alia accidentia, ut dictum est.[11]

---

[5] *Luke* 24, 31
[6] See Guitmund, *De corp. et sanguine Christi* 2. PL 149, 1449
[7] 3a. 77, 2
[8] In the body of the article
[9] In the body of the article

Secondly, a glorious body, which appears at will, disappears also at will after the apparition: we read in the last chapter of *Luke*, that the Lord *vanished out of their sight.*[5] What appears in the sacrament, however, under the form of flesh lasts a long time; indeed one reads of it at times as being locked up and by the advice of many bishops being reserved in a ciborium;[6] now it would be quite wrong to treat Christ in such a way if he were there in his natural form.

We must then conclude that, while original quantitative dimensions remain, a miraculous change takes place in the other accidental quantities, for example, the shape and colour, etc., so that flesh or blood appears or even a child. And, as we have already said, there is no deception in all this, because it all happens in order to express a certain truth, and the miraculous appearance is to show that the body and blood of Christ are really present in this sacrament. Thus we see that as long as the quantitative dimensions, which are the foundation of the other accidents (as will be seen in the next question),[7] remain, the body of Christ remains really present in this sacrament.

Hence: 1. When such an apparition occurs, the sacramental species sometimes still remain in their entirety, sometimes only the more important ones, as we have just said.[8]

2. In these appearances, as has just been said,[9] Christ's natural form is not seen, but a form miraculously produced either in the eyes of the beholders or even in the dimensions themselves of the sacrament, as we have just said.[10]

3. The dimensions of the bread and wine remain consecrated; the miraculous change takes place in them with regard to the other accidents, as has just been said.[11]

---

[10]ibid
[11]ibid

Quæstio 77. de accidentibus remanentibus in hoc sacramento

Deinde considerandum est de accidentibus remanentibus in hoc sacramento. Et circa hoc quæruntur octo:

1. utrum accidentia quæ remanent sint sine subjecto;
2. utrum quantitas dimensiva sit subjectum aliorum accidentium;
3. utrum hujusmodi accidentia possunt immutare aliquod corpus extrinsecum;
4. utrum possunt corrumpi:
5. utrum ex eis aliquid possit generari;
6. utrum possint nutrire;
7. de fractione panis consecrati;
8. utrum vino consecrato possit aliquid admisceri.

articulus 1. *utrum accidentia remaneant in hoc sacramento sine subjecto*

AD PRIMUM sic proceditur.[1] 1. Videtur quod accidentia non remaneant in hoc sacramento sine subjecto. Nihil enim inordinatum aut fallax debet esse in hoc sacramento veritatis. Sed accidentia esse sine subjecto est contra rerum ordinem, quem Deus naturæ indidit. Videtur etiam ad quamdam fallaciam pertinere: cum accidentia* sint signa naturæ subjecti. Ergo in hoc sacramento non sunt accidentia sine subjecto.

2. Præterea, fieri non potest, etiam miraculose, quod definitio rei ab ea separetur, vel quod uni rei conveniat definitio alterius, puta quod homo, manens homo, sit animal irrationale. Ad hoc enim sequeretur contradictoria esse simul: *hoc* enim *quod significat nomen rei, est definitio*,[2] ut dicitur in *Meta.* Sed ad definitionem accidentis pertinet quod sit in subjecto: ad definitionem vero substantiæ, quod per se subsistat non in subjecto. Non potest ergo miraculose fieri quod in hoc sacramento sint accidentia sine subjecto.

3. Præterea, accidens individuatur ex subjecto. Si ergo accidentia remanent in hoc sacramento sine subjecto, non erunt individua, sed universalia. Quod patet esse falsum: quia sic non essent sensibilia, sed intelligibilia tantum.

---

*Piana: *naturaliter*, naturally

[1]cf 3a. 75, 5. 1 *Sent.* 47, 4; IV 12, 1, 1. *CG* IV, 62, 63 & 65. *Quodl.* III, 1, 1 ad 1; IX, 3, 1. *Contra Græc.* 8. *In Matt.* 26. *In* 1 *Cor.* 11, *lect.* 5

Question 77. the accidents which remain in this sacrament

Let us now take up the question of the accidents which remain in this sacrament. There are eight points of inquiry:

1. have the accidents which remain no subject in which to inhere?
2. is the dimensive quantity the subject in which the other accidents inhere?
3. can these accidents change other bodies?
4. can they disintegrate?
5. can anything be produced out of them?
6. are they able to nourish?
7. on the breaking of the consecrated bread.
8. can anything be mixed with the consecrated wine?

article 1. *have the accidents which remain no subject in which to inhere?*

THE FIRST POINT:[1] 1. It seems that the accidents do not remain in this sacrament without a subject. There should be nothing out of order or deceptive in this sacrament of truth. But for accidents to be without a subject is against the natural order of things for which God is responsible. Likewise, there is something deceptive about it, because accidents are signs which reveal the nature of the subject in which they inhere. Therefore, in this sacrament, the accidents are not without a subject.

2. Moreover, not even by a miracle could a thing be separated from what defines it, or have applied to it what defines something quite different; for example that a man while remaining such could be an irrational animal. For then you would have contradictions co-existing; as Aristotle says, *the name of a thing signifies its definition.*[2] Now part of the very definition of an accident is that it exists in a subject, whereas it is of the definition of a substance that it exists independently and not in a subject. Therefore not even by a miracle can it come to pass for accidents in this sacrament to exist without a subject.

3. Furthermore, an accident receives its individuation from the subject in which it inheres. If then accidents remain in the sacrament outside any subject, they will not be individuated but rather universal. But that is obviously not the case, because were it so, they would not be object of our sense-knowledge, but only of intellectual knowledge.

---

[2] *Metaphysics* III, 7. 1012a23

4. Præterea, accidentia per consecrationem hujus sacramenti non adipiscuntur aliquam compositionem. Sed ante consecrationem non erant composita neque ex materia et forma, neque ex *quo est* et *quod est*. Ergo etiam post consecrationem non sunt composita altero horum modorum. Quod est inconveniens: quia sic essent simpliciora quam angeli, cum tamen hæc accidentia sint sensibilia. Non ergo accidentia remanent in hoc sacramento sine subjecto.

SED CONTRA est quod Gregorius dicit, in Homilia Paschali, quod *species sacramentales sunt illarum rerum vocabula quæ ante fuerunt, scilicet panis et vini.*[3] Et ita, cum non remaneat substantia panis et vini, videtur quod hujusmodi species sint sine subjecto.

RESPONSIO: Dicendum quod accidentia panis et vini, quæ sensu deprehenduntur in hoc sacramento remanere post consecrationem, non sunt sicut in subjecto in substantia panis et vini, quæ non remanet, ut supra habitum est.[4] Neque etiam in forma substantiali, quæ non manet; et, si remaneret, *subjectum esse non posset*, ut patet per Boëtium, in libro *de Trin.*[5] Manifestum est etiam quod hujusmodi accidentia non sunt in substantia corporis et sanguinis Christi sicut in subjecto: quia substantia humani corporis nullo modo potest his accidentibus affici; neque etiam est possibile quod corpus Christi, gloriosum et impassibile existens, alteretur ad suscipiendas hujusmodi qualitates.

Dicunt autem quidam[6] quod sunt, sicut in subjecto, in aere circumstante. Sed nec hoc esse potest. Primo quidem, quia aër non est hujusmodi accidentium susceptivus. Secundo, quia hujusmodi accidentia non sunt ubi est aër. Quinimmo ad motum harum specierum aër depellitur. Tertio, quia accidentia non transeunt de subjecto in subjectum: ut scilicet idem accidens numero quod primo fuit in uno subjecto, postmodum fiat in alio. Accidens enim numerum accipit a subjecto. Unde non potest esse quod, idem numero manens, sit quandoque in hoc, quandoque in alio subjecto. Quarto quia, cum aër non spolietur accidentibus propriis, simul haberet

---

[3]cf Gratian, *Decretum* 3, 2, 34 *Species*. Richter-Friedberg I, 1324. Lanfranc, *De corp. et sang. Dom.* 20. PL 150, 436

[4]3a. 75, 2

[5]*De Trinitate* I, 2. PL 64, 1250

[6]e.g. Abelard; cf William of St Thierry, *Disputatio adv. Abælardum*, 9. PL 180, 280

[a]*Quod est* is the immediate subject of existence. It is the nature or essence—the *quo est*—as terminated, finished, and then actuated by existence. The *quod est* is sometimes called the '*suppositum*' or 'hypostasis', the *quo est* is the form, or at times the nature or essence composed of matter and form, by which the '*suppositum*' has

4. Again, as a result of the consecration of this sacrament, the accidents do not acquire any new addition to their being. Now, prior to the consecration they were not composed of matter and form, nor could we distinguish in them between that which exists and its nature or essence.[a] Therefore, after the consecration, they do not have either of these kinds of composition. But that raises an awkward difficulty—it means that they are less affected by composition than are the angels, and yet they are only corporeal. We should not then allow that the accidents remain in this sacrament without inhering in a subject.

ON THE OTHER HAND, Gregory in an Easter sermon says, *the sacramental species are named after those realities which previously existed, namely, the bread and wine.*[3] So, since the substance of the bread and wine no longer exists, it would appear that these species exist without a subject.

REPLY: The accidents of the bread and wine, which our senses tell us remain in this sacrament after the consecration, do not inhere in the substance of the bread and wine as their subject, seeing that the substance of the bread and wine is no longer there, as we saw above.[4] Nor do they inhere in the substantial form, because that too has gone, and, even if it did remain, *it could not be a subject*, as is clear from Boëthius.[5] Now it is obvious that those accidents do not inhere in the substance of Christ's body and blood, because the substance of the human body as such could not be affected by accidents of this kind, and it is further impossible that Christ's body, now glorious and immune from suffering change, should so be altered as to receive these qualities.

Some theologians[6] think that these accidents inhere in the atmosphere around the sacrament. But this is not possible. First of all, it is incapable of receiving such accidents. Second, these accidents are not actually where the air is; indeed, if you move these species, the atmosphere is displaced. Third, accidents do not pass from one subject of inherence to another, as if the very same accident which was previously in one subject could afterwards be in another. You see, accidents receive their individuation from the subject in which they inhere. It is quite impossible, then, for the same numerically identical accident to be in this subject now and afterwards in that one. Fourth, since the air is not deprived of its own proper accidents, it would be simultaneously affected by its own proper accidents and by

---

meaning, and which the intelligence can express as idea or concept. All this applies properly to substance, not to accident. Accident is properly merely a *quo est*, a form, supervening to the inner form or nature, and affecting a substance, which substance can alone be properly said to be the thing that exists.

accidentia propria et aliena. Nec potest dici quod hoc fiat miraculose virtute consecrationis, quia verba consecrationis hoc non significant; quæ tamen non efficiunt nisi significatum.

Et ideo relinquitur quod accidentia in hoc sacramento manent sine subjecto. Quod quidem virtute divina fieri potest. Cum enim effectus magis dependeat a causa prima quam a causa secunda, potest Deus, qui est prima causa substantiæ et accidentis, per suam infinitam virtutem conservare in esse accidens subtracta substantia, per quam conservabatur in esse sicut per propriam causam: sicut etiam alios effectus naturalium causarum potest producere sine naturalibus causis, sicut corpus humanum formavit in utero Virginis sine virili semine.

1. Ad primum ergo dicendum quod nihil prohibet aliquid esse ordinatum secundum communem legem naturæ, cujus tamen contrarium est ordinatum secundum speciale privilegium gratiæ, ut patet in resurrectione mortuorum, et in illuminatione cæcorum: prout etiam in rebus humanis quædam aliquibus conceduntur ex speciali privilegio præter communem legem. Et ita, licet sit secundum communem naturæ ordinem quod accidens sit in subjecto, ex speciali tamen ratione, secundum ordinem gratiæ, accidentia sunt in hoc sacramento sine subjecto, propter rationes supra inductas.[7]

2. Ad secundum dicendum quod, cum ens non sit genus, hoc ipsum quod est esse, non potest esse essentia vel substantiæ vel accidentis. Non ergo definitio substantiæ est 'ens per se sine subjecto', nec definitio accidentis 'ens in subjecto', sed quidditati seu essentiæ substantiæ 'competit habere esse non in subjecto'; quidditati autem sive essentiæ accidentis 'competit habere esse in subjecto'. In hoc autem sacramento non datur accidentibus quod ex vi suæ essentiæ sint sine subjecto, sed ex divina virtute sustentante. Et ideo non desinunt esse accidentia, quia nec separatur ab eis definitio accidentis, nec competit eis definitio substantiæ.

3. Ad tertium dicendum quod hujusmodi accidentia acquisierunt esse individuum in substantia panis et vini, qua conversa in corpus et sanguinem Christi, remanent virtute divina accidentia in illo esse individuato quod prius habebant. Unde sunt singularia et sensibilia.

---

[7]3a. 75, 5

[b]This is a very compressed piece of metaphysics. Being is not a genus, applying equally and univocally, to its inferiors and differentiated by the addition of extrinsic determinants, as animal is applied to man and brute. It is an analogous concept, applying in different senses to its inferiors and differentiated by intrinsic adaptation to each case. God is the supreme analogue of being and created beings in their hierarchy of value are the lesser analogues. God is he whose essence is existence. The creature as such is defined as that the essence of which is not existence. To affirm

accidents foreign to it. Nor can you say that all this happens miraculously in virtue of the consecration, because the words of consecration do not signify this and they only effect what they signify.

We are left to conclude that the accidents in this sacrament do not inhere in any subject. God's power is able to bring this about. Seeing that all effects depend more on the first cause than on secondary causes, God, who is the first cause of both substance and accident, by using his infinite power, is able to conserve an accident in being, even when the substance which hitherto as its immediate cause was keeping it in existence has disappeared. In this way also he is able to produce what are the effects of other natural causes without actually employing these causes, as when he formed a human body in the Virgin's womb without male seed.

Hence: 1. There is no reason why the common law of nature should not arrange things in one way, yet for a contrary arrangement to be quite in order because of some special privilege of grace. Examples of this are the resurrection of the dead and the giving of sight to the blind; and in human affairs, too, look how some people are granted special privileges beyond the ordinary law. So it is that although the common order of nature prescribes that an accident should inhere in a subject, we have here, for a special reason and in the order of grace, accidents without a subject. We have already mentioned what the reasons for this are.[7]

2. Seeing that being is not a genus, existence cannot be of the essence of either substance or accident.[b] It is not right then to define substance as 'that which exists of itself without inhering in a subject' or to define accident as 'that which exists in a subject'; one should say that to the definition or essence of a substance 'it pertains to have existence without inhering in a subject', and that to the definition or essence of an accident, 'it pertains to have existence in a subject'. Now in this sacrament the fact that the accidents exist without actually inhering in a subject is not because their essence has been changed but because they are being kept in existence by God. Hence they do not cease to be accidents; they are not deprived of their definition as accident, nor is the definition of substance attributed to them.

3. These accidents acquired their individual existence in the substance of the bread and wine; when it was changed into the body and blood of Christ, the accidents remained by divine power in that individual existence which they already had. Hence they are concrete realities and can be by the object of sense-knowledge.

---

the analogy of being is to affirm that God is he who is and that the creature is that which of itself is not.

4. Ad quartum dicendum quod accidentia hujusmodi, manente substantia panis et vini, non habebant ipsa esse nec alia accidentia; sed substantia eorum habebat* hujusmodi esse per ea, sicut nix est alba per albedinem. Sed post consecrationem ipsa accidentia quæ remanent, habent esse. Unde sunt composita ex *esse* et *quod est*, sicut in Prima Parte de angelis dictum est.[8] Et cum hoc habent compositionem partium quantitativarum.

articulus 2. utrum in hoc sacramento quantitas dimensiva panis vel vini sit aliorum accidentium subjectum

AD SECUNDUM sic proceditur:[1] 1. Videtur quod in hoc sacramento quantitas dimensiva panis vel vini non sit aliorum accidentium subjectum. Accidentis enim† non est accidens: nulla enim forma potest esse subjectum, cum subjici pertineat ad proprietatem materiæ. Sed quantitas dimensiva est quoddam accidens. Ergo quantitas dimensiva non potest esse subjectum aliorum accidentium.

2. Præterea, sicut quantitas individuatur ex substantia, ita etiam et alia accidentia. Si ergo quantitas dimensiva panis aut vini remanet individuata secundum esse prius habitum in quo conservatur, pari ratione et alia accidentia remanent individuata secundum esse quod prius habebant in substantia. Non ergo sunt in quantitate dimensiva sicut in subjecto, cum omne accidens individuetur per suum subjectum.

3. Præterea, inter alia accidentia panis et vini quæ remanent, deprehenduntur etiam sensu rarum et densum. Quæ non possunt esse in quantitate dimensiva præter materiam existente: quia rarum est quod habet parum de materia sub dimensionibus magnis; densum autem quod habet multum de materia sub dimensionibus parvis, ut dicitur in *Physic.*[2] Ergo videtur quod quantitas dimensiva non possit esse subjectum accidentium quæ remanent in hoc sacramento.

4. Præterea, quantitas a subjecto separata videtur esse quantitas mathematica, quæ non est subjectum qualitatum sensibilium. Cum ergo

---

*Piana: *subjecta eorum habebant*, it was their subjects that had existence
†Piana: *subjectum enim accidentis*, for the subject of an accident

[8] 1a. 50, 2 ad 3. cf 3a. 75, 5 ad 4
[1] cf IV *Sent.* 1, 1, iii. *CG* IV, 63 & 65. *Quodl.* VII, 4, 3. *In Matt.* 26. *In* I *Cor.* 11, *lect.* 5
[2] *Physics* IV, 9. 217b10

[c] St Thomas here quietly admits that the metaphysical status of the accidents (at least of the basic accident—quantity, as the next article will show) has undergone a change. What was merely form, *quo*, is now behaving as if it were hypostasis, *suppositum*, a *quod* now possessing existence. Hitherto the accidents were real, not because they existed, but because they inhered in the real substance which alone possessed existence. Now the quantity seems real, as itself possessing existence.

4. These accidents, as long as the substance of the bread and wine remained, had not themselves got existence, indeed, no accidents have existence; for it was their substance that existed, which existed in this way or in that because of them. Thus we say that snow exists as white (or is white) because of its whiteness. But after the consecration the accidents which remain do have existence. Hence, they are now composed of *existence* and *that which exists*,[c] as we affirmed in the *Prima Pars* about the angels.[8] And along with this they are also composed of quantitative parts.

article 2. in this sacrament is the dimensive quantity of the bread and wine the subject in which the other accidents inhere?

THE SECOND POINT:[1] 1. It would seem that in this sacrament the dimensions of the bread and wine are not the subject in which the other accidents inhere. It is not natural for accident to support accident, seeing that no form can be a subject.[a] To be a subject pertains rather to the nature of matter. But the dimensive quantity is an accident. Therefore, it cannot be a subject receiving other accidents.

2. Moreover, just as quantity is individuated by the substance, so also are the other accidents. If then the quantity of the bread and wine remains individuated according to the existence which it first had and in which it is conserved,[b] for the same reason the other accidents remain individuated in the existence which was previously theirs in the substance. It follows that the dimensive quantity is not their subject, because the subject of an accident is the source of its individuation.

3. Furthermore, among the other accidents of the bread and wine which remain after the change, our very senses experience density and tenuousness. But these quantities cannot be found in quantity apart from matter, because tenuousness means that there is little matter in great volume and density means that there is much matter in small volume, as Aristotle says.[2] It follows then that the dimensive quantity cannot be the subject which receives the accidents which remain in this sacrament.

4. Again, quantity separated from a subject would appear to be mathematical quantity, and this is not the subject of qualities perceptible by our

---

[a]We are here concerned with bodily substance and its forms—the substantial form which has the primal matter as its subject, and the accidental forms which have the composite of primal matter and substantial form as their subject. The angels are pure forms and such pure forms are the subject of accidental forms.

[b]This way of speaking is to be understood in the light of the replies in the previous article.

accidentia quæ remanent in hoc sacramento sint sensibilia, videtur quod non possint esse in hoc sacramento sicut in subjecto in quantitate* panis et vini remanente post consecrationem.

SED CONTRA est quod qualitates non sunt divisibiles nisi per accidens, scilicet ratione subjecti. Dividuntur autem qualitates remanentes in hoc sacramento per divisionem quantitatis dimensivæ: sicut patet ad sensum. Ergo quantitas dimensiva est subjectum accidentium quæ remanent in hoc sacramento.

RESPONSIO: Dicendum quod necesse est dicere accidentia alia quæ remanent in hoc sacramento esse sicut in subjecto in quantitate dimensiva panis vel vini remanente. Primo quidem, per hoc quod ad sensum apparet aliquod quantum esse ibi coloratum et aliis accidentibus affectum: nec in talibus sensus decipitur.

Secundo, quia prima dispositio materiæ est quantitas dimensiva; unde et Plato posuit primas differentias materiæ *magnum* et *parvum*. Et quia primum subjectum est materia, consequens est quod omnia alia accidentia referantur ad subjectum mediante quantitate dimensiva, sicut et primum subjectum coloris dicitur superficies esse: ratione cujus quidam posuerunt dimensiones esse substantias corporum, ut dicitur in *Meta.*[3] Et quia, subtracto subjecto, remanent accidentia secundum esse quod prius habebant, consequens est quod omnia accidentia remaneant fundata super quantitatem dimensivam.

Tertio quia, cum subjectum sit principium individuationis accidentium, oportet id quod ponitur aliquorum accidentium subjectum esse, aliquo modo esse individuationis principium. Est enim de ratione individui quod non possit in pluribus esse. Quod quidem contingit dupliciter. Uno modo, quia non est natum in aliquo esse; et hoc modo formæ immateriales separatæ, per se subsistentes, sunt etiam per seipsas individuæ. Alio modo, ex eo quod forma substantialis vel accidentalis est quidem nata in aliquo esse, non tamen in pluribus; sicut hæc albedo, quæ est in hoc corpore.

Quantum igitur ad primum, materia est individuationis principium omnibus formis inhærentibus: quia, cum hujusmodi formæ, quantum est de

---

*Piana: *dimensiva*, in the dimensive quantity

[3]*Metaphysics* II, 5. 1001b26

[c]The point is that the dimensive quantity which remains is now separate from its subject, e.g. from bread, and is therefore an abstraction.

[d]We can distinguish between a subject in which a form is merely received, and a subject which receives a form and also sustains it in being. The first and second arguments in the body of the article show that quantity is a receiving subject, the

senses. Now seeing that the accidents which remain in this sacrament are reached by sense-knowledge, it follows that in this sacrament they have not got as their subject the dimensive quantity of the bread and wine that still remains after the consecration.[c]

ON THE OTHER HAND, qualities are divisible not in themselves, but only because the subject in which they are is divisible. Now the qualities which remain in this sacrament are divided whenever the dimensive quantity is divided; our senses tell us that. Therefore, the dimensive quantity is the subject of the accidents which remain in this sacrament.

REPLY: It has to be admitted that the other accidents which remain in this sacrament have as their subject[d] the dimensive quantity of the bread and wine which remains. First of all, what appears to our senses is something extended which is coloured and is affected by other accidental qualities; in those matters our senses are not deceived.

Secondly, its dimensive quantity is the very first accident which affects a material thing; for this reason Plato stated that the first differences in material things were *large* and *small*. And because the material substance is the basic subject in which all the accidents are received, it follows that all the other accidents cling to the substance through the medium of the quantity; for this reason we say that the immediate recipient of colour is the extended surface. This led some people to think that the dimensions of a body were its very substance, as we read in Aristotle.[3] Now, since in the Eucharist the substance of the bread disappears and the accidents remain in being precisely as they were before, it follows that they remain clinging to the quantity as their subject.

Thirdly, since accidents derive their individuation from the subject which receives them, whatever is claimed as the subject of any accidents must be in some way the source of their individuation; the very notion of individuation involves not being in a number of subjects. This can happen in two ways. First, it may be that the individuated reality is not such as to be received in any subject at all; it is because of this that spiritual forms, separated from matter and subsisting of themselves, are also individuated in themselves. Second, a substantial or an accidental form is indeed geared to being in a subject that receives it, but not to be in a plurality of subjects; for example, this particular whiteness is in this particular bodily thing.

With regard to the first point (i.e. being or not-being in a subject), the primal matter is the source of individuation for all forms that inhere in a

---

third argument (a very tortuous one) shows that it is most probably also a subject that sustains the other accidents in their being.

se, sint natæ in aliquo esse sicut in subjecto, ex quo aliqua earum recipitur in materia, quæ non est in alio, jam nec ipsa forma sic existens potest in alio esse. Quantum autem ad secundum, dicendum est quod individuationis principium est quantitas dimensiva. Ex hoc enim aliquid est natum esse in uno solo, quod illud est in se indivisum et divisum ab omnibus aliis. Divisio autem accidit substantiæ ratione quantitatis, ut dicitur in *Physic.*[4] Et ideo ipsa quantitas dimensiva est quoddam individuationis principium in hujusmodi formis, inquantum scilicet diversæ formæ numero sunt in diversis partibus materiæ. Unde et ipsa quantitas dimensiva secundum se habet quandam individuationem; ita quod possumus imaginari plures lineas* ejusdem speciei differentes positione, quæ cadit in ratione hujus quantitatis; convenit enim dimensioni quod sit *quantitas positionem habens*. Et ideo potius quantitas dimensiva potest esse subjectum aliorum accidentium quam e converso.

1. Ad primum ergo dicendum quod accidens per se non potest esse subjectum alterius accidentis, quia non per se est. Secundum vero quod est in alio, unum accidens dicitur esse subjectum alterius, inquantum unum accidens recipitur in subjecto alio mediante, sicut superficies dicitur esse subjectum coloris. Unde, quando accidenti datur divinitus ut per se sit, potest etiam per se alterius accidentis esse subjectum.

2. Ad secundum dicendum quod alia accidentia, etiam secundum quod erant in substantia panis, individuabantur mediante quantitate dimensiva, sicut dictum est.[5] Et ideo potius quantitas dimensiva est subjectum aliorum accidentium remanentium in hoc sacramento quam e converso.

3. Ad tertium dicendum quod rarum et densum sunt quædam qualitates consequentes corpora ex hoc quod habent multum vel parum de materia sub dimensionibus; sicut etiam omnia alia accidentia consequuntur ex principiis substantiæ. Et sicut, subtracta substantia, divina virtute conservantur alia accidentia; ita, subtracta materia, divina virtute conservantur qualitates materiam consequentes, sicut rarum et densum.

4. Ad quartum dicendum quod quantitas mathematica non abstrahit a materia intelligibili, sed a materia sensibili, ut dicitur *Meta.*[6] Dicitur autem materia sensibilis ex hoc quod subjicitur sensibilibus qualitatibus. Et ideo manifestum est quod quantitas dimensiva quæ remanet in hoc sacramento sine subjecto non est quantitas mathematica.

---

*Piana: *separatas*, many separate lines

[4] *Physics* II, 10 & 13. 183a33; b16. cf St Thomas, *In Physic.* I, *lect.* 3

[5] In the body of the article

[6] *Metaphysics* VI, 10. 1036a11

[e] The point is that mathematical quantity is withdrawn from the condition of being sensed; the dimensive quantity of the sacrament is withdrawn from the underlying subject which was sensed through it and through the succeeding accidents.

subject. Since these forms are naturally meant to be received in something as their subject, as soon as they are found in primal matter, which itself exists in no deeper ground of being, they are incapable of being in anything else. With regard to the second point (i.e. not being in a plurality of subjects) the source of individuation is dimensive quantity itself. The reason why a thing is in one thing and in one thing only is because that thing, undivided in itself, is divided off from everything else. Now it is because of its quantity that a substance is divided off from everything else, as Aristotle teaches.[4] Hence the dimensive quantity itself is a source of individuation for all such forms as are received in a subject; all these forms are numerically distinct because they are received in different parts of matter. So it is that dimensive quantity in itself has a certain individuation; we can imagine many lines of the same kind, but all different because of their position; and this position is part of the very idea of this quantity. For it is of the very definition of a dimension to be *quantity having position*. This is the reason why it is more likely that quantity should be the subject that sustains the other accidents than that it should not be such.

Hence: 1. No accident of itself can be the subject which sustains another accident in being, because its own being is not independently enjoyed. In so far, however, as it is in a subject, one accident can be the subject of another, in the sense that the second accident is received in the sustaining subject through the medium of the first. In this sense the surface is said to be the subject of colour. Hence, when it is miraculously granted to an accident to enjoy its being independently, it can be the immediate subject which sustains another accident.

2. As we said,[5] even when they were in the substance of the bread the other accidents were individuated because of the dimensive quantity. For this reason it is most likely that it should be their sustaining subject when they remain on in this sacrament.

3. Tenuousness and density are certain qualities which bodies have from the fact that there is much or little matter underlying the dimensions; in thus flowing from the sources of the substance they are on a par with all the other accidents. Just as the other accidents are miraculously kept in being when the substance has been withdrawn, so too, when the matter has been withdrawn, the qualities which have their source in matter, such as tenuousness and quantity, are miraculously conserved.

4. Mathematical quantity does not abstract from intelligible matter but from matter that is open to sense-knowledge, as Aristotle teaches.[6] That matter is said to be open to sense-knowledge because it is the subject of qualities that can be sensed. Hence it is clear that the dimensive quantity which remains without any subject in this sacrament is not mathematical quantity.[e]

articulus 3. *utrum species quæ remanent in hoc sacramento, possint immutare aliquod extrinsecum*

AD TERTIUM sic proceditur:[1] 1. Videtur quod species quæ remanent in hoc sacramento, non possint immutare aliquid extrinsecum. Probatur enim in *Meta.*[2] quod formæ quæ sunt in materia, fiunt a formis quæ sunt in materia, non autem a formis quæ sunt sine materia: eo quod simile agit sibi simile. Sed species sacramentales sunt species sine materia: quia remanent sine subjecto, ut ex dictis[3] patet. Non ergo possunt immutare materiam exteriorem, inducendo aliquam formam.

2. Præterea, cessante actione primi* agentis, necesse est quod cesset actio instrumenti: sicut, quiescente fabro, non movetur martellus. Sed omnes formæ accidentales agunt instrumentaliter in virtute formæ substantialis tanquam principalis agentis. Cum ergo in hoc sacramento non remaneat forma substantialis panis et vini, sicut supra habitum est,[4] videtur quod formæ accidentales remanentes agere non possunt ad immutationem exterioris materiæ.

3. Præterea, nihil agit extra† suam speciem: quia effectus non potest esse potior causa. Sed species sacramentales omnes sunt accidentia. Non ergo possunt exteriorem materiam immutare, ad minus ad formam substantialem.

SED CONTRA est quod, si non possent immutare exteriora corpora, non possent sentiri: sentitur enim aliquid per hoc quod immutatur sensus a sensibili, ut dicitur *De Anima.*[5]

RESPONSIO: Dicendum quod, quia unumquodque agit inquantum est ens actu, consequens est quod unumquodque sicut se habet ad esse ita se habet ad agere. Quia igitur, secundum prædicta,[6] speciebus sacramentalibus datum est divina virtute ut remaneant in suo esse quod habebant substantia panis et vini existente, consequens est quod etiam remaneant in suo agere. Et ideo omnem actionem quam poterant agere substantia panis et vini existente, possunt etiam agere substantia panis et vini transeunte in corpus et sanguinem Christi. Unde non est dubium quod possunt immutare exteriora corpora.

1. Ad primum ergo dicendum quod species sacramentales, licet sint formæ sine materia existentes, retinent tamen idem esse quod habebant

---

*Piana: *principalis*
†Piana: *ultra*

[1]cf IV *Sent.* 12, 1, 2, i & ii. *Resp. de* XXXVI *Artic.* 35
[2]*Metaphysics* VI, 8. 1033b5
[3]3a. 77, 1

article 3. can the species which remain in this sacrament change outside things?

THE THIRD POINT:[1] 1. It would appear that the species which remain in this sacrament cannot set up a change in an outside thing. Aristotle[2] has established that forms which are in matter are brought into being by other forms in matter and not by forms which exist apart from matter, the general rule being that like causes like. Now the sacramental species are forms that are apart from matter, because they have no subject, as we have seen.[3] They cannot then, by introducing a new form, bring about a change in anything else.

2. Moreover, when a principal cause ceases to act, the action of its instrument is necessarily brought to a halt; for example, when the carpenter rests, the hammer is idle. But all accidental forms act as instruments of the substantial form as of a principal cause. Now, since in this sacrament the substantial form of the bread and wine does not remain, as we showed earlier,[4] it seems that the accidental forms which remain cannot act to bring about any change in other things.

3. Furthermore, nothing acts beyond the limits of its own kind, because no effect can transcend its cause. Now the sacramental species are all accidents. They cannot then produce a change in any external thing; at any rate they cannot produce substantial form.

ON THE OTHER HAND, if they were unable to produce any change outside themselves, they could never be perceived by our senses; sense-knowledge is the result of our senses being acted upon by the object which is sensed, as Aristotle has shown.[5]

REPLY: Seeing that everything acts in so far as it is actually in being, it follows that the relation of a thing to its activity will correspond to its relation to its being. Since therefore, according to what has been said,[6] it has been miraculously granted to the sacramental species to remain in the being that was theirs when the substance of the bread and wine was still existing, it follows that they continue in their activity. And therefore, every action which they were able to have when the substance of the bread and wine was still there, they can now exercise although the substance of the bread and wine has passed into the body and the blood of Christ. There is then no doubt that they can bring about a change in other things.

Hence: 1. The sacramental species, although they are forms existing apart from matter, retain the same being which was theirs when they were

---

[4] 3a. 75, 6
[5] *De Anima* II, 7. 419a17. Also 12. 424a21
[6] 3a. 77, 1 ad 3

prius in materia. Et ideo secundum suum esse assimilantur formis quæ sunt in materia.

2. Ad secundum dicendum quod ita actio formæ accidentalis dependet ab actione formæ substantialis, sicut esse accidentis dependet ab esse substantiæ. Et ideo, sicut divina virtute datur speciebus sacramentalibus ut possint esse sine substantia, ita datur eis ut possint agere sine forma substantiali, virtute Dei, a quo sicut a primo agente dependet omnis actio formæ et substantialis et accidentalis.

3. Ad tertium dicendum quod immutatio quæ est ad formam substantialem, non fit a forma substantiali immediate, sed mediantibus qualitatibus activis et passivis, quæ agunt in virtute formæ substantialis. Hæc autem virtus instrumentalis conservatur in speciebus sacramentalibus divina virtute sicut et prius erat. Et ideo possunt agere ad formam substantialem instrumentaliter; per quem modum aliquid potest agere ultra suam speciem, non quasi virtute propria, sed virtute principalis agentis.

articulus 4. utrum species sacramentales corrumpi possint

AD QUARTUM sic proceditur:[1] 1. Videtur quod species sacramentales corrumpi non possint. Corruptio enim accidit per separationem formæ a materia. Sed materia panis non remanet in hoc sacramento, ut ex supra dictis patet.[2] Ergo hujusmodi species non possunt corrumpi.

2. Præterea, nulla forma corrumpitur nisi per accidens, corrupto subjecto: unde formæ per se subsistentes incorruptibiles sunt, sicut patet in substantiis spiritualibus. Sed species sacramentales sunt formæ sine subjecto. Ergo corrumpi non possunt.

3. Præterea, si corrumpuntur, aut hoc erit naturaliter, aut miraculose. Sed non naturaliter quia non est ibi assignare aliquod corruptionis subjectum, quod maneat corruptione terminata. Similiter etiam nec miraculose, quia miracula quæ sunt in hoc sacramento, fiunt virtute consecrationis, per quam species sacramentales conservantur; non est autem idem causa conservationis et corruptionis. Ergo nullo modo species sacramentales corrumpi possunt.

SED CONTRA est quod sensu deprehenditur hostias consecratas putrefieri et corrumpi.

---

[1]cf IV *Sent.* 12, 1, 2, iii. *CG* IV, 66. *Resp. de Art.* XXXVI, 35
[2]3a. 75, 4, 8

in matter. So it is that in their being they are on a par with forms which are in matter.

2. The activity of an accidental form depends on the activity of a substantial form in the same way as the being of an accident depends on the being of a substance. And therefore, just as it is miraculously granted to the sacramental species to continue in being without the support of substance, so it is given to them to act without a substantial form. This happens through the power of God, from whom as from the first cause all activity, either of substantial or of accidental form, depends.

3. The change which leads up to a substantial form is not brought about immediately by substantial form, but through the medium of active and passive qualities, which act in virtue of substantial form. And this instrumental power is conserved by divine power in the sacramental species just as it was. Thus it is that they can act instrumentally towards the production of substantial form. In this way a thing can act beyond the limits of its own kind, not indeed through its own power but by the power of the principal cause.

article 4. can the sacramental species cease to exist by decomposition?

THE FOURTH POINT:[1] 1. It would appear that the sacramental species cannot be destroyed by decomposition. Decomposition can occur only by the separation of form from matter. But the matter of the bread no longer remains in this sacrament, as we have seen.[2] Therefore, these species cannot be destroyed by decomposition.

2. Moreover, no form ceases to be by its own decomposition, but because the subject which has it disintegrates; hence forms which subsist in independence cannot cease to be by decomposition, as we see in the spiritual substances. Now the sacramental species are forms without any subject. Therefore, they cannot cease to be by decomposition.

3. Furthermore, if they do cease by decomposition, this will have to be either something natural or a miracle. But it cannot be something natural, because there is no underlying subject for the process of disintegration which would be still there when the process was over. Nor can it be by a miracle, because all the miracles which pertain to this sacrament take place in virtue of the consecration, because of which the sacramental species are conserved in being; and it cannot be that the same cause is responsible for a thing's being and its ceasing to be. Hence, there is no way in which the sacramental species can cease by decomposition.

ON THE OTHER HAND, we observe with our senses that consecrated hosts go bad and decompose.

RESPONSIO: Dicendum quod corruptio est motus ex esse in non esse. Dictum est autem supra[3] quod species sacramentales retinent idem esse quod prius habebant substantia panis et vini existente. Et ideo, sicut esse horum accidentium poterat corrumpi substantia panis et vini existente, ita etiam potest corrumpi illa substantia abeunte.

Poterant autem hujusmodi accidentia primo corrumpi dupliciter; uno modo per se, alio modo per accidens. Per se quidem, sicut per alterationem qualitatum, et augmentum vel diminutionem quantitatis: non quidem per modum augmenti vel diminutionis, qui invenitur in solis corporibus animatis, qualia non sunt substantia panis et vini, sed per additionem vel divisionem. Nam, sicut dicitur in *Meta.*,[4] per divisionem una dimensio corrumpitur et fiunt duæ, per additionem autem e converso ex duabus fit una. Et per hunc modum manifeste possunt corrumpi hujusmodi accidentia post consecrationem: quia et ipsa quantitas dimensiva remanens potest divisionem et additionem recipere; et, cum sit subjectum qualitatum sensibilium, sicut dictum est,[5] potest etiam esse subjectum alterationis earum, puta si alteretur color aut sapor panis aut vini.

Alio modo poterant corrumpi per accidens, per corruptionem subjecti. Et hoc modo possunt corrumpi etiam post consecrationem. Quamvis enim subjectum non remaneat, remanet tamen esse quod habebant hujusmodi accidentia in subjecto, quod quidem est proprium et conforme subjecto. Et ideo hujusmodi esse potest corrumpi a contrario agente, sicut corrumpebatur substantia panis vel vini: quæ etiam non corrumpebatur nisi præcedente alteratione circa accidentia.

Distinguendum tamen est inter utrumque prædictarum corruptionum. Quia, cum corpus Christi et sanguis succedant in hoc sacramento substantiæ panis et vini, si fiat talis immutatio ex parte accidentium quæ non suffecisset ad corruptionem panis et vini, propter talem immutationem non desinit corpus et sanguis Christi esse sub hoc sacramento: sive fiat immutatio ex parte qualitatis, puta cum modicum immutatur color aut sapor vini aut panis; sive ex parte quantitatis, sicut cum dividitur panis aut vinum in tales partes quod adhuc in eis possit salvari natura panis aut vini. Si vero fiat tanta immutatio quod fuisset corrupta substantia panis aut vini, non remanent corpus et sanguis Christi sub hoc sacramento. Et hoc tam ex parte qualitatum, sicut cum ita immutatur color et sapor et aliæ qualitates panis aut vini quod nullo modo posset compati naturas panis aut vini: sive etiam ex parte quantitatis, puta si pulverizetur panis, vel vinum

---

[3] 3a. 77, 3
[4] *Metaphysics* II, 4. 1002a34
[5] 3a. 77, 2

REPLY: Decomposition is change from being to not being. We have said above[3] that the sacramental species keep the same being which was theirs when the substance of the bread and wine was still existing. And hence, just as the being of those accidents was able to cease by decomposition when the substance of the bread and wine still existed, so also it is able to cease after that substance has departed.

There were two ways in which these accidents could have ceased to be, directly and indirectly. Directly, as by alteration as to the qualities, or by growth or diminution as to the quantity, not indeed by that growth or diminution which is found only in living things, for the substance of bread and wine is not living, but by addition or division. As Aristotle says,[4] by division one dimension is destroyed and two result, and, on the contrary, by addition out of two dimensions one comes into being. It is quite clear that in this way the Eucharistic accidents can cease to be after the consecration, because the dimensive quantity which remains on can be divided or can be added to. And, because the quantity is now become the subject of the bodily qualities, as we have seen,[5] it can be the subject in which their change takes place, for example, an alteration in the colour or taste of bread or wine.

There is another way in which these accidents could have ceased to be, this time indirectly, because of the disintegration of their subject. And they can also cease to be in this way, even after the consecration. Although it is true that their subject is no longer there, the being which these accidents had when they were inhering in their subject still remains—a being which is proper to this subject and in keeping with it. And so this sort of being can be destroyed by an agent in opposition to it, which would have caused the substance of the bread and wine to disintegrate; indeed this disintegration could not take place except by means of an alteration first taking place in the accidents.

We must, however, make a distinction between these two types of ceasing-to-be. Since the body and blood of Christ have succeeded to the substance of bread and wine in this sacrament, if the change that takes place in the accidents is such that it would not suffice to cause bread and wine to cease to be, the body and blood of Christ do not cease to be sacramentally present: this is true whether the change be in some quality, for example, when the colour or taste of wine or bread is slightly changed, or in the quantity, when the bread or wine is so divided into parts that the nature of bread and wine would still be able to be preserved. If, however, the change is so great that the substance of bread or wine would be destroyed were it there, the body and blood of Christ are no longer sacramentally present. This is true whether it be a change in the qualities, as when the colour and taste and other qualities of bread and wine are so changed that they can no longer be the connatural accidents of bread and

in minimas* partes dividatur, ut jam non remaneant species panis vel vini.

1. Ad primum ergo dicendum quod, quia ad corruptionem per se pertinet quod auferatur esse rei inquantum esse alicujus formæ est in materia, consequens est quod per corruptionem separetur forma a materia. Si vero hujusmodi esse non esset in materia, simile tamen ei quod est in materia, posset per corruptionem auferri etiam materia non existente: sicut accidit in hoc sacramento, ut ex dictis patet.[6]

2. Ad secundum dicendum quod species sacramentales, licet sint formæ non in materia, habent tamen esse quod prius in materia habebant.

3. Ad tertium dicendum quod corruptio illa specierum non est miraculosa, sed naturalis: præsupponit tamen miraculum quod est factum in consecratione, scilicet quod illæ species sacramentales retineant esse sine subjecto quod prius habebant in subjecto; sicut et cæcus miraculose illuminatus naturaliter videt.

articulus 5. utrum ex speciebus sacramentalibus aliquid possit generari

AD QUINTUM sic proceditur:[1] 1. Videtur quod ex speciebus sacramentalibus nihil possit generari. Omne enim quod generatur ex aliqua materia generatur: ex nihilo enim nihil generatur, quamvis ex nihilo fiat aliquid per creationem. Sed speciebus sacramentalibus non subest aliqua materia nisi corporis Christi, quod est incorruptibile. Ergo videtur quod ex speciebus sacramentalibus nihil possit generari.

2. Præterea, ea quæ non sunt unius generis non possunt ex invicem fieri: non enim ex albedine fit linea. Sed accidens et substantia differunt genere. Cum ergo species sacramentales sint accidentia, videtur quod ex eis non possit aliqua substantia generari.

3. Præterea, si ex eis generatur aliqua substantia corporea non erit sine accidente. Si ergo ex speciebus sacramentalibus generatur aliqua substantia corporea, oportet quod ex accidente generetur substantia et accidens, duo scilicet ex uno: quod est impossibile. Ergo impossibile est quod ex speciebus sacramentalibus aliqua substantia corporea generetur.

SED CONTRA est quod ad sensum videri potest ex speciebus sacramentalibus aliquid generari; vel cinerem, si comburantur, vel vermes, si putrefiant, vel pulverem, si conterantur.

---

*Piana: *minutas*

[6]In the body of the article

[1]cf IV *Sent.* 12, 1, 2, iv. *CG* IV, 66. *Quodl.* IX, 5 ad 3. *In* 1 *Cor.* 11, *lect.* 4

wine; or a change in the quantity, as when bread is reduced to dust or wine is divided into the tiniest parts, so that the appearances of bread and wine no longer remain.

Hence: 1. Since direct ceasing-to-be by decomposition means that a thing's existence is taken from it, in so far as it exists as having form in matter, it follows that by decomposition form is separated from matter. If, however, this existence is not actually in matter, but of the same kind as the existence of a material thing, it can be taken away by a disintegrating power even when the matter is no longer there. This is what happens in this sacrament, as we have just said.[6]

2. The sacramental species, although they are forms no longer in matter, hold on to the being which was formerly theirs in matter.

3. The ceasing-to-be of the species is nothing miraculous but quite natural; however, it presupposes the miracle which took place at the consecration, namely, that these sacramental species hold on to the being which they had when they inhered in a subject. In the same way a blind man who is miraculously given his sight, sees naturally.

article 5. can anything be generated from the sacramental species?

THE FIFTH POINT:[1] 1. It seems that nothing can be generated from the sacramental species. Whatever is generated is produced from matter; from nothing nothing is generated, although from nothing something is produced by creation. But there is no matter underlying the sacramental species except the matter of the body of Christ and it is outside the world of change. It would seem then that nothing can be generated from the sacramental species.

2. Moreover, things that are not in the same genus cannot be produced from one another; you cannot make a line out of whiteness. But accident and substance belong to different genera. Since then the sacramental species are accidents, it seems impossible that any substance should be produced from them.

3. Furthermore, if any bodily substance were to be generated from them, it would not be deprived of accidents. If, therefore, any bodily substance is produced from the sacramental species, you will have accident producing substance and accident, two things from one, which is not possible. Therefore, it is impossible that a bodily substance should be produced from the sacramental species.

ON THE OTHER HAND, with our very senses we can observe something being produced from the sacramental species—ashes, if they are burned, or worms if they go rotten, or dust if they are ground fine.

RESPONSIO: Dicendum quod, cum *corruptio unius sit generatio alterius*, ut dicitur in *De Generat.*,[2] necesse est quod ex speciebus sacramentalibus aliquid generetur cum corrumpantur, ut dictum est.[3] Non enim sic corrumpuntur ut omnino dispereant,* quasi in nihilum redigantur, sed manifeste aliquid sensibile eis succedit.

Quomodo autem ex eis aliquid generari possit, difficile est videre. Manifestum est enim quod ex corpore et sanguine Christi, quæ ibi veraciter sunt, non generatur aliquid; cum sint incorruptibilia. Si autem substantia panis aut vini remaneret in hoc sacramento, vel eorum materia, facile esset assignare quod ex eis generatur illud sensibile quod succedit, ut quidam posuerunt. Sed hoc est falsum, ut supra habitum est.[4]

Et ideo quidam[5] dixerunt quod ea quæ generantur, non fiunt ex speciebus sacramentalibus, sed ex aëre circumstante. Quod quidem multipliciter apparet esse impossibile. Primo quidem, quia ex eo generatur aliquid quod prius alteratum et corruptum apparet. Nulla autem alteratio et corruptio prius apparuit in aëre circumstante. Unde ex eo vermes aut cineres non generantur. Secundo, quia natura aëris non est talis quod ex eo per tales alterationes talia generentur. Tertio, quia potest contingere in magna quantitate hostias consecratas comburi vel putrefieri: nec esset possibile tantum de corpore terreo ex aëre generari, nisi magna vel valde sensibili inspissatione aëris facta. Quarto, quia idem potest accidere corporibus solidis circumstantibus, puta ferro aut lapidibus: quæ integra remanent post prædictorum generationem. Unde hæc positio stare non potest: quia contrariatur ei quod ad sensum apparet.

Et ideo alii[6] dixerunt quod redit substantia panis et vini in ipsa corruptione specierum, et sic ex substantia panis et vini redeunte generantur cineres aut vermes aut aliquid hujusmodi. Sed hæc positio non videtur esse possibilis. Primo quidem quia, si substantia panis et vini conversa est in corpus et sanguinem, ut supra habitum est,[7] non potest substantia panis vel vini redire nisi corpore aut sanguine Christi iterum converso in substantiam panis et vini, quod est impossibile: sicut, si aër sit conversus in ignem, non potest aër redire nisi iterum ignis convertatur in aërem. Si vero substantia panis aut vini sit annihilata, non potest iterum redire, quia quod in nihilum decidit, non redit idem numero: nisi forte dicatur redire prædicta substantia, quia Deus de novo creat† novam substantiam loco primæ. Secundo

---

*Piana: *dispereant*, wasted

†Piana adds *aliam*, another

[2]*De Generatione et Corruptione* I, 3. 318a23

[3]3a. 77, 4

[4]3a. 75, 2, 4, 8

[5]cf note 6 to Art. I

[6]cf Innocent III, *De Sacro Altaris Mysterio* 4, 11. PL 217, 863. Alexander of Hales, *Summa Theologica* 4, 53, 5. Bonaventure, *In* IV *Sent.* 12, 3, 2

REPLY: Seeing that the *disintegration of one thing is the production of something else*,[2] as Aristotle says, it follows that when the sacramental species decompose, which we saw they do,[3] something must be generated from them. Because they are not so destroyed that they disappear completely, as if they were annihilated; it is obvious that something which we can see has taken their place.

But how anything can be generated from them is very hard to see. It is clear that nothing can be generated from the body and blood of Christ which are really there; they are immune from substantial change. If the substance of the bread and wine remained in this sacrament or even their primal matter, it would be easy to point to them as allowing for the generation of the new substance that we see. Some people have actually held for this. But it is not true that they remain, as we saw earlier.[4]

This has led others[5] to conclude that the substances which come into being are produced, not from the sacramental species, but from the air that surrounds them. But there are many reasons which show that this is impossible. First of all, because whatever is generated arises from what is first seen to change and to become decomposed. But no change or decomposition is to be seen in the surrounding air. Hence it is not from it that the worms or the ashes are generated. Then again, the nature of air is not such that by such changes it should yield such results. Thirdly, it can happen that a large quantity of consecrated hosts is burned or becomes decomposed; now it is not possible that so much earthly matter should arise from air or without a most striking condensation. Fourthly, the same thing could happen to the solid bodies that are close by, for example, to iron or stones; yet these remain whole and entire after such a process of generation. This position cannot, then, be allowed; it runs counter to the evidence of our senses.

Others[6] then went on to say that the substance of the bread and wine returns when the species decompose; in this way, ashes or worms or suchlike are produced from the returning substance of the bread and wine. But this does not seem to be a tenable position. First, indeed, because if the substance of the bread and wine has been changed into the body and the blood, as we saw above,[7] they cannot come back unless the body and blood of Christ are again changed into the substance of bread and wine, which is quite impossible; just as, if air is changed into fire, the air cannot come back unless the fire is again changed into air. And in the hypothesis that the substance of the bread and wine is annihilated, it cannot come back, because whatever is reduced to nothingness cannot return numerically the same. One might, of course, say that God by a fresh creation creates a new substance in place of the first. Secondly, this would seem impossible

---

[7] 3a. 75, 2, 4

videtur hoc esse impossibile, quia non est dare quando substantia panis redeat. Manifestum est enim ex supra dictis[8] quod, manentibus speciebus panis et vini, manet corpus et sanguis Christi, quæ non sunt simul cum substantia panis et vini in hoc sacramento, secundum præhabita.[9] Unde substantia panis et vini non potest redire, speciebus sacramentalibus manentibus. Similiter etiam nec eis cessantibus: quia jam substantia panis et vini esset sine propriis accidentibus, quod est impossibile. Nisi forte dicatur quod in ipso ultimo instanti corruptionis specierum redit, non quidem substantia panis et vini, quia illud idem instans est in quo primo habent esse substantiæ generatæ ex speciebus: sed materia panis et vini magis quasi de novo creata diceretur quam rediens,[10] proprie loquendo. Et secundum hoc, posset sustineri prædicta positio.

Verum, quia non rationabiliter videtur dici quod miraculose aliquid accidat in hoc sacramento nisi ex ipsa consecratione, ex qua non est quod materia creetur vel redeat; melius videtur dicendum quod in ipsa consecratione miraculose datur quantitati dimensivæ panis et vini quod sit primum subjectum subsequentium formarum. Hoc autem est proprium materiæ. Et ideo ex consequenti datur prædictæ quantitati dimensivæ omne id quod ad materiam pertinet. Et ideo quidquid posset generari ex materia panis* si esset, totum potest generari ex prædicta quantitate dimensiva panis vel vini, non quidem novo miraculo, sed ex vi miraculi prius facti.

1. Ad primum ergo dicendum quod, quamvis non sit ibi materia ex qua aliquid generetur, quantitas tamen dimensiva supplet vicem materiæ, ut dictum est.

2. Ad secundum dicendum quod illæ species sacramentales sunt quidem accidentia, habent tamen actum et vim substantiæ, ut dictum est.[11]

3. Ad tertium dicendum quod quantitas dimensiva panis et vini et retinet naturam propriam, et accipit miraculose vim et proprietatem substantiæ. Et ideo potest transire in utrumque, id est in substantiam et dimensionem.

articulus 6. utrum species sacramentales possint nutrire

AD SEXTUM sic proceditur.[1] 1. Videtur quod species sacramentales non possint nutrire. Dicit enim Ambrosius, *Non iste panis est qui vadit in corpus; sed panis vitæ æternæ, qui animæ nostræ substantiam fulcit.*[2] Sed omne quod

---

*Piana: *vel vini si adesset*, or of the wine were it there

[8]3a. 77, 4; 76, 6 ad 3

[9]3a. 75, 2

[10]See Peter of Tarentaise. *In* IV *Sent.* 12, 3, 2

[11]In the body of the article and in 77, 3

because you cannot point to any particular moment when the substance of the bread come back. It is clear from what we have already said[8] that as long as the species of the bread and wine remain the body and blood of Christ are also there. But, as we have seen,[9] they do not co-exist with the substance of the bread and wine. The substance of the bread and wine cannot then return as long as the sacramental species remain. Nor, likewise, when they have ceased to be, because then you would have the substance of bread and wine without its connatural accidents, which is impossible. Someone may perhaps say that in the last instant of the decomposition of the species there comes back, not indeed the substance of the bread and wine, because that is the very instant in which the substances generated from the species first begin to exist, but the primal matter of the bread and wine. Properly speaking, however, this primal matter should rather be spoken of as newly created than as returning.[10] In this qualified sense the position could be defended.

Now, it does not seem reasonable to say that anything happens miraculously in this sacrament except as a result of the consecration, and you cannot point to it as the cause of matter being created or of its coming back. It seems better then to say this: by the consecration itself the dimensive quantity becomes miraculously the subject of all subsequent forms. Now there you have something which is proper to matter. And as a result, everything that pertains to matter is granted to this dimensive quantity. And so, everything that could be generated from the matter of the bread if it were there, can now be generated from the dimensive quantity of the bread and wine. There is no new miracle; it all happens as a result of the original one.

Hence: 1. Although there is no matter there from which anything can be generated, the dimensive quantity supplies for the matter, as we have just seen.

2. These sacramental species are indeed accidents, but they have the status and the power of substance, as we have just said.[11]

3. The dimensive quantity of the bread and wine retains its proper nature, but it miraculously receives the power and the property of substance. Hence it can turn into both, that is, into the substance and quantity.

article 6. can the sacramental species nourish?

THE SIXTH POINT:[1] 1. It would seem that the sacramental species cannot nourish. Ambrose says, *this is not the sort of bread that becomes part of our body; it is the bread of eternal life that stays up the substance of our soul.*[2] Now

[1]cf IV *Sent.* 12, 1, 2, v. *CG* IV, 66. *In* 1 *Cor.* 11, *lect.* 4

[2]*De Sacramentis* 5, 4. PL 16, 471

nutrit, vadit in corpus. Ergo panis iste non nutrit. Et eadem ratio est de vino.

2. Præterea, sicut dicitur in *De Generat.*, *ex eisdem nutrimur ex quibus sumus.*[3] Species autem sacramentales sunt accidentia, ex quibus homo non constat: non enim accidens est pars substantiæ. Ergo videtur quod species sacramentales nutrire non possunt.

3. Præterea, Philosophus dicit, in *De Anima*, quod *alimentum nutrit prout est quædam substantia, auget autem prout est aliquid quantum.*[4] Sed species sacramentales non sunt substantia. Ergo non possunt nutrire.

SED CONTRA est quod Apostolus, loquens de hoc sacramento, dicit: *Alius quidem esurit, alius autem ebrius est:*[5] ubi dicit Glossa quod *notat illos qui, post celebrationem sacri mysterii et consecrationem panis et vini, suas oblationes vindicabant, et, aliis non communicantes, sibi solis sumebant, ita ut inde etiam inebriarentur.* Quod quidem non potest contingere si sacramentales species non nutrirent. Ergo species sacramentales nutriunt.

RESPONSIO: Dicendum quod hæc quæstio difficultatem non habet, præcedenti quæstione soluta. Ex hoc enim, ut dicitur in *De Anima*,[6] cibus nutrit, quod convertitur in substantiam nutriti. Dictum est autem[7] quod species sacramentales possunt converti in substantiam aliquam quæ ex eis generatur. Per eandem autem rationem possunt converti in corpus humanum, per quam possunt converti in cineres vel in vermes. Et ideo manifestum est quod nutriunt.

Quod autem quidam[8] dicunt, quod non vere nutriunt, quasi in corpus humanum convertantur, sed reficiunt et confortant quadam sensuum immutatione, sicut homo confortatur ex odore cibi et inebriatur ex odore vini, ad sensum patet esse falsum. Talis enim refectio non diu sufficit homini, cujus corpus, propter continuam deperditionem, restauratione indiget. Et tamen homo diu sustentari posset, si hostias et vinum consecratum sumeret in magna quantitate.

Similiter etiam non potest stare quod quidam dicunt, quod species sacramentales nutriunt per formam substantialem panis et vini, quæ remanet. Tum quia non remanet, ut supra habitum est.[9] Tum quia non est actus formæ nutrire, sed magis materiæ, quæ accipit formam nutriti,

---

[3]*De Generatione et Corruptione* II, 8. 335a10
[4]*De Anima* II, 4. 416b12
[5]I *Corinthians* II, 21. *Glossa Lombardi.* PL 191, 1639
[6]*De Anima* II, 4. 416b9
[7]3a. 77, 5
[8]Alger of Liège. *De Sacramento Corporis et Sanguinis Domini* II, 1. PL 180, 811. William of Paris, *De Sacramento Eucharistiæ* I

whatever nourishes us becomes part of our body. Therefore the bread does not nourish. And the same thing goes for the wine.

2. Moreover, as Aristotle says, *those things nourish us which go to make up our being.*[3] But the sacramental species are accidents and man is not made up of accidents, seeing that accident is not part of substance. It would seem then that the sacramental species cannot nourish us.

3. Furthermore, Aristotle says, *food gives nourishment in so far as it is substance, it causes growth in so far as it is something extended.*[4] Now, the sacramental species are not anything substantial. Therefore, they cannot provide nourishment.

ON THE OTHER HAND, St Paul, speaking of this sacrament, says, *one goes hungry whilst another is drunk.*[5] A gloss on this says, *he is pointing to those who, after the celebration of the sacred mystery and the consecration of the bread and wine, claimed back their offerings, and, not sharing them with others, took them all by themselves and so much so that they even got drunk as a result.* Now this could not happen if the sacramental species were unable to give nourishment. We conclude, therefore, that they do.

REPLY: There is no difficulty about this question in the light of the solution to the previous one. It is by the fact that food is changed into the substance of the one who is nourished that it gives nourishment, as Aristotle says.[6] Now we have seen[7] that the sacramental species can be changed into a substance which is generated from them. For the same reason then that they can be changed into ashes or into worms they can also be changed into the human body. Hence it is quite clear that they do nourish.

Some[8] have the idea that they do not really nourish, in the sense of being changed into the human body, but that they only afford refreshment and strength by bringing about a certain change of feeling, in the way a man feels stronger from the very smell of food and has a feeling of euphoria from the smell of wine; but this is easily shown to be false. Such a refreshment cannot support a man for any length of time, because the human body is all the time being used up and has to be restored. And on the other hand, if a man were to consume a large quantity of consecrated hosts and wine, he could be kept going for a long time.

And what others hold about the sacramental species nourishing through the substantial form of the bread and wine which would remain over cannot be accepted. First of all, this does not remain over, as we saw earlier on.[9] Then again, it is not form that makes nourishment but rather matter, which takes on the form of the one who is nourished whilst the form of food

[9] 3a. 75, 6

recedente forma nutrimenti. Unde dicitur in *De Anima*,[10] quod nutrimentum in principio est dissimile, in fine autem simile.

1. Ad primum ergo dicendum quod, facta consecratione, dupliciter potest dici 'panis' in hoc sacramento. Uno modo, ipsæ species panis, quæ retinent nomen prioris substantiæ, ut Gregorius dicit, in Homilia Paschali.[11] Alio modo, potest dici panis ipsum corpus Christi, quod est panis mysticus *de cælo descendens*. Ambrosius ergo, cum dicit quod *iste panis non transit in corpus*, accipit 'panem' secundo modo: quia scilicet corpus Christi non convertitur in corpus hominis, sed reficit mentem ejus. Non autem loquitur de pane primo modo dicto.

2. Ad secundum dicendum quod species sacramentales, etsi non sint ea ex quibus corpus hominis constat, tamen in ea convertuntur, sicut dictum est.[12]

3. Ad tertium dicendum quod species sacramentales, quamvis non sint substantia, habent tamen virtutem substantiae, ut dictum est.[13]

articulus 7. utrum species sacramentales frangantur in hoc sacramento

AD SEPTIMUM sic proceditur:[1] 1. Videtur quod species sacramentales non frangantur in hoc sacramento. Dicit enim Philosophus, in *Meteor.*,[2] quod corpora dicuntur frangibilia propter determinatam dispositionem pororum. Quod non potest attribui sacramentalibus speciebus. Ergo sacramentales species non possunt frangi.

2. Præterea, fractionem sequitur sonus. Sed species sacramentales non sunt sonabiles: dicit enim Philosophus, *De Anima*,[3] quod sonabile est corpus durum habens superficiem levem. Ergo species sacramentales non franguntur.

3. Præterea, ejusdem videtur esse manducari, frangi et masticari. Sed verum corpus Christi est quod manducatur: secundum illud *Joan.*, *Qui manducat meam carnem et bibit meum sanguinem.*[4] Ergo corpus Christi est quod frangitur et masticatur. Unde et in confessione Berengarii dicitur, *Consentio sanctæ Romanæ Ecclesiæ, et corde et ore profiteor panem et vinum quæ in altari ponuntur, post consecrationem verum corpus et sanguinem Christi esse, et in veritate manibus sacerdotum tractari, frangi et fidelium dentibus atteri.*[5] Non ergo fractio debet attribui sacramentalibus speciebus.

---

[10]*De Anima* II, 4. 416b6

[11]See Lanfranc, *De Corpore et Sanguine Domini* 20. PL 150, 436. Gratian, *Decretum* 3, 2, 34 *Species*. Richter-Friedberg 1, 1324

[12]In the body of the article

[13]3a. 77, 3 ad 3, 5 ad 2

[1]cf IV *Sent.* 12, 1, 3, i & ii. *CG* IV, 67. *In* I *Cor.* 11, *lect.* 5

disappears. For this reason Aristotle[10] says that what provides nourishment is initially different but eventually the same.

Hence: 1. After the consecration there are two ways in which we can speak of 'bread' in this sacrament. First, the species hold on to the name of the original substance, as Gregory explains in an Easter sermon.[11] Second, the body of Christ itself can be called bread; it is the mystical bread that *comes down from heaven*. Therefore, when Ambrose says that *this bread does not become part of our body*, he is taking 'bread' in the second sense and his meaning is that the body of Christ is not changed into our body but that it refreshes our soul. He is not talking about bread in the first sense.

2. The sacramental species, although they are not the elements that naturally go to make up the human body, are yet changed into it, as we have just seen.[12]

3. The sacramental species, although they are not substance, have, all the same, the power of substance, as we saw earlier.[13]

article 7. is it the sacramental species that are broken in this sacrament?

THE SEVENTH POINT:[1] 1. It would seem that it is not the sacramental species that are broken in this sacrament. According to Aristotle,[2] bodies are said to be breakable because of the way their pores are arranged. But there is no question of this where the sacramental species are concerned. Therefore, they cannot be broken.

2. Moreover, when fraction takes place sound is produced. Now the sacramental species are incapable of producing sound, because, as Aristotle says,[3] sound is produced by a hard body which has a light surface. Therefore, it is not the species that are broken.

3. Furthermore, it is the same thing that is eaten, broken and masticated. Now it is the actual body of Christ that is eaten; as the text of *John* has it, *he who eats my flesh and drinks my blood*.[4] It is, therefore, the body of Christ that is broken and masticated. And so we read in Berengarius's profession of faith, *I agree with the holy Roman Church, and with heart and lips I profess that the bread and wine that are placed on the altar are, after the consecration, the actual body and blood of Christ which are really handled by the priests, broken, and torn by the teeth of the faithful*.[5] The fraction then ought not to be attributed to the sacramental species.

---

[2]*Meteorologica* IV, 9. 386a14
[3]*De Anima* II, 8. 419b9
[4]*John* 6, 55, 57
[5]cf Gratian, *Decretum* 3, 2, 42 *Ego Berengarius*. Richter-Friedberg I, 1328

SED CONTRA est quod fractio fit per divisionem quanti. Sed nullum quantum ibi dividitur nisi species sacramentales: quia neque corpus Christi, quod est incorruptibile; neque substantia panis, quæ non manet. Ergo species sacramentales franguntur.

RESPONSIO: Dicendum quod apud antiquos circa hoc multiplex fuit opinio. Quidam[6] enim dixerunt quod non erat in hoc sacramento fractio secundum rei veritatem, sed solum secundum aspectum intuentium. Sed hoc non potest stare. Quia in hoc sacramento veritatis sensus non decipitur circa ea quorum judicium ad ipsum pertinet: inter quæ est fractio, per quam ex uno fiunt multa, quæ quidem sunt sensibilia communia, ut patet in *De Anima*.[7]

Unde alii[8] dixerunt quod erat ibi vera fractio sine substantia existente. Sed hoc etiam sensui contradicit. Apparet enim in hoc sacramento aliquid quantum, prius unum existens, postea in multa partitum: quod quidem oportet esse subjectum fractionis.

Non autem potest dici quod ipsum corpus Christi verum frangatur. Primo quidem, quia est incorruptibile et impassibile. Secundo, quia est totum sub qualibet parte, ut supra habitum est:[9] quod est quidem contra rationem ejus quod frangitur.

Unde relinquitur quod fractio sit sicut in subjecto in quantitate dimensiva panis, sicut et alia accidentia. Et sicut species sacramentales sunt sacramentum corporis Christi veri, ita fractio hujusmodi specierum est sacramentum Dominicæ passionis, quæ fuit in corpore Christi vero.

1. Ad primum ergo dicendum quod, sicut in speciebus sacramentalibus remanet rarum et densum, ut supra dictum est,[10] ita etiam remanet ibi porositas: et per consequens frangibilitas.

2. Ad secundum dicendum quod densitatem sequitur duritia. Et ideo, ex quo in speciebus sacramentalibus remanet densitas, consequens est quod remaneat ibi duritia: et per consequens sonabilitas.

3. Ad tertium dicendum quod illud quod manducatur in propria specie, ipsum et frangitur et masticatur in sua specie. Corpus autem Christi non manducatur in sua specie, sed in specie sacramentali. Unde super illud

---

[6]Pseudo-Abelard, *Epitome Theologiæ* 29. PL 178, 1742. Pseudo-Hugh of St Victor, *Summa Sententiarum* 5, 8. PL 176, 144

[7]*De Anima* II, 6. 418a11

[8]Pseudo-Hugh of St Victor, loc cit

[9]3a. 76, 3

[10]3a. 77, 2 ad 3

[a]St Thomas sees the quantity of the bread as doing all the substance of bread would have done were it there. In that sense the quantity is the substance, the thing, which is broken.

ON THE OTHER HAND, breaking means dividing what is extended. But we have nothing extended and divisible here except the sacramental species, because the body of Christ is now removed from all possibility of change and the substance of the bread is no longer present. Consequently, it must be the sacramental species that are broken.

REPLY: The old theologians had many opinions on this subject. Some of them[6] said that objectively there was no fraction at all in this sacrament but that there only seemed to be one. But you cannot say that. This is the very sacrament of truth and there is no room here for our senses to be deceived in that which is their proper concern. Fraction is a case in point; from one arise many—there you have an object which is reached by more than one sense, as Aristotle teaches.[7]

Others[8] then were led to say that there is a genuine fraction but that there is no substance there at all.[a] But this also goes against the evidence of our senses.[b] We see in this sacrament something extended which at first is one and is afterwards divided into many, and this it is which must be the thing which is broken.

Now it cannot be that it is the actual body of Christ which is broken. First, it is outside all change and we can do nothing to it. Second, it is present in all its completeness under every part of the quantity, as we saw above,[9] and that runs counter to the whole idea of being broken into parts.

It remains then that the fraction takes place in the dimensive quantity of the bread, where all the other accidents also find their subject. And just as the sacramental species are the sign of the real body of Christ, so the fraction of these species is the sign of our Lord's passion which he endured in his actual body.

Hence: 1. Just as qualities of tenuousness and density remain in the sacramental species, as we saw above,[10] so too does porousness and in consequence brittleness.

2. Hardness is a consequence of density. And so, as a result of the density remaining in the sacramental species, the hardness remains also and consequently the capability of producing sound.

3. Whatever is eaten as under its natural form, is broken and chewed as under its natural form. But the body of Christ is not eaten as under its natural form, but as under the sacramental species. For this reason,

---

[b]Actually, the evidence of our senses is concerned with quantity and the other accidents, not with substance. It is our intelligence which reaches substance as such; our intelligence enlightened by faith shows that the substance of the bread is no longer there; our intelligence enlightened by theology knows that the dimensive quantity is now behaving as if it were substance.

Joan. vi, *Caro non prodest quidquam,*[11] dicit Augustinus, *Hoc est intelligendum secundum illos qui carnaliter intelligebant. Carnem quippe sic intellexerunt quo modo in cadavere dilaniatur, aut in macello venditur.*[12] Et ideo ipsum corpus Christi non frangitur, nisi secundum speciem sacramentalem. Et hoc modo intelligenda est confessio Berengarii: ut fractio et contritio dentium referatur ad speciem sacramentalem, sub qua vere est corpus Christi.

articulus 8. *utrum vino consecrato possit aliquis liquor misceri*

AD OCTAVUM sic proceditur:[1] 1. Videtur quod vino consecrato non possit aliquis liquor misceri. Omne enim quod miscetur alicui, recipit qualitatem ipsius. Sed nullus liquor potest recipere qualitatem sacramentalium specierum: quia accidentia illa sunt sine subjecto, ut dictum est.[2] Ergo videtur quod nullus liquor possit permisceri speciebus sacramentalibus vini.

2. Præterea, si aliquis liquor permisceatur illis speciebus, oportet quod ex his fiat aliquod unum. Sed non potest fieri aliquod unum neque ex liquore, qui est substantia, et speciebus sacramentalibus, quæ sunt accidentia; neque ex liquore et sanguine Christi, qui, ratione suæ incorruptibilitatis, neque additionem recipit neque diminutionem. Ergo nullus liquor potest admisceri vino consecrato.

3. Præterea, si aliquis liquor admisceatur vino consecrato, videtur quod etiam ipsum efficiatur consecratum: sicut aqua quæ admiscetur aquæ benedictæ, efficitur etiam benedicta. Sed vinum consecratum est vere sanguis Christi. Ergo etiam liquor permixtus esset sanguis Christi. Et ita aliquid fieret sanguis Christi aliter quam per consecrationem: quod est inconveniens. Non ergo vino consecrato potest aliquis liquor permisceri.

4. Præterea, si duorum unum totaliter corrumpatur, non erit mixtio, ut dicitur in *De Generat.*[3] Sed ad permixtionem cujuscumque liquoris videtur corrumpi species sacramentalis vini, ita quod sub ea desinat esse sanguis Christi. Tum quia magnum et parvum sunt differentiæ quantitatis et diversificant ipsam, sicut album et nigrum colorem. Tum etiam quia liquor permixtus, cum non habeat obstaculum, videtur undique diffundi per totum: et ita desinit ibi esse sanguis Christi, qui non est ibi simul cum alia substantia. Non ergo aliquis liquor potest permisceri vino consecrato.

---

[11] *John* 6, 64
[12] *Tract* 27 *on John* 5. PL 35, 1617
[1] cf IV *Sent.* 12, 1, 2, vi. *Quodl.* X, 1, 3
[2] 3a. 77, 1
[3] *De Generatione et Corruptione* I, 10. 327b2

Augustine, commenting on the text of *John*, *the flesh availeth nothing*,[11] says, *understand this as spoken of the flesh in the way some people understood Christ carnally. They thought of eating his flesh as if it had been treated like butcher's meat.*[12] The body of Christ in itself is not broken, but only in its sacramental appearance. And this is the sense in which we should understand Berengarius's profession of faith;[c] the fraction and the chewing with the teeth refer to the sacramental species, underneath which the body of Christ is really present.

article 8. *can a liquid be mixed with the consecrated wine?*

THE EIGHTH POINT:[1] 1. It would seem that you cannot mix any other liquid with the consecrated wine. Whatever is mixed with something else takes on its quality. But no liquid can take on the quality of the sacramental species, seeing that they are accidents without any subject, as we said above.[2] It seems then that no liquid can be mixed with the consecrated wine.

2. Moreover, if any liquid did mix with these species, that would mean having some sort of unity as a result. But no unity can arise from a liquid, which is substance, and the sacramental species, which are accidents; nor from a liquid and the blood of Christ, because the blood of Christ, being outside all possibility of change, cannot take on a new quantity. Therefore no liquid can be mixed with the consecrated wine.

3. Furthermore, if any liquid were to mix with the consecrated wine, the liquid itself would become consecrated; just as the ordinary water which is mixed with holy water becomes itself blessed. But the consecrated wine is actually the blood of Christ. It would then follow that the liquid which had mixed with it would be the blood of Christ. You would then have some thing becoming the blood of Christ in some other way than by consecration—an impossible supposition. It is not then possible for any other liquid to be mixed with the consecrated wine.

4. Again, if one of the two elements completely disappears you have not got a mixture, as Aristotle teaches.[3] Now if you add any liquid to the wine the sacramental species are destroyed so that the blood of Christ ceases to be present. There are two reasons for this: first, large and little are differences in quantity and make for different quantities, just as black and white in regard to colours. Second, the liquid which is mixed, since it finds no obstacle, spreads right through the whole, and so the blood of Christ ceases to be present, because it cannot co-exist with another substance. It follows then that no liquid can be mixed with the consecrated wine.

[c]One may regret that the profession of faith which Berengarius had to subscribe to was so unsubtle.

SED CONTRA est quod ad sensum patet alium liquorem vino permisceri posse post consecrationem, sicut et ante.

RESPONSIO: Dicendum quod istius quæstionis veritas manifesta est ex præmissis. Dictum est enim supra[4] quod species in hoc sacramento remanentes, sicut adipiscuntur virtute consecrationis modum essendi substantiæ, ita etiam adipiscuntur modum agendi et patiendi: ut scilicet agere et pati possint quidquid ageret vel pateretur substantia si ibi præsens existeret. Manifestum est autem quod, si esset ibi substantia vini, liquor aliquis posset ei permisceri.

Hujus tamen permixtionis diversus esset effectus et secundum formam liquoris, et secundum quantitatem. Si enim permisceretur aliquis liquor in tanta quantitate quod posset diffundi per totum vinum, totum fieret permixtum. Quod autem est commixtum ex duobus, neutrum miscibilium est, sed utrumque transit in quoddam tertium ex his compositum. Unde sequeretur quod vinum prius existens non remaneret, si liquor permixtus esset alterius speciei. Si autem esset ejusdem speciei liquor adjunctus, puta si vinum permisceretur vino, remaneret quidem eadem species, sed non remaneret idem numero vinum. Quod declarat diversitas accidentium, puta si unum vinum esset album, et aliud rubeum.

Si vero liquor adjunctus esset tam parvæ quantitatis quod non posset perfundi per totum, non fieret totum vinum permixtum, sed aliqua pars ejus. Quæ quidem non remaneret eadem numero, propter permixtionem extraneæ materiæ. Remaneret tamen eadem specie, non solum si parvus liquor permixtus esset ejusdem speciei, sed etiam si esset alterius speciei: quia gutta aquæ multo vino permixta transit in speciem vini, ut dicitur in *De Generatione*.[5]

Manifestum est autem ex prædictis[6] quod corpus et sanguis Christi remanent in hoc sacramento quandiu illæ species manent eædem in numero: consecratur enim hic panis et hoc vinum. Unde si fiat tanta permixtio liquoris cujuscumque quod pertingat ad totum vinum consecratum et fiat permixtum, et erit aliud numero, et non remanebit ibi sanguis Christi. Si vero fiat tam parva alicujus liquoris adjunctio quod non possit diffundi per totum, sed usque ad aliquam partem specierum, desinet esse sanguis Christi sub illa parte vini consecrati, remanebit tamen sub alia.

1. Ad primum ergo dicendum quod Innocentius III dicit, in quadam decretali, quod *ipsa accidentia vinum appositum videntur afficere, quia, si aqua*

---

[4]3a. 77, 3
[5]*De Generatione et Corruptione* I, 5. 321a33
[6]3a. 77, 4

ON THE OTHER HAND we have the evidence of our senses that another liquid can be mixed with the wine after the consecration just as effectively as before it.

REPLY: The answer to all this question is clear from what has already been established. We saw above[4] that the species which remain in this sacrament take on, as a result of the consecration, the mode of being of substance and also its mode of action and of being acted upon. They can now do and have done to them exactly what the substance could do and have done to it were it present. Now, it is clear that if the substance of wine were still there, it would be possible that a liquid could be mixed with it.

The effect, however, of this mixing will depend upon the nature of the liquid used and also upon the quantity of liquid employed. If some liquid were to be mixed in such a quantity that it could penetrate through the whole of the wine, the whole thing would become a mixture. Now a mixture that results from two elements fusing together is neither of those two, but is a third thing arising from their coming together. It follows then that the wine originally existing no longer remains, if the liquid mixed with it is of another species. If, however, the added liquid is of the same species, for example if wine is mixed with wine, the same species will be preserved, but the same numerical wine will be no longer there. The difference in the accidents shows this clearly; for example, if one of the wines is white and the other is red.

If, however, the added liquid is so small in quantity that it cannot spread right through the wine, only a part and not all the wine will become a mixture. And this part will not remain numerically the same, because of the extraneous matter now mixed with it. It will, however, remain specifically the same, not only when the small amount of liquid added is of the same species but even when it is of a different species, because a drop of water, when mingled with a lot of wine, itself becomes wine, as Aristotle points out.[5]

Now it is clear from what we said above[6] that the body and blood of Christ remain in this sacrament as long as the sacramental species remain numerically the same; what is consecrated is this bread and this wine. We conclude therefore that if the amount of liquid added (no matter what its nature may be) is such as to spread right through the consecrated wine and to become mixed with it, you will have something numerically different from the original wine and the blood of Christ will no longer be there. But if the amount of the liquid which is added is so small that it cannot penetrate throughout all the wine, but only reaches as far as part of the species, the blood of Christ will cease to be present under that part of the species, but will continue to be present under the other part.

Hence: 1. Innocent III in a certain decretal says, *it seems that the accidents do affect the wine that is added, because, if you were to add water, it would take*

fuerit apposita, vini saporem assumeret. Contingit igitur accidentia mutare subjectum, sicut et subjectum contingit accidentia permutare. Cedit quippe natura miraculo, et virtus supra consuetudinem operatur.[7] Hoc tamen non est sic intelligendum quasi idem numero accidens quod prius fuit in vino ante consecrationem, postmodum fiat in vino apposito: sed talis permutatio fit per actionem. Nam accidentia vini remanentia retinent actionem substantiæ, secundum prædicta:[8] et ita immutando afficiunt liquorem appositum.

2. Ad secundum dicendum quod liquor appositus vino consecrato nullo modo miscetur substantiæ sanguinis Christi. Miscetur tamen speciebus sacramentalibus; ita tamen quod, permixtione facta, corrumpuntur prædictæ species, vel in toto vel in parte, secundum modum quo supra dictum est quod ex speciebus illis potest aliquid generari.[9] Et si quidem corrumpantur in toto, nulla jam remanet quæstio: quia jam totum erit uniforme. Si autem corrumpantur in parte, erit quidem una dimensio secundum continuitatem quantitatis, non tamen una secundum modum essendi: quia una pars ejus est sine subjecto, alia erit in subjecto; sicut, si aliquod corpus constituatur ex duobus metallis, erit unum corpus secundum rationem quantitatis, non tamen unum secundum speciem naturæ.

3. Ad tertium dicendum quod, sicut Innocentius III dicit, in decretali prædicta, *si post calicis consecrationem aliud vinum mittatur in calicem, illud quidem non transit in sanguinem, neque sanguini commiscetur: sed, accidentibus prioris vini commixtum, corpori quod sub eis latet undique circumfunditur, non madidans circumfusum.*[10] Quod quidem intelligendum est quando non fit tanta permixtio liquoris extranei quod sanguis Christi desinat esse sub toto. Tunc enim 'undique' dicitur 'circumfundi', non quia tangat sanguinem Christi secundum ejus proprias dimensiones: sed secundum dimensiones sacramentales, sub quibus continetur. Nec est simile de aqua benedicta: quia illa benedictio nullam immutationem facit circa substantiam aquæ, sicut facit consecratio vini.

4. Ad quartum dicendum quod quidam posuerunt quod, quantumcumque parva fiat extranei liquoris permixtio, substantia sanguinis Christi desinet esse sub toto. Et hoc ratione inducta. Quæ tamen non cogit. Quia magnum et parvum diversificant quantitatem dimensivam non quantum ad ejus essentiam, sed quantum ad determinationem mensuræ.

Similiter etiam liquor appositus adeo potest esse parvus quod sua

---

[7] *Decretalia Gregorii IX*, 3, 41, 6 *Cum Marthæ*. Richter-Friedberg II, 639
[8] In the body of the article
[9] 3a. 77, 5
[10] *Regesta* v. *Ep*. 121. PL 214, 1121

on the taste of wine. It does then happen that accidents change a substance, just as it normally happens that a substance causes accidental changes. Nature yields to miracle and a power more than normal is at work.[7] Do not, however, understand this as meaning that the numerically identical accident which was in the wine from before the consecration is later found also in the wine that is added; no, the change is the result of action. The accidents of wine that remain on now keep the action which belonged to the substance, as we have seen;[8] it is in this way by causing a change that they affect the liquid which is added.

2. The liquid that is added to the consecrated wine does not mix at all with the substance of the blood of Christ. It mixes, however, with the sacramental species; and in such a way that, when the mixture has taken place, the species cease to be, either wholly or in part, in the way in which we said above that it is possible for something to be produced from these species.[9] And if they completely cease to be no question arises, because the whole thing is now uniform. If, however, they cease to be in part, you will have one dimension from the point of view of the quantity which is continuous, but it will not be one if you consider the way in which it exists, because one part of the dimension is without any subject and the other part is inhering in a subject. It is then like when something coalesces from two metals; you have one thing from the point of view of the quantity, but it is not one from the point of view of the specific natures involved.

3. As Innocent III says, in the decretal we have just quoted from, *if, after the consecration of the chalice, more wine is put into the chalice, it is not changed into the blood, nor is it mixed with the blood; but mingling with the accidents of wine already there, it is poured in all about what lies under them, but does not soak into it.*[10] We are to take this as happening when the quantity of the liquid mingled is not so great that the blood of Christ ceases to be present under every single part of the whole. In that case we speak of the mingled liquid as being 'poured all about', not that it touches the blood of Christ in the dimensions of the blood, but according to the sacramental dimensions under which the blood is contained. There is no parity with holy water; the blessing of holy water brings about no change with regard to the substance of the water, as the consecration of wine does.

4. Some people held that no matter how small the quantity of liquid mixed might be, the substance of Christ's blood would cease to be under every single part of the whole. They held this view for the reason given in the objection. But it is not a compelling argument. First, great and little do not make for an essential difference in dimensive quantity but only for a difference in its determinate measure.

Likewise, the added liquid can be so small in its dimensions that its very smallness prevents it from penetrating through the whole; it is not just

parvitate impeditur ne diffundatur per totum, et non solum dimensionibus: quæ, licet sint sine subjecto, tamen obstant alteri liquori sicut et substantia si ibi esset, secundum ea quæ præmissa sunt.

that the dimensions of the original wine do not allow this, which although they are without any substance of their own, resist the added liquid in the way that substance would if it were there, in accordance with what we have said at the beginning of the article.

Quæstio 78. de forma hujus sacramenti

Deinde considerandum est de forma hujus sacramenti. Et circa hoc quæruntur sex:

1. quæ sit forma hujus sacramenti;
2. utrum sit conveniens forma consecrationis panis;
3. utrum sit conveniens forma consecrationis sanguinis;
4. de virtute utriusque formæ;
5. de veritate locutionis;
6. de comparatione unius formæ ad aliam.

articulus 1. *utrum hæc sit forma hujus sacramenti, 'Hoc est corpus meum', et, 'Hic est calix sanguinis mei'*

AD PRIMUM sic proceditur:[1] 1. Videtur quod hæc non sit forma hujus sacramenti, 'Hoc est corpus meum', et 'Hic est calix sanguinis mei'. Illa enim verba videntur pertinere ad formam sacramenti quibus Christus corpus suum et sanguinem consecravit. Sed Christus ante benedixit panem acceptum, et postea dixit, *Accipite et comedite: hoc est corpus meum*, ut habetur *Matth.* xxvi;[2] et similiter fecit de calice.[3] Ergo prædicta verba non sunt forma hujus sacramenti.

2. Præterea, Eusebius dicit quod *invisibilis sacerdos visibiles creaturas in suum corpus convertit, dicens: Accipite et comedite, hoc est corpus meum.*[4] Ergo totum hoc videtur pertinere ad formam sacramenti. Et eadem ratio est de verbis pertinentibus ad sanguinem.

3. Præterea, in forma Baptismi exprimitur persona ministri et actus ejus, cum dicitur, 'Ego te baptizo'. Sed in præmissis verbis nulla fit mentio de persona ministri, nec de actu ejus. Ergo non est conveniens forma sacramenti.

4. Præterea, forma sacramenti sufficit ad perfectionem sacramenti: unde sacramentum baptismi quandoque perfici potest solis verbis formæ prolatis, et omnibus aliis prætermissis. Si ergo prædicta verba sunt forma hujus sacramenti, videtur quod aliquando possit hoc sacramentum perfici his solis verbis prolatis, et omnibus aliis prætermissis quæ in missa dicuntur. Quod tamen videtur esse falsum: quia, ubi verba alia prætermitterentur, prædicta verba acciperentur ex persona sacerdotis proferentis, in cujus corpus et sanguinem panis et vinum non convertuntur. Non ergo prædicta verba sunt forma hujus sacramenti.

---

[1]cf IV *Sent.* 8, 2, 1, i, ii & iii; 2, i; 4, iii. *In Matt.* 26. *In* I *Cor.* 11, *lect.* 5

[2]*Matthew* 26, 26 [3]*Matthew* 26, 27, 28

[4]cf Gratian, *Decretum* 3, 2, 35 *Quia corpus.* Richter-Friedberg I, 1325. See note 8 to 73, 5

Question 78. the form of this sacrament

We now come to study the form of this sacrament. On this topic there are six points of inquiry:

1. what is the form of this sacrament?
2. is the form of consecration for the bread a suitable one?
3. is the form of consecration of the blood a suitable one?
4. on the efficaciousness of each of these forms.
5. is the manner of expression adequate?
6. a comparison of the two forms.

article 1. *is the form of this sacrament the words, 'This is my body', and, 'This is the chalice of my blood'?*

THE FIRST POINT:[1] 1. It would seem that the words, 'This is my body', and 'This is the chalice of my blood', are not the form of this sacrament. Whatever words Christ used to consecrate his body and his blood are the words that constitute the form of this sacrament. But Christ first of all blessed the bread that he had taken; it was only afterwards that he said, *Take, eat; this is my body*;[2] and he acted in like manner with the chalice.[3] Hence, these words are not the form of this sacrament.

2. Moreover, Eusebius says that the *invisible priest changes visible created things into his body, saying: take, eat; this is my body.*[4] The whole of this phrase then would seem to be the form of the sacrament. And the same can be said of the words that refer to the blood.

3. Furthermore, in the form of Baptism the person of the minister and his action are expressed, when the words 'I baptize you' are said. But in the above-mentioned formula there is no mention made of the person of the minister or of his action. Therefore, it is not an appropriate form for this sacrament.

4. Again, the form of a sacrament is all that is required to bring the sacrament to completion: for that reason the sacrament of Baptism is at times validly performed when only the words of the form are said and all others are omitted. If then you say that the aforementioned words are the form of this sacrament, it will follow that at times this sacrament is validly celebrated by the utterance of these words only, leaving out all the others which are said at Mass. But this does not seem to be the case, because, if all the other words are left out, the aforementioned words will be taken as spoken in the person of the priest who utters them; but the bread and wine are not changed into his body and blood. These words are not, then, the form of this sacrament.

SED CONTRA est quod Ambrosius dicit, *Consecratio fit verbis et sermonibus Domini Jesu. Nam per reliqua omnia quæ dicuntur, laus Deo refertur, oratione petitur pro populo, pro regibus, pro cæteris. Ubi autem sacramentum conficitur, jam non suis sermonibus sacerdos utitur, sed utitur sermonibus Christi. Ergo sermo Christi hoc conficit sacramentum.*[5]

RESPONSIO: Dicendum quod hoc sacramentum ab aliis sacramentis differt in duobus. Primo quidem quantum ad hoc, quod hoc sacramentum perficitur in consecratione materiæ; alia vero sacramenta perficiuntur in usu materiæ consecratæ. Secundo, quia in aliis sacramentis consecratio materiæ consistit solum in quadam benedictione, ex qua materia consecrata accipit instrumentaliter quandam spiritualem virtutem, quæ per ministrum, qui est instrumentum animatum, potest ad instrumenta inanimata procedere. Sed in hoc sacramento consecratio materiæ consistit in quadam miraculosa conversione substantiæ, quæ a solo Deo perfici potest. Unde minister in hoc sacramento perficiendo non habet alium actum nisi prolationem verborum.

Et quia forma debet esse conveniens rei, ideo forma hujus sacramenti differt a formis aliorum sacramentorum in duobus. Primo quidem, quia formæ aliorum sacramentorum important usum materiæ, puta baptizationem vel consignationem: sed forma hujus sacramenti importat solam consecrationem materiæ, quæ in transubstantiatione consistit; puta cum dicitur, 'Hoc est corpus meum', vel 'Hic est calix sanguinis mei'. Secundo, quia formæ aliorum sacramentorum proferuntur ex persona ministri, sive per modum exercentis actum, sicut cum dicitur, 'Ego te baptizo', vel 'Ego te confirmo', sive per modum imperantis, sicut in sacramento ordinis dicitur, 'Accipe potestatem, etc.'; sive per modum deprecantis, sicut cum in sacramento extremæ unctionis dicitur, 'Per istam unctionem et nostram intercessionem, etc.' Sed forma hujus sacramenti profertur* ex persona ipsius Christi loquentis: ut detur intelligi quod minister in perfectione hujus sacramenti nihil agit nisi quod profert verba Christi.

---

*Piana: *quasi*, as if, just as

[5]*De Sacramentis* IV, 4. PL 16, 459. cf Gratian, *Decretum* 3, 2, 55 *Panis est*. Richter-Friedberg I, 1334

[a]The natural subordination of matter to mind (or spirit) is already to be observed in this first blessing of the matter. At the moment of application (the actual baptizing or anointing), an even further degree of subordination (and of full instrumental use) is to be seen. In blessing the matter the bishop or priest acts as a principal cause, though in virtue of ordination; in applying the matter they act as an instrumental cause.
[b]i.e. as a principal cause.

[c]St Thomas thought that the words uttered by the bishop at the moment of presenting the ordinand with the chalice and paten were the form of ordination. Whatever may have been the form of ordination in the Latin Church in St Thomas's time and later, it is now, since Pius XII's declaration, the consecratory formula pronounced by

ON THE OTHER HAND, we find Ambrose saying, *the consecration is brought about by the words and discourses of the Lord Jesus. Everything else that is said is to offer praise to God or to make petition for the people, for kings, for all. But at the point where the sacrament is effected, the priest does not use his own words, but the words of Christ. And so it is the word of Christ that accomplishes this sacrament.*[5]

REPLY: There are two respects in which this sacrament differs from the others. First, this sacrament is fully established when the matter is consecrated; the other sacraments are brought to completion only when the consecrated matter is being used. Second, in the other sacraments the consecration of the matter consists merely in a certain blessing, as a result of which the consecrated matter receives an instrumental spiritual power; this derives from the minister who is a living instrument able to reach to inanimate instruments.[a] But in this sacrament the consecration of the matter consists in a miraculous change of the substance, which only God can bring about.[b] So it is that the minister has no other act in effecting this sacrament than to pronounce the words.

Now since the form of a thing ought to be in accordance with its nature, it follows that the form of this sacrament differs from the forms of the other sacraments in two respects. First of all, the forms of the other sacraments imply that the matter is actually being used, as, for example, Baptism and Confirmation; but the form of this sacrament implies only that the matter is being consecrated, and this is the transubstantiation which takes place when the priest says the words, 'This is my body', or 'This is the chalice of my blood'. Secondly, the forms of the other sacraments are pronounced by the minister speaking in his own person, either as exercising some action, as when he says, 'I baptize you', or 'I confirm you'; or as conveying a charge, as when in the sacrament of Order the words are uttered, 'Receive the power, etc.';[c] or as calling on God's mercy, as when in the sacrament of the Last Anointing he says, 'By this anointing and our intercession, etc.'. But in this sacrament the form is pronounced as in the person of Christ himself speaking; by this we are to understand that the part played by the minister in the effecting of this sacrament is the mere utterance of the words of Christ.[d]

---

the bishop with outstretched hands over the candidates. In the early western church and always in the eastern church it was this. The Church has power to change the sacramental sign or, at least, to expand it, if the basic significance can be safeguarded.

[d]The priest utters the words of Christ by his own power of utterance. But at that moment he plays an instrumental rôle in the effecting of the transubstantiation. Christ the priest, offering the body and the blood, is through the priest, changing bread and wine into that body and blood. Christ the priest is thus present to the human priest.

1. Ad primum ergo dicendum quod circa hoc est multiplex opinio. Quidam[6] enim dixerunt quod Christus, qui habebat potestatem excellentiæ in sacramentis, absque omni forma verborum hoc sacramentum perfecit; et postea verba protulit sub quibus alii postea consecrarent. Quod videntur sonare verba Innocentii III dicentis, *Sane dici potest quod Christus virtute divina confecit, et postea formam expressit sub qua posteri benedicerent.*[7] Sed contra hoc expresse sunt verba Evangelii, in quibus dicitur quod Christus *benedixit*: quæ quidem benedictio aliquibus verbis facta est. Unde prædicta verba Innocentii sunt opinative magis dicta quam determinative.

Quidam[8] autem dixerunt quod benedictio illa facta est quibusdam aliis verbis nobis ignotis. Sed nec hoc stare potest. Quia benedictio consecrationis nunc perficitur per recitationem eorum quæ tunc acta sunt. Unde, si tunc per hæc verba non est facta consecratio, nec modo fieret.

Et ideo alii[9] dixerunt quod illa benedictio eisdem etiam verbis facta est quibus modo fit, sed Christus ea bis protulit: primo quidem secrete, ad consecrandum; secundo manifeste, ad instruendum. Sed nec hoc stare potest. Quia sacerdos consecrat proferens hæc verba, non ut a Christo in occulta benedictione dicta, sed ut publice prolata. Unde, cum non habeant vim hujusmodi verba nisi ex Christi prolatione, videtur quod etiam Christus manifeste ea proferens consecraverit.

Et ideo alii[10] dixerunt quod Evangelistæ non semper eundem ordinem in recitando servaverunt quo res sunt gestæ: ut patet per Augustinum.[11] Unde intelligendum est ordinem rei gestæ sic exprimi posse, *Accipiens panem, benedixit dicens, 'Hoc est corpus meum', et deinde fregit et dedit discipulis suis.* Sed idem sensus potest esse in verbis Evangelii non mutatis. Nam hoc participium 'dicens' concomitantiam quandam importat verborum prolatorum ad ea quæ præcedunt. Non autem oportet quod hæc concomitantia intelligatur solum respectu verbi ultimi prolati, quasi Christus tunc ista verba protulerit quando dedit discipulis suis: sed potest intelligi concomitantia respectu totius præcedentis, ut sit sensus, *dum benediceret et frangeret et daret discipulis suis, hæc verba dixit, 'Accipite, etc.'*

2. Ad secundum dicendum quod in his verbis, 'Accipite et comedite', intelligitur usus materiæ consecratæ, qui non est de necessitate hujus

---

[6]Præpositinus of Cremona, *Summa* 4, *de Eucharistia*

[7]Innocent III, *De Sacro Altaris Mysterio* IV, 6. PL 217, 859

[8]ibid. Odo of Cambrai, *In canonem Missæ* 3. PL 160, 1061

[9]Stephen of Autun, *De Sacramento Altaris* 14. PL 172, 1245

[10]Innocent III, *De Sacro Altaris Mysterio* 4, 6. PL 217, 589. William of Auxerre, *Summa Aurea* 4, *De Eucharistia* 2

[11]*De Consensu Evangelistarum* 2, 21, 30, 34. PL 34, 1102, 1111, 1123

Hence: 1. There are many opinions on this matter. Some theologians[6] thought that Christ, whose sacramental power was supreme, consecrated this sacrament without using any form of words at all; it was only afterwards that he gave the words which others were to use thereafter. This seems to be what Innocent III means when he says, *it can be said that Christ consecrated by divine power and later on gave the form which others were to use in consecrating.*[7] But the words of the Gospel are clearly opposed to this view; we read that Christ *blessed*, and that means he used certain words. So, we are to take Innocent's words as expressing an opinion and not as authoritative teaching.

Some[8 e] held that the blessing was made with some other words that we do not now know. But this position also cannot be sustained. The blessing which we now use to consecrate consists of a recital of what was done then. Hence, if these were not the words which were then effective of the consecration, they would not be so now.

And so others[9] went on to say that Christ blessed with the same words that we now use, but that he uttered them twice; first, secretly, in order to consecrate; again, openly, to let us know what had happened. But this view also is unacceptable. The priest consecrates by uttering these words, not as having been pronounced by Christ in some secret consecration, but as he expressed them publicly. Seeing that these words derive all their efficaciousness from their first utterance by Christ, it must be that he consecrated when he spoke them openly.

Others[10] then said that the evangelists did not always keep the same order in their narrative in which the events actually occurred; this view is found in Augustine.[11] We should understand the order of events as follows, *taking bread he blessed it saying, this is my body, and then he broke it and gave it to his disciples*. But there is no need to make any change in the words of the Gospel in order to have this sense. The participle *saying* implies a certain concomitance of the words uttered with what goes before it. This concomitance is not necessarily restricted to the last part of the preceding phrase, as if Christ said the words at the moment of actually giving to his disciples; the concomitance can be understood as referring to the whole preceding statement, so that the sense is, *when he blessed and broke and gave to his disciples, he said these words, 'Take ye, etc.'*

2. The words, 'Take ye and eat', have to do with the use of the consecrated matter, and we saw earlier[12] that in this sacrament actual use is

[e]The liturgical scholar, Dom Gregory Dix, in his *The Shape of the Liturgy*, held that Christ consecrated by the normal Jewish blessing (*Berakah*) over the bread and wine.

sacramenti, ut supra habitum est.[12] Et ideo nec hæc verba sunt de substantia formæ.

Quia tamen ad quandam perfectionem sacramenti pertinet materiæ consecratæ usus, sicut operatio non est prima, sed secunda perfectio rei; ideo per omnia hæc verba exprimitur tota perfectio hujus sacramenti. Et hoc modo Eusebius intellexit his verbis confici sacramentum, quantum ad primam et secundam perfectionem ipsius.

3. Ad tertium dicendum quod in sacramento baptismi minister aliquem actum exercet circa usum materiæ, qui est de essentia sacramenti: quod non est in hoc sacramento. Et ideo non est similis ratio.

4. Ad quartum dicendum quod quidam dixerunt hoc sacramentum perfici non posse prædictis verbis prolatis et aliis prætermissis, præcipue quæ sunt in canone missæ. Sed hoc patet esse falsum. Tum ex verbis Ambrosii supra inductis. Tum etiam quia canon missæ non est idem apud omnes, nec secundum omnia tempora, sed diversa sunt a diversis apposita.

Unde dicendum est quod, si sacerdos sola verba prædicta proferret cum intentione conficiendi hoc sacramentum, perficeretur hoc sacramentum: quia intentio faceret ut hæc verba intelligerentur quasi ex persona Christi prolata, etiam si verbis præcedentibus hoc non recitaretur. Graviter tamen peccaret sacerdos sic conficiens hoc sacramentum, utpote ritum Ecclesiæ non servans. Nec est simile de baptismo, quod est sacramentum necessitatis: defectum autem hujus sacramenti potest supplere spiritualis manducatio, ut Augustinus dicit.[13]

articulus 2. utrum hæc sit conveniens forma consecrationis panis, 'Hoc est corpus meum'

AD SECUNDUM sic proceditur:[1] 1. Videtur quod hæc non sit conveniens forma consecrationis panis, 'Hoc est corpus meum'. Per formam enim sacramenti debet exprimi sacramenti effectus. Sed effectus qui fit in consecratione panis, est conversio substantiæ panis in corpus Christi: quæ magis exprimitur per hoc verbum 'fit', quam per hoc verbum 'est'. Ergo in forma consecrationis deberet dici, 'Hoc fit corpus meum'.

2. Præterea, Ambrosius dicit, *Sermo Christi hoc conficit sacramentum. Quis sermo Christi? Hic quo facta sunt omnia: jussit Dominus et facta sunt cæli et terra.*[2] Ergo et forma hujus sacramenti convenientior esset per verbum imperativum, ut diceretur, 'Hoc sit corpus meum'.

---

[12] 3a. 74, 7
[13] cf 3a. 73, 3 ad 1
[1] cf 3a. 75, 2. IV *Sent.* 8, 2, 1, iii & iv. *In Matt.* 26. *In* 1 *Cor.* 11, *lect.* 5
[2] *De Sacramentis* IV, 4

not an sesential part of the sacrament. So it is that these words are not an essential part of the form.

Since, however, the use of the consecrated matter does make for a certain perfection of the sacrament, in the way that the operation of a thing though not its basic perfection is still a secondary one, it follows that by all these words is expressed the complete perfection of this sacrament. It was in this way that Eusebius took it that the sacrament involved the use of all these words: he was thinking of its basic and its secondary perfection.

3. In the sacrament of Baptism the minister in using the matter performs a certain action which is part of the essence of that sacrament; this is not the case in the Eucharist. And so there is no argument from analogy.

4. Some theologians said that this sacrament could not be validly celebrated by reciting the aforementioned words only, leaving out the others, especially those found in the canon of the Mass. But this is obviously not the case. First of all, there is the text of Ambrose we have quoted above. Then again, the Canon of the Mass is not the same everywhere, nor has it been the same at all times, but different churches have made their own additions.

We must then conclude that if a priest were to say these words only, with the intention of effecting the sacrament, it would be validly consecrated; his intention would suffice to make the words mean that they were spoken in the person of Christ, even if this were not stated by reciting the foregoing words. But a priest so consecrating would gravely sin in not keeping the rite of the Church. The case is not the same in Baptism which cannot be dispensed with, but the lack of this sacrament can be made up for by spiritual communion, as Augustine teaches.[13]

article 2. is the form of consecration of the bread, 'This is my body', a suitable one?

THE SECOND POINT:[1] 1. It would seem that the words, 'This is my body', are not suitable as the form of consecration of the bread. The form of a sacrament ought to show what the effect of the sacrament is. But the effect which is brought about by the consecration of the bread is the change of the substance of the bread into the body of Christ; and this is more exactly expressed by the term 'is becoming' than by the term 'is'. It follows that in the form of consecration one ought to say, 'This is becoming my body'.

2. Moreover, Ambrose says, *a word of Christ consecrates this sacrament. What word of Christ? This word by which all things were made: the Lord commanded and the heavens and the earth were made.*[2] The form of this sacrament would then be better expressed in the imperative, thus, 'Be this my body'.

3. Præterea, per subjectum hujus locutionis importatur illud quod convertitur; sicut per prædicatum importatur conversionis terminus. Sed sicut est determinatum id in quod fit conversio, non enim fit conversio nisi in corpus Christi, ita est determinatum id quod convertitur, non enim convertitur in corpus Christi nisi panis. Ergo, sicut ex parte prædicati ponitur nomen, ita ex parte subjecti debet poni nomen, ut dicatur, 'Hic panis est corpus meum'.

4. Præterea, sicut id in quod terminatur conversio est determinatæ naturæ, quia est corpus; ita etiam est determinatæ personæ. Ergo, ad determinandam personam, debet dici, 'Hoc est corpus Christi'.

5. Præterea, in verbis formæ non debet poni aliquid quod non sit de substantia ejus. Inconvenienter ergo additur in quibusdam libris hæc conjunctio 'enim' quæ non est de substantia formæ.

SED CONTRA est quod Dominus hac forma in consecrando est usus, ut patet *Matth.* xxvi.[3]

RESPONSIO: Dicendum quod hæc est conveniens forma consecrationis panis. Dictum est enim[4] quod hæc consecratio consistit in conversione substantiæ panis in corpus Christi. Oportet autem formam sacramenti significare id quod in sacramento efficitur. Unde et forma consecrationis panis debet significare ipsam conversionem panis in corpus Christi. In qua tria considerantur: scilicet ipsa conversio, et terminus a quo, et terminus ad quem.

Conversio autem potest considerari dupliciter: uno modo, ut in *fieri*; alio modo, ut in *facto esse*. Non autem debuit significari conversio in hac forma ut in fieri, sed ut in facto esse. Primo quidem, quia hæc conversio non est successiva, ut supra habitum est,[5] sed instantanea; in hujusmodi autem mutationibus fieri non est nisi factum esse. Secundo, quia ita se habent formæ sacramentales ad significandum effectum sacramenti, sicut se habent formæ artificiales ad repræsentandum effectum artis. Forma autem artificialis est similitudo ultimi effectus in quem fertur intentio artificis; sicut forma artis in mente ædificatoris est forma domus ædificatæ principaliter, ædificationis autem per consequens. Unde et in hac forma debet exprimi conversio ut in facto esse, ad quod fertur intentio.

Et quia ipsa conversio exprimitur in hac forma ut *in facto esse*, necesse est quod extrema conversionis significentur ut se habent *in facto esse* conversionis. Tunc autem terminus in quem habet propriam naturam

---

[3] *Matthew* 26, 26
[4] 3a. 78, 1
[5] 3a. 75, 7

3. Furthermore, the subject of the consecratory phrase is concerned with the thing that is changed, just as the predicate is concerned with the term of the change. Now, just as the term of the change is something determinate, namely, the body of Christ, so too what is changed is something determinate, namely, the bread. It follows then that, just as in the predicate a name is stated, so also a name should be stated in the subject and the form should be, 'This bread is my body'.

4. Again, just as the term of the change has a definite nature, for it is a body, so too it belongs to a definite person. Therefore, to show who this definite person is, the form ought to say, 'This is the body of Christ'.

5. Finally, nothing should be included in the words of the form which is not absolutely essential. The conjunction 'for' found in some missals is, then, an undesirable addition, see ng that it is not essential to the form.

ON THE OTHER HAND, our Lord used this form where consecrating, as appears in *Matthew*.[3]

REPLY: This is a suitable form for the consecration of the bread. We have said[4] that this consecration consists in the change of the substance of the bread into the body of Christ. Now the form of any sacrament should signify what happens when the sacrament is celebrated. And so the form of consecration of the bread ought to signify the actual change of the bread into the body of Christ. Now in this change three things are to be considered, the change itself, what is as the starting point and what is as the point of rest.

The change itself can be envisaged in two ways; first of all, as the actual *process of becoming*, and then, as the *fact of having become*. Now the Eucharistic form ought to signify the change not as the actual process of becoming but as the fact of having become. The first reason for saying this is because the Eucharistic change is not successive but instantaneous, as we saw above,[5] and in changes of this kind the becoming is telescoped into the having become. Secondly, sacramental forms signify the sacramental effect after the manner in which the idea in the mind of a craftsman represents the effect he produces. Now the craftsman's idea bears on the final effect he intends; for example, the idea in a builder's mind is principally of the house as built, and only secondarily of the actual building of it. And so in the Eucharistic form the change should be expressed as accomplished, for this is what is intended.

And because in the Eucharistic form the change is expressed as it is seen identified with the actual *having become*, it follows that what is as the starting point and what is as the point of rest should be signified as they are found at the moment of the actual *having become*. At that moment

suæ substantiæ: sed terminus a quo non manet secundum suam substantiam, sed solum secundum accidentia, quibus sensui subjacet, et ad sensum determinari potest. Unde convenienter terminus conversionis a quo exprimitur per pronomen demonstrativum relatum ad accidentia sensibilia, quæ manent. Terminus autem ad quem exprimitur per nomen significans naturam ejus in quod fit conversio: quod quidem est totum corpus Christi, et non sola caro ejus, ut dictum est.[6] Unde hæc forma est convenientissima, 'Hoc est corpus meum'.

1. Ad primum ergo dicendum quod fieri non est ultimus effectus hujus consecrationis, sed factum esse, ut dictum est.[7] Et ideo hoc potius exprimi debet in forma.

2. Ad secundum dicendum quod sermo Dei operatus est in creatione rerum, qui etiam operatur in hac consecratione: aliter tamen et aliter. Nam hic operatur sacramentaliter, id est secundum vim significationis. Et ideo oportet in hoc sermone significari ultimum effectum consecrationis per verbum substantivum indicativi modi et præsentis temporis. Sed in creatione rerum operatus est solum effective: quæ quidem efficientia est per imperium suæ sapientiæ. Et ideo in creatione rerum exprimitur sermo Dominicus per verbum imperativi modi: secundum illud *Gen.* i, *Fiat lux, et facta est lux.*[8]

3. Ad tertium dicendum quod terminus a quo in ipso facto esse conversionis non retinet naturam suæ substantiæ, sicut terminus ad quem. Et ideo non est simile.

4. Ad quartum dicendum quod per hoc pronomen 'meum', quod includit demonstrationem primæ personæ, quæ est persona loquentis, sufficienter exprimitur persona Christi, ex cujus persona hæc proferuntur, ut dictum est.[9]

5. Ad quintum dicendum quod hæc conjunctio 'enim' apponitur in hac forma secundum consuetudinem Romanæ Ecclesiæ a beato Petro Apostolo derivatam.[10] Et hoc propter continuationem ad verba præcedentia. Et ideo non est de forma, sicut nec præcedentia formam.

articulus 3. *utrum hæc sit conveniens forma consecrationis vini, 'Hic est calix sanguinis mei, etc.'*

AD TERTIUM sic proceditur:[1] 1. Videtur quod hæc non sit conveniens forma consecrationis vini, 'Hic est calix sanguinis mei, novi et æterni testamenti,

---

[6] 3a. 76, 1 ad 2
[7] In the body of the article
[8] *Genesis* 1, 3
[9] 3a. 78, 1
[10] cf Innocent III, loc cit. PL 217, 858. *Decretalia Gregorii IX*, III, 41, 6 *Cum Marthæ*. Richter-Friedberg II, 638

what is the terminus of the change exists in its substantial nature; but what is as the starting point of the change exists no longer in its substantial nature, but only in its accidental appearances which relate it to our senses and make it knowable to them. And so it is very suitable to designate what is as the starting point by a demonstrative pronoun in reference to the corporeal accidents which remain. What we have as the end of the change is designated by a noun signifying the nature of the thing in which the change culminates; and this is the whole body of Christ and not merely his flesh, as we saw earlier.[6] We conclude then that the form 'This is my body' is the most suitable one.

Hence: 1. Becoming is not the final effect of this consecration, but having become, as we have just said.[7] And so it is rather the latter that should find expression in the form.

2. The word of God was effective in the first creation of things and that self-same word is effective here, but the mode of operation is different. Here it works through a sacramental mystery, it is effective through a sign. And so it is that the form should signify the final effect of consecration by the verb to be, in the indicative mood and the present tense. In the creation of things God's word was purely and simply effective; it worked through the command of his wisdom. For that reason the word of the Lord at the creation of things is expressed by a verb in the imperative mood; as the text of *Genesis* has it, *let there be light, and there was light.*[8]

3. What is as the starting point in the change does not retain its substantial nature when the actual having become is reached, but what is as the point of rest does do so. You cannot compare the two.

4. The pronoun 'my', which includes a pointing to the first person, which is the person speaking, sufficiently indicates the person of Christ, on whose behalf the words are uttered, as we saw already.[9]

5. The conjunction *for* is found in the form used by the Roman Church and it goes back to blessed Peter the Apostle.[10] It is put in to establish continuity with the preceding words. Hence it is not really part of the form, just as the words which precede the form are not part of the form.

article 3. is the form for the consecration of the wine, 'This is the chalice of my blood, etc.', a suitable one?

THE THIRD POINT:[1] 1. It would seem that the following words are not suitable as a form for the consecration of the wine, 'This is the chalice of my blood, of the new and eternal testament, the mystery of faith, which

[1]cf IV *Sent.* 8, 2, 2, i, ii & iii. *In Matt.* 26. *In* I *Cor.* 11, *lect.* 6

mysterium fidei, qui pro vobis et pro multis effundetur in remissionem peccatorum'. Sicut enim panis convertitur in corpus Christi ex vi consecrationis, ita et vinum in sanguinem Christi, sicut ex prædictis[2] patet. Sed in forma consecrationis panis ponitur in recto corpus Christi, nec aliquid aliud additur. Inconvenienter ergo in hac forma ponitur sanguis Christi in obliquo, et additur 'calix' in recto, cum dicitur, 'Hic est calix sanguinis mei'.

2. Præterea, non sunt majoris efficaciæ verba quæ proferuntur in consecratione panis quam ea quæ proferuntur in consecratione vini, cum utraque sint verba Christi. Sed statim dicto, 'Hoc est corpus meum', est perfecta consecratio panis. Ergo statim cum dictum est, 'Hic est calix sanguinis mei', est perfecta consecratio sanguinis. Et ita ea quæ consequuntur non videntur esse de substantia formæ: præsertim cum pertineant ad proprietates hujus sacramenti.

3. Præterea, Testamentum novum pertinere videtur ad internam inspirationem: ut patet ex hoc quod Apostolus, *ad Heb.* viii,[3] introducit verba quæ habentur in *Jerem.* xxxi, *Consummabo super domum Israel testamentum novum, dando leges meas in mentibus eorum.*[4] Sacramentum autem exterius visibiliter agitur. Inconvenienter ergo in forma sacramenti dicitur, 'novi Testamenti'.

4. Præterea, 'novum' dicitur aliquid ex eo quod est prope principium sui esse. Æternum autem non habet principium sui esse. Ergo inconvenienter dicitur 'novi et æterni', quia videtur contradictionem implicare.

5. Præterea, occasiones erroris sunt hominibus subtrahendæ: secundum illud *Isaiæ* lvii: *Auferte offendicula de via populi mei.*[5] Sed quidam erraverunt æstimantes mystice solum esse corpus et sanguinem Christi in hoc sacramento. Ergo in hac forma inconvenienter ponitur 'mysterium fidei'.

6. Præterea, supra[6] dictum est quod, sicut Baptismus est sacramentum fidei, ita Eucharistia est sacramentum caritatis. Ergo in hac forma magis debuit poni 'caritas' quam 'fides'.

7. Præterea, totum hoc sacramentum, et quantum ad corpus et quantum ad sanguinem, est memoriale Dominicæ passionis: secundum illud I *Cor.* xi, *Quotiescumque manducabitis panem hunc et calicem bibetis, mortem Domini annuntiabitis.*[7] Non ergo magis debuit in forma consecrationis sanguinis fieri mentio de passione Christi et de ejus fructu, quam in forma consecrationis corporis; præsertim cum, *Luc.* xxii, Dominus dixerit, *Hoc est corpus meum, quod pro vobis tradetur.*[8]

---

[2]3a. 76, 1, 2
[3]*Hebrews* 8, 8–10
[4]*Jeremiah* 31, 31–3
[5]*Isaiah* 57, 14
[6]3a. 73, 3 ad 3
[7]1 *Corinthians* 11, 26
[8]*Luke* 22, 19

will be shed for you and for many for the remission of sins'. It is by virtue of the consecration that the bread is changed into the body of Christ and it is likewise by the consecration that the wine is changed into Christ's blood, as we have seen.[2] But in the form of consecration of the bread the body of Christ is spoken of directly and nothing else is added. It is, then, not desirable that in this form the blood of Christ should be spoken of indirectly, and that the word 'chalice' should be added and spoken of directly, when the priest says, 'This is the chalice of my blood'.

2. Moreover, the words that are uttered in the consecration of the bread are not of greater efficacy than the words that are pronounced in the consecration of the wine; they are all the words of Christ. But immediately 'This is my body' is said, the consecration of the bread is effected. Therefore, immediately 'This is the chalice of my blood' is uttered the consecration of the wine is accomplished. It follows that all the subsequent words do not pertain to the substance of the form. A further reason for saying this is that these words are concerned with the properties of this sacrament.

3. Furthermore, the new testament belongs to the world of interior inspiration, as we see from the fact that the Apostle, in the epistle to the *Hebrews*,[3] quotes the words which are found in *Jeremiah*, *I will establish a new covenant with the house of Israel*, *I will put my laws into their minds*.[4] But a sacrament is something that is done externally in a visible fashion. The words then 'of the New Testament' are out of keeping with the form of any sacrament.

4. Again, a thing is said to be new when it is close to the beginning of its existence. But what is eternal has no beginning of its existence. It is, then, quite unsuitable to say 'new and eternal'; it seems to involve a contradiction.

5. Moreover, occasions for misunderstanding should be removed from people; we read in *Isaiah*, *remove every obstruction from my people's way*.[5] Now some people have erred in thinking that the body and blood of Christ are only mystically in this sacrament. Therefore, it is not desirable to have the words 'mystery of faith' in the Eucharistic form.

6. Furthermore, we have already seen[6] that just as Baptism is the sacrament of faith, so the Eucharist is the sacrament of charity. Therefore, in the form of the Eucharist 'charity' should be mentioned rather than 'faith'.

7. Again, this whole sacrament, both as to the body as well as to the blood, is a memorial of the Lord's passion; as the text of *Corinthians* put it, *as often as you eat this bread and drink the cup, you proclaim the Lord's death*.[7] There is no greater reason then why the passion of Christ and its fruit should be mentioned in the form of consecration of the blood and not in that of the body, especially as the Lord said, *this is my body which is given for you*.[8]

8. Præterea, passio Christi, ut supra habitum est,[9] ad sufficientiam profuit omnibus, quantum vero ad efficaciam profuit multis. Debuit ergo dici quod 'effundetur pro omnibus', aut 'pro multis', sine hoc quod adderetur 'pro vobis'.

9. Præterea, verba quibus hoc sacramentum conficitur, efficaciam habent ex institutione Christi. Sed nullus Evangelista recitat Christum hæc omnia verba dixisse. Ergo non est conveniens forma consecrationis vini.

SED CONTRA est quod Ecclesia, ab Apostolis instructa, utitur hac forma in consecratione vini.

RESPONSIO: Dicendum quod circa hanc formam est duplex opinio. Quidam[10] enim dixerunt quod de substantia formæ hujus est hoc solum quod dicitur, 'Hic est calix sanguinis mei', non autem ea quæ sequuntur. Sed hoc videtur inconveniens: quia ea quæ sequuntur, sunt quædam determinationes prædicati, id est sanguinis Christi; unde pertinent ad integritatem locutionis.

Et propter hoc sunt alii qui melius dicunt quod omnia sequentia sunt de substantia formæ, usque ad hoc quod postea sequitur, 'Hoc quotiescumque feceritis', quæ pertinent ad usum hujus sacramenti, unde non sunt de substantia formæ. Et inde est quod sacerdos eodem ritu et modo, scilicet tenendo calicem in manibus, omnia hæc verba profert. *Lucæ* etiam xxii interponuntur verba sequentia verbis primis, cum dicitur, *Hic calix novum testamentum est in sanguine meo.*[11]

Dicendum est ergo quod omnia prædicta verba sunt de substantia formæ: sed per prima verba, 'Hic est calix sanguinis mei', significatur ipsa conversio vini in sanguinem, eo modo quo dictum est[12] in forma consecrationis panis; per verba autem sequentia designatur virtus sanguinis effusi in passione, quæ operatur in hoc sacramento. Quæ quidem ad tria ordinatur. Primo quidem et principaliter ad adipiscendam æternam hereditatem: secundum illud *Heb.* x, *Habemus fiduciam in introitu sanctorum per sanguinem ejus.*[13] Et ad hoc designandum dicitur, 'novi et æterni Testamenti'. Secundo, ad justitiam gratiæ, quæ est per fidem: secundum illud *Rom.* iii, *Quem proposuit Deus propitiatorem per fidem in sanguine ejus, ut sit ipse justus, et justificans eum qui ex fide est Jesu Christi.*[14] Et quantum ad hoc subditur, 'mysterium fidei'. Tertio autem,

---

[9]3a. 48, 2
[10]Alexander of Hales, *Summa Theologica* 4, 33, 4, 3, 1. Bonaventure, *In* IV *Sent.* 8, 2, 1, 2. Peter of Tarentaise, *In* IV *Sent.* 3, 2
[11]*Luke* 22, 20
[12]3a. 78, 2

8. Also, the passion of Christ, as we saw earlier on,[9] was sufficient to save all men and was efficacious in regard to many. The form then ought rather to read 'which will be shed for all', or to read 'for many' without the addition of 'for you'.

9. Finally, the words by which this sacrament is consecrated derive their efficacy from Christ's institution. But none of the evangelists tells us that Christ said all these words. Therefore, the form of consecration of the wine is not a suitable one.

ON THE OTHER HAND, the Church, taught by the Apostles, uses this form.

REPLY: There are two opinions with regard to this form. Some people[10] have thought that the only essential part of the form is the words, 'This is the chalice of my blood', and that what follows is not necessary. But this does not seem to be true, because the words that follow give us further knowledge about the predicate, that is, the blood of Christ; and so they are part of the complete phrase.

Because of this others more correctly hold that everything that follows is part of the essential form up to the words, 'as often as you do this . . .' which, being concerned with the usage of the sacrament, are not part of the form. This is the reason why the priest says all these words using the while the same rite and manner, i.e. holding the chalice in his hands. And in the text of *Luke* these following words are interposed among the words of the first phrase; we read, *this cup is the new covenant in my blood.*[11]

We should conclude then that all these words belong to the essence of the form; the opening words, 'This is the chalice of my blood', signify the actual change of the wine into the blood, in the same way that we explained earlier[12] with regard to the form of consecration of the bread; the words that follow signify the power of Christ's blood which was shed in his passion—which power is now at work in this sacrament. This power is productive of three effects. The first and greatest effect is that it gains an eternal inheritance for us; as the text of *Hebrews* puts it, *we have confidence to enter the sanctuary by the blood of Jesus.*[13] The words of the form 'of the new and eternal testament' signify just this. The second effect is justification which is ours through grace and which is brought about by faith; as the text of *Romans* puts it, *whom God put forward as an expiation by his blood, to be received by faith . . . to prove that he himself is righteous and that he justifies him who has faith in Jesus.*[14] This is the reason for adding the words 'the mystery of faith'. The third effect is that

[13]*Hebrews* 10, 19
[14]*Romans* 3, 25, 26

ad removendum impedimenta utriusque prædictorum, scilicet peccata, secundum illud *Heb.* ix, *sanguis Christi emundabit conscientias nostras ab operibus mortuis*,[15] id est a peccatis. Et quantum ad hoc subditur, 'qui pro vobis et pro multis aliis* effundetur in remissionem peccatorum'.

1. Ad primum ergo dicendum quod, cum dicitur, 'Hic est calix sanguinis mei', est locutio figurativa, et potest dupliciter intelligi. Uno modo, secundum metonymiam, quia ponitur continens pro contento, ut sit sensus, 'Hic est sanguis meus contentus in calice'. De quo fit hic mentio, quia sanguis Christi in hoc sacramento consecratur inquantum est potus fidelium, quod non importatur in ratione sanguinis; et ideo oportuit hic designari per vas huic usui accommodatum.

Alio modo potest intelligi secundum metaphoram, prout per calicem similitudinare intelligitur passio Christi, quæ ad similitudinem calicis inebriat, secundum illud *Thren.* iii, *Replevit me amaritudinibus, inebriavit me absynthio*:[16] unde et ipse Dominus passionem suam calicem nominat, *Matth.* xxvi, dicens, *Transeat a me calix iste*,[17] ut sit sensus, 'Hic est calix passionis meæ'. De qua fit mentio in sanguine seorsum a corpore consecrato, quia separatio sanguinis a corpore fuit per passionem.

2. Ad secundum dicendum quod quia, ut dictum est,[18] sanguis seorsum consecratus expresse passionem Christi repræsentat, ideo potius in consecratione sanguinis fit mentio de effectu passionis quam in consecratione corporis, quod est passionis subjectum. Quod etiam designatur in hoc quod Dominus dicit, *quod pro vobis tradetur*, quasi dicat, 'quod pro vobis passioni subjicietur'.

3. Ad tertium dicendum quod testamentum est dispositio hereditatis. Hereditatem autem cælestem Deus disposuit hominibus dandam per virtutem sanguinis Jesu Christi: quia, ut dicitur *Heb.* ix, *Ubi est testamentum, mors necesse est intercedat testatoris*.[19] Sanguis autem Christi dupliciter est hominibus exhibitus. Primo quidem, in figura: quod pertinet ad vetus Testamentum. Et ideo Apostolus ibidem concludit, *Unde nec primum Testamentum sine sanguine dedicatum est*,[20] quod patet ex hoc quod, sicut dicitur *Exod.* xxiv, *lecto omni mandato Legis a Moyse, omnem populum aspersit, dicens, Hic est sanguis testamenti quod mandavit ad vos Deus*.[21]

---

*Piana omits *aliis*, as in the Canon of the Mass

[15]*Hebrews* 9, 14

[16]*Lamentations* 3, 15

[17]*Matthew* 26, 39

[18]Above ad 1; 76, 2 ad 1

[19]*Hebrews* 9, 16

[20]*Hebrews* 9, 18

[21]*Exodus* 24, 7–8

[a]The name of one thing put for that of another related to it.

[b]St Thomas's thought here, like that of the author of *Hebrews*, moves round the two ideas of a last will and testament and of an alliance or covenant. There is an analogy, because in both cases the ratification is associated with death, in the first case the

it takes away our sins which come between us and the first two effects just mentioned; the text of *Hebrews* says, *the blood of Christ will purify your conscience from dead works*,[15] that is, from sins. This is signified by the words, 'which for you and for many others will be poured out for the remission of sins'.

Hence: 1. When the priest says, 'This is the chalice of my blood', he is using a figurative expression which can be understood in two ways. First, it could be an instance of metonymy,[a] making that which contains stand for that which is contained, so that the meaning would be, 'This is my blood contained in the chalice'. The chalice is mentioned here, because the blood of Christ in this sacrament is consecrated as the drink of the faithful, and that is something not involved in the idea of blood as such; so the blood of Christ is rightly here designated by the vessel that is used for drinking.

There is another way in which these words can also be metaphorically understood; chalice may be understood as a symbol of the passion of Christ, in the sense of the text of *Lamentations*, *he has filled me with bitterness, he has sated me with wormwood*;[16] it was in this sense that our Lord himself spoke of his passion as a chalice when he said, *let this cup pass from me*;[17] the meaning, then, would be, 'This is the chalice of my passion'. The passion is mentioned in connection with the blood which is consecrated separately from the body, because it was by his passion that his blood was actually separated from his body.

2. As we have said,[18] because the separate consecration of the blood explicitly represents the actual passion of Christ, it is at the consecration of the blood that the effect of Christ's passion is mentioned rather than at the consecration of his body, which was the subject of that passion. But that is alluded to by our Lord's saying *which will be given for you*, as if he were to say, 'which will be subjected to a passion for your sakes'.

3. A testament is an arrangement about an inheritance. Now God has arranged that men should have a heavenly inheritance which will be theirs through the power of the blood of Christ; because, as we read in *Hebrews*, *where a will is involved, the death of the one who made it must be established.*[19] Now the blood of Christ is given to men in two ways. First of all, in figure; that is the Old Testament situation. For this reason, the apostle draws the conclusion in the same passage that *even the first covenant was not ratified without blood*,[20 b] as is clear from the text of *Exodus*, that when Moses had read *all the commandments of the Law, he sprinkled all the people saying, Behold the blood of the covenant which the Lord has made with you.*[21]

---

death of the testator, in the second case the death of a sacrificial victim. The N.T. Greek word *diatheke* (and the Latin word *testamentum* here) means both will and covenant. The latter idea is closer to the real thought of *Hebrews*.

Secundo autem est exhibitus in rei veritate: quod pertinet ad novum Testamentum. Et hoc est quod Apostolus ibidem præmittit, dicens: *Ideo novi Testamenti mediator est Christus, ut, morte intercedente, repromissionem accipiant qui vocati sunt æternæ hereditatis.*[22] Dicitur ergo hic *sanguis novi Testamenti*, quia jam non in figura, sed in veritate exhibetur. Unde subditur, *qui pro vobis effundetur*. Interna autem inspiratio ex sanguinis virtute procedit secundum quod passione Christi justificamur.

4. Ad quartum dicendum quod hoc testamentum est novum ratione exhibitionis. Dicitur autem æternum, tam ratione æternæ Dei præordinationis; quam etiam ratione æternæ hereditatis, quæ per hoc testamentum disponitur. Ipsa etiam persona Christi, cujus sanguine testamentum disponitur, est æterna.

5. Ad quintum dicendum quod 'mysterium' hic ponitur, non quidem ad excludendum rei veritatem, sed ad ostendendam occultationem. Quia et ipse sanguis Christi occulto modo est in hoc sacramento; et ipsa passio Christi occulte fuit figurata in veteri Testamento.

6. Ad sextum dicendum quod dicitur 'sacramentum fidei',* quasi fidei objectum: quia quod sanguis Christi secundum rei veritatem sit in hoc sacramento, sola fide tenetur. Ipsa etiam passio Christi per fidem justificat. Baptismus autem dicitur 'sacramentum fidei' quia est quædam fidei protestatio. Hoc autem est 'sacramentum caritatis' quasi figurativum et effectivum.

7. Ad septimum dicendum quod, sicut dictum est,[23] sanguis seorsum consecratus a corpore expressius repræsentat passionem Christi. Et ideo in consecratione sanguinis fit mentio de passione Christi et fructu ipsius, potius quam in consecratione corporis.

8. Ad octavum dicendum quod sanguis passionis Christi non solum habet efficaciam in Judæis electis, quibus exhibitus est sanguis veteris Testamenti, sed etiam in gentilibus; nec solum in sacerdotibus, qui hoc efficiunt sacramentum, vel aliis qui sumunt, sed etiam in illis pro quibus offertur. Ideo signanter dicit, 'pro vobis' Judæis, 'et pro multis', scilicet gentilibus; vel, 'pro vobis' manducantibus, 'et pro multis' pro quibus offertur.

9. Ad nonum dicendum quod Evangelistæ non intendebant tradere formas sacramentorum, quas in primitiva Ecclesia oportebat esse occultas, ut dicit Dionysius, in fine *Ecclesiasticæ Hierarchiæ*.[24] Sed intenderunt historiam de Christo texere.

---

*Piana: *mysterium fidei*, a mystery of faith

[22] *Hebrews* 9, 15 [23] Above ad 2

[24] *Ecclesiastical Hierarchy* 7, 3, 10. PG 3, 565

[c] To be justified is to be made holy, to be re-born as a child of God and to be made to stand before the Father, clinging to Christ by faith, being made one with him in appropriating his love for his Father, his merit, his atonement.

Then, secondly, the blood of Christ is given to men in actual reality; this is the New Testament situation. This is what the Apostle was saying earlier on in our passage, *hence he (Christ) is the mediator of a new covenant, so that those who are called may receive the promised eternal inheritance, since a death has occurred, etc.*[22] So it is here called 'the blood of the new testament', because it is now given not in figure, but in actual reality. So the addition is made, 'which will be poured forth for you'. As regards interior inspiration, that is brought about by the power of Christ's blood when we are being justified[c] by the passion of Christ.

4. This testament is new by reason of the time it was actually established. But it is said to be eternal because God had ordained it from all eternity and also because the inheritance for which it makes arrangement is an eternal one.[d] Likewise, the person of Christ, by whose blood the testament is sealed, is an eternal one.

5. The term 'mystery' is used here, not in order to rule out factual reality, but to show that it is hidden. The blood of Christ is present in this sacrament in a hidden way, and the passion of Christ was prefigured in a hidden way in the Old Testament.

6. The Eucharist is called 'the sacrament of faith', in the sense of being an object of faith; it is only by faith that we can know that the blood of Christ is in this sacrament in actual fact. And, also, the passion of Christ justifies us through our faith in it. But Baptism is said to be 'the sacrament of faith' because it is a profession of faith. The Eucharist is 'the sacrament of charity' because it symbolizes charity and brings it about.

7. As we have already said,[23] the blood consecrated separately from the body gives us a more vivid representation of Christ's passion. So it is that in the consecration of the blood rather than in that of the body, mention is made of the passion of Christ and of what it causes.

8. The blood of the passion of Christ is efficacious not merely in regard to the chosen Jews who had been given the blood of the old testament but also in regard to the Gentiles; it is efficacious not merely for priests who consecrate the Eucharist, or for those who receive it, but also for those for whom it is offered. So Christ deliberately says 'for you'—Jews, 'and for many'—Gentiles; or 'for you', who are partaking of the Eucharist, 'and for many', those namely for whom it is offered.

9. It was not the intention of the Evangelists to record the sacramental forms, which the early Church had to keep secret, as Dionysius tells us, at the end of his *Ecclesiastical Hierarchy*.[24] Their intention was to give us the history of Christ. And yet, however, almost all these words can be

[d]And also because it is the final economy governing the relations between God and man till the end of time.

Et tamen omnia hæc verba fere ex diversis Scripturæ locis accipi possunt. Nam quod dicitur, 'Hic est calix', habetur *Luc.* xxii[25] et I *Cor.* xi.[26] *Matt.* autem xxvi dicitur, 'Hic est sanguis meus novi Testamenti, qui pro multis effundetur in remissionem peccatorum'.[27] Quod autem additur, 'æterni', et iterum, 'mysterium fidei', ex traditione Domini habetur, quæ ad Ecclesiam per Apostolos pervenit: secundum illud I *Cor.* xi, *Ego accepi a Domino quod et tradidi vobis.*[28]

articulus 4. utrum prædictis verbis formarum insit aliqua vis creata effectiva consecrationis

AD QUARTUM sic proceditur:[1] 1. Videtur quod prædictis verbis formarum non insit aliqua vis creata effectiva consecrationis. Dicit enim Damascenus, *Sola virtute Spiritus Sancti fit conversio panis in corpus Christi.*[2] Sed virtus Spiritus Sancti est virtus increata. Ergo nulla virtute creata horum verborum conficitur sacramentum hoc.

2. Præterea, opera miraculosa non fiunt aliqua virtute creata, sed sola virtute divina, ut in *Prima Parte* habitum est.[3] Sed conversio panis et vini in corpus et sanguinem Christi est opus non minus miraculosum quam creatio rerum, vel etiam formatio corporis Christi in utero virginali, quæ quidem nulla virtute creata fieri potuerunt. Ergo neque hoc sacramentum consecratur virtute creata aliqua dictorum verborum.

3. Præterea prædicta verba non sunt simplicia, sed ex multis composita; nec simul, sed successive proferuntur. Conversio autem prædicta, ut supra dictum est,[4] fit in instanti: unde oportet quod fiat per simplicem virtutem. Non ergo fit per virtutem horum verborum.

SED CONTRA est quod Ambrosius dicit, *Si tanta est vis in sermone Domini Jesu ut inciperet esse quod non erat, quanto magis operativus est ut sint quæ erant, et in aliud commutentur? Et sic quod erat panis ante consecrationem, jam corpus Christi est post consecrationem, quia sermo Christi creaturam mutat.*[5]

---

[25] *Luke* 22, 20
[26] I *Corinthians* 11, 25
[27] *Matthew* 26, 28
[28] I *Corinthians* 11, 23
[1] cf IV *Sent.* 8, 2, 3. *In Matt.* 26
[2] *De Fide Orthodoxa* IV, 13. PG 94, 1141, 1145
[3] 1a. 110, 4
[4] 3a. 75, 7
[5] *De Sacramentis* 4, 4. PL 16, 459

drawn from different parts of scripture. The expression 'this is the chalice' is found in *Luke*[25] and in 1 *Corinthians*.[26] In *Matthew* we find 'this is my blood of the new testament, which will be poured out for many for the remission of sins'.[27] The additions 'eternal' and 'mystery of faith' come from our Lord from whom they came to the Church through the Apostles; as the text of 1 *Corinthians* puts it, *for I received from the Lord what I also delivered to you.*[28]

article 4. in the words of the Eucharistic forms is there any created power which produces the consecration?

THE FOURTH POINT:[1] 1. It would seem that in the words referred to there is not any created power which produces the consecration. St John Damascene says, *it is only by the power of the Holy Ghost that the change of the bread into the body of Christ takes place.*[2] But the power of the Holy Ghost is something uncreated. Hence, it is not by any created power in these words that this sacrament is consecrated.

2. Moreover, miracles are not wrought by any created power, but only by the power of God, as we saw in the *Prima Pars.*[3] Now, the change of the bread and wine into the body and blood of Christ is something not less miraculous than the original creation of things or than the formation of Christ's body in a virgin's womb, and by no created power could these have come about. Hence, neither is this sacrament consecrated by any created power in the above-mentioned words.

3. Furthermore, these words are not a unity but are composed of many elements; nor are they uttered all together, but one after another. But the Eucharistic change, as we saw earlier on,[4] takes place in an instant; so it must be brought about by a power that is one and undivided. It cannot then be produced by any power that would be in these words.

ON THE OTHER HAND we have Ambrose saying, *if an utterance of Christ can have in it such power that what had no existence now begins to be, how much easier is it for it, while keeping in being things that were, to change them into something else?*[a] *And so it is that what was bread before the consecration is now the body of Christ after the consecration, because the utterance of Christ has changed the created thing.*[5]

---

[a]How close the mind of Ambrose here is to the thought of St Thomas on the nature of the unique change which is transubstantiation. The bread is not annihilated; its being passes into the being of Christ's body. St Thomas, of course, would hardly regard this as easier than creation. Yet it is on the same metaphysical plane.

RESPONSIO: Dicendum quod quidam dixerunt nullam virtutem creatam esse nec in prædictis verbis ad transubstantionem faciendam, nec etiam in aliis sacramentorum formis, vel etiam in ipsis sacramentis ad inducendos sacramentorum effectus. Quod, sicut supra dictum est,[6] et dictis Sanctorum repugnat et derogat dignitati sacramentorum Novæ Legis. Unde, cum hoc sacramentum sit præ cæteris dignius, sicut supra dictum est,[7] consequens est quod in verbis formalibus hujus sacramenti sit quædam virtus creata ad conversionem hujus sacramenti faciendam: instrumentalis tamen, sicut et in aliis sacramentis, sicut supra dictum est.[8] Cum enim hæc verba ex persona Christi proferantur, ex ejus mandato consequuntur virtutem instrumentalem a Christo: sicut et cætera ejus facta vel dicta habent instrumentaliter salutiferam virtutem, ut supra habitum est.[9]

1. Ad primum ergo dicendum quod, cum dicitur sola virtute Spiritus Sancti panem in corpus Christi converti, non excluditur virtus instrumentalis quæ est in forma hujus sacramenti: sicut, cum dicitur quod solus faber facit cultellum, non excluditur virtus martelli.

2. Ad secundum dicendum quod opera miraculosa nulla creatura potest facere quasi agens principale; potest tamen ea facere instrumentaliter, sicut ipse tactus manus Christi sanavit leprosum. Et per hunc modum verba ejus convertunt panem in corpus Christi. Quod quidem non potuit in conceptione corporis Christi, qua corpus Christi formabatur, ut aliquid a corpore Christi procedens haberet instrumentalem virtutem ad ipsius corporis formationem. In creatione etiam non fuit aliquod extremum in quod instrumentalis actio creaturæ posset terminari. Unde non est simile.

3. Ad tertium dicendum quod prædicta verba quibus fit consecratio, sacramentaliter operantur. Unde vis conversiva quæ est in formis horum sacramentorum, sequitur significationem, quæ in prolatione ultimæ dictionis terminatur. Et ideo in ultimo instanti prolationis verborum prædicta verba consequuntur hanc virtutem, in ordine tamen ad præcedentia. Et hæc virtus est simplex ratione significati;* licet in ipsis verbis exterius prolatis sit quædam compositio.

---

*Piana: *simplicis*

[6] 3a. 62, 1
[7] 3a. 65, 3
[8] 3a. 62, 3 & 4
[9] 3a. 48, 6

[b] An instrumental power is found in all the sacraments. In the other sacraments the instrumental power elevates the whole sacramental sign, matter and form, and is productive of the sacramental character or of a modification of it and thereby of sanctifying grace in the soul. In the Eucharist the instrumental power is limited to the words of the form and is productive of the presence of the body and blood of Christ. It is the body and blood of Christ—and the whole Christ—under the appearances of bread and wine, that produces grace in the soul. Does Christ, at the

REPLY: Some theologians have held that there is no created power either in the Eucharistic words to produce the transubstantiation, or in the other sacramental forms or the other sacraments to produce the sacramental effects. This view, as we saw above,[6] runs counter to what has been affirmed by the Fathers and takes away from the dignity of the sacraments of the New Law. Now, seeing that this sacrament is of greater dignity than all the others, as we said above,[7] it follows that in the formal words of this sacrament there is a certain created power which brings about the sacramental change;[b] it is, however, an instrumental power, as is the case in all the sacraments, as was also said earlier on.[8] Now since these words are uttered as being the words of Christ himself, it is by his will they derive from Christ an instrumental power; in the same way his other deeds and utterances have instrumentally a saving power, as we saw above.[9]

Hence: 1. When we say that it is by the power of the Holy Ghost and by it alone that the bread is changed into the body of Christ, we do not rule out the presence of an instrumental power in the form of this sacrament; just like when we say that it is only the craftsman who makes the knife, we do not exclude all power from the hammer.

2. No creature, acting as a principal cause, can bring about miraculous effects; but it can cause them instrumentally, as was the case when the very touch of the hand of Christ healed the leper. And it is in this way that his words change the bread into the body of Christ. But this could not be the case in the formation of Christ's body at his conception, because there could not be anything proceeding from Christ's body to be endowed with instrumental power for the production of that very body. Likewise, in creation there was nothing for the instrumental action of a creature to play on.[c] Thus the argument from analogy breaks down.

3. The above-mentioned words by which the consecration is brought about work in a sacramental way. This means that the power of changing which is found in the formal part of these sacramental signs, depends on the sign fully signifying, and that only happens at the utterance of the last syllable. It is because of this that it is only at the last instant of the utterance of the words that the words are endowed with this power, in relation of course to all that went before that last instant. This power is one because what the words signify is one; admittedly, the actual words themselves externally uttered do constitute a complexity.

---

moment when we receive the sacrament, instrumentally use these appearances? Perhaps St Thomas never asked the question.

[c]All creaturely activity, whether connatural or instrumental, is within a field of action and thus presupposes other things to be acted on. The action of creating presupposes absolutely nothing.

articulus 5. utrum prædictæ locutiones sint veræ

AD QUINTUM sic proceditur:[1] 1. Videtur quod prædictæ locutiones non sint veræ. Cum enim dicitur, 'Hoc est corpus meum', ly* 'hoc' est demonstrativum substantiæ. Sed secundum prædicta,[2] quando profertur hoc pronomen 'hoc', adhuc est substantia panis: quia transubstantiatio fit in ultimo prolationis verborum. Sed hæc est falsa, 'Panis est corpus Christi'. Ergo etiam hæc est falsa, 'Hoc est corpus meum'.

2. Præterea, hoc pronomen 'hoc' facit demonstrationem ad sensum. Sed species sensibiles quæ sunt in hoc sacramento neque sunt ipsum corpus Christi, neque sunt accidentia corporis Christi. Ergo hæc locutio non potest esse vera, 'Hoc est corpus meum'.

3. Præterea, hæc verba, sicut supra dictum est,[3] sua significatione efficiunt conversionem panis in corpus Christi. Sed causa effectiva præintelligitur effectui. Ergo significatio horum verborum præintelligitur conversioni panis in corpus Christi. Sed ante conversionem hæc est falsa, 'Hoc est corpus meum'. Ergo simpliciter est judicandum quod sit falsa. Et eadem ratio est de hac locutione, 'Hic est calix sanguinis mei, etc.'

SED CONTRA est quod hæc verba proferuntur ex persona Christi, qui de se dicit, *Joan.* xiv, *Ego sum veritas.*[4]

RESPONSIO: Dicendum quod circa hoc multiplex fuit opinio. Quidam[5] enim dixerunt quod in hac locutione, 'Hoc est corpus meum', hæc dictio 'hoc' importat demonstrationem ut conceptam, non ut exercitam: quia tota ista locutio sumitur materialiter, cum recitative proferatur; recitat enim sacerdos Christum dixisse, 'Hoc est corpus meum'.

Sed hoc stare non potest. Quia secundum hoc, verba non applicarentur ad materiam corporalem præsentem, et ita non perficeretur sacramentum: dicit enim Augustinus, *super Joan., Accedit verbum ad elementum et fit sacramentum.*[6] Et ex hoc totaliter non evitatur difficultas hujus quæstionis: quia eædem rationes manent circa primam prolationem qua Christus hæc verba protulit; qua re manifestum est quod non materialiter, sed significative sumebantur. Et ideo dicendum est quod etiam quando proferuntur a sacerdote, significative, et non tantum materialiter accipiuntur. Nec obstat quod sacerdos etiam recitative profert quasi a Christo dicta.

---

*'*ly*', a translation of the Arabic article '*el*'

[1]IV *Sent.* 8, 2, 1, iv. *In Matt.* 26. *In* 1 *Cor.* 11, *lect.* 5

[2]3a. 78, 1, 4 ad 3 [3]3a. 78, 4 ad 3 [4]*John* 14, 6

[5]Innocent III, *De Sacro Altaris Mysterio* 4, 17. PL 217, 868. Præpositinus, *Summa* 4, *de Eucharistia*

[6]*Tractatus super Joannem* 80, 3. PL 35, 1840

article 5. are these formulas really true?

THE FIFTH POINT:[1] 1. It would seem that these formulas are not really true. When we say, 'This is my body', the word 'this' points to some substance. But from what we have just seen,[2] when the pronoun 'this' is pronounced, the substance of bread is still there; because the transubstantiation is effected only at the last moment of the utterance of the words. But it is false to say, 'This bread is the body of Christ'. Therefore, it is also false to say, 'This is my body'.

2. Moreover, the pronoun 'this' refers to what is the object of sense-experience. But the sense phenomena in this sacrament are neither the actual body of Christ, nor are they the accidents of the body of Christ. Hence, it cannot be true to say, 'This is my body'.

3. Furthermore, as we have just seen,[3] it is in dependence on their actually signifying it, that these words bring about the change of the bread into the body of Christ. But what brings anything about can be thought of prior to its effect. Therefore the significance of these words is complete prior to the change of the bread into the body of Christ. But prior to the actual change it would be false to say, 'This is my body'. We should conclude then quite simply that the formula is not true. A similar line of reasoning applies to the formula, 'This is the chalice of my blood, etc.'

ON THE OTHER HAND, these words are pronounced in the person of Christ, who says of himself, *I am the truth.*[4]

REPLY: There have been many opinions on this matter. Some theologians[5] said that in the formula, 'This is my body', the word 'this' does not actually refer to anything present, but refers to something we are thinking about; the whole phrase is to be taken materially, since it is uttered as recording something; the priest records that Christ said, 'This is my body'.

This view, however, cannot be sustained. If it were so, the words would have no reference to any present bodily material, and so there would be no sacrament; as Augustine says, in his commentary on *John*, *The word associated with the bodily element is what makes the sacrament.*[6] And actually the embarrassment of the question is not completely evaded; because the same difficulties would apply to the original utterance of these words by Christ; because it is evident that they were employed by him in no merely material sense, but as having signifying power. So we ought to conclude that when the priest utters them, they are to be understood as having signifying power and not in a purely material sense. Nor should you object that when the priest utters them he is simply recording them, as words that were said by Christ. Remember that the power of Christ

Quia propter infinitam virtutem Christi, sicut ex contactu carnis suæ vis regenerativa pervenit non solum ad illas aquas quæ Christum tetigerunt, sed ad omnes ubique terrarum per omnia futura sæcula; ita etiam ex prolatione ipsius Christi hæc verba virtutem consecrativam sunt consecuta a quocumque sacerdote dicantur, ac si Christus ea præsentialiter proferret.

Et ideo alii[7] dixerunt quod hæc dictio 'hoc' in hac locutione facit demonstrationem, non ad sensum, sed ad intellectum: ut sit sensus, 'Hoc est corpus meum', id est 'Significatum per hoc est corpus meum'.

Sed nec hoc stare potest. Quia, cum in sacramentis hoc efficiatur quod significatur, non fieret per hanc formam ut corpus Christi sit in hoc sacramento secundum veritatem, sed solum sicut in signo. Quod est hæreticum, ut supra dictum est.[8]

Et ideo alii dixerunt quod hæc dictio 'hoc' facit demonstrationem ad sensum, sed intelligitur hæc demonstratio non pro illo instanti locutionis quo profertur hæc dictio, sed pro ultimo instanti locutionis: sicut, cum aliquis dicit, 'Nunc taceo', hoc adverbium 'nunc' facit demonstrationem pro instanti immediate sequenti locutionem; est enim sensus, 'Statim dictis his verbis, taceo'.

Sed nec hoc stare potest. Quia secundum hoc, hujus locutionis est sensus, 'Corpus meum est corpus meum'. Quod prædicta locutio non facit: quia hoc fuit etiam ante prolationem verborum. Unde neque hoc prædicta locutio significat.

Et ideo aliter dicendum est quod, sicut prædictum est,[9] hæc locutio habet virtutem factivam conversionis panis in corpus Christi. Et ideo comparatur ad alias locutiones, quæ habent solum vim significativam et non factivam, sicut comparatur conceptio intellectus practici, quæ est factiva rei, conceptioni intellectus nostri speculativi, quæ est accepta a rebus: nam *voces sunt signa intellectuum*,[10] secundum Philosophum. Et ideo, sicut conceptio intellectus practici non præsupponit rem conceptam, sed facit eam, ita veritas hujus locutionis non præsupponit rem significatam, sed facit eam: sic enim se habet verbum Dei ad res factas per verbum. Hæc autem conversio non fit successive, sed in instanti, sicut dictum est.[11] Et ideo oportet quidem intelligere prædictam locutionem secundum ultimum instans prolationis verborum: non tamen ita quod

[7]cf Alexander of Hales, *Summa Theologica* 4, 32, 3, 2, 1

[8]3a. 75, 1

[9]3a. 78, 4

[10]*De Interpretatione* or *Perihemerneias* 1, 1. 16a3

[11]3a. 75, 7

[a]At the moment of Christ's being baptized, the sacrament of Baptism was instituted.

is not limited, and just as from the touch of his flesh a regenerative power passed not merely to the actual waters which touched Christ, but to any water anywhere until the end of time;[a] so also from their first utterance by Christ these words have possessed the same consecratory power, provided they are spoken by a priest, as if Christ himself were actually amongst us pronouncing them.

For these reasons other theologians[7] said that the word 'this' in the Eucharistic formula does here and now point to something, not to what is before our senses, but to what is descried by our intelligence; the meaning of 'This is my body' would be 'What is signified by this is my body'.

But this position also is not tenable. Remember that in the sacraments what is signified is actually brought about, but this understanding of the form would mean that the body of Christ is not actually in the sacrament, but only there as in a sign. It is an heretical position, as we saw above.[8]

Other theologians, therefore, went on to say that the word 'this' does actually point to something present to our senses, but it points to it not at the instant of speaking when the word is uttered, but at the last instant of the phrase; for example, when someone says, 'Now I am silent', the adverb 'now' refers to the instant immediately after the utterance; the sense is, 'Immediately after these words I am silent'.

But this position also cannot be sustained. In this view, the meaning of the formula would be, 'My body is my body'. But that is not the purport of the formula, because that was the fact even before the words were uttered. And so this is not the meaning of the phrase.

We must then arrive at another conclusion. As we saw above,[9] this formula is endowed with power to change the bread into Christ's body. And so it is compared with other statements, which merely affirm something but do not bring about a change, in the way that an idea in our practical intelligence, which actually brings something into being, is to be compared with an idea in our speculative intelligence which arises in our mind from the impact of reality; as Aristotle says, *the spoken words correspond to ideas.*[10] So it is that, just as the idea in the practical intelligence does not presuppose the thing we are thinking about, but rather brings it into existence, so the truth of the Eucharistic formula does not presuppose the thing it signifies but rather causes it; it is in this way that the word of God is related to the things called into being by that word. Now this change does not take place successively but in an instant, as we said above.[11] Hence we should understand the Eucharistic formula as taken at the last instance of the utterance of the words; not, however, that we

---

He touched the water; the water touched him. At every Christian baptism he touches the water, though the water no longer touches him.

præsupponatur ex parte subjecti id quod est terminus conversionis, scilicet quod corpus Christi sit corpus Christi; neque etiam illud quod fuit ant- conversionem, scilicet panis; sed id quod communiter se habet quantum ad utrumque, scilicet contentum in generali sub istis speciebus. Non enim faciunt hæc verba quod corpus Christi sit corpus Christi; neque quod panis sit corpus Christi; sed quod contentum sub his speciebus, quod prius erat panis, sit corpus Christi. Et ideo signanter non dicit Dominus, 'Hic panis est corpus meum', quod esset secundum intellectum secundæ opinionis; neque, 'Hoc corpus meum est corpus meum', quod esset secundum intellectum tertiæ; sed in generali, 'Hoc est corpus meum', nullo nomine apposito ex parte subjecti, sed solo pronomine, quod significat substantiam in communi sine qualitate, id est forma determinata.

1. Ad primum ergo dicendum quod hæc dictio 'hoc' demonstrat substantiam, sed absque determinatione propriæ naturæ, sicut dictum est.[12]

2. Ad secundum dicendum quod hoc pronomen 'hoc' non demonstrat ipsa accidentia, sed substantiam sub accidentibus contentam, quæ primo fuit panis, et postea est corpus Christi: quod, licet non informetur his accidentibus, tamen sub eis continetur.

3. Ad tertium dicendum quod significatio hujus locutionis præintelligitur rei significatæ ordine naturæ, sicut causa naturaliter est prior effectu: non tamen ordine temporis, quia hæc causa simul habet secum suum effectum. Et hoc sufficit ad veritatem locutionis.

articulus 6. *utrum forma consecrationis panis consequatur effectum suum antequam perficiatur forma consecrationis vini*

AD SEXTUM sic proceditur:[1] 1. Videtur quod forma consecrationis panis non consequatur effectum suum quousque perficiatur forma consecrationis vini. Sicut enim per consecrationem panis incipit esse corpus Christi sub hoc sacramento, ita per consecrationem vini incipit esse sanguis. Si ergo verba consecrationis panis haberent effectum suum ante consecrationem vini, sequeretur quod in hoc sacramento inciperet esse corpus Christi exsangue. Quod est inconveniens.

2. Præterea, unum sacramentum unum habet complementum: unde, licet in Baptismo sint tres immersiones, non tamen prima immersio consequitur suum effectum quousque tertia fuerit terminata. Sed totum hoc

[12]In the body of the article

[1]cf IV *Sent.* 8, 2, 4, i; 11, 2, 1, i ad 4. *In Matt.* 26. *In* I *Cor.* 11, *lect.* 6

should take as being the subject the thing that is the term of the conversion, and mean by the words that the body of Christ is the body of Christ; nor should we take as the subject the thing that was there before the change took place, namely, the bread; but we should understand what is common to both before and after the change, namely, what is contained (without further determining what it is) under the species. For these words do not bring about that the body of Christ is the body of Christ; nor that bread is the body of Christ; but that what is contained under these species, which was once bread, should now be Christ's body. And so our Lord significantly did not say, 'This bread is my body', which would be in line with the way the second opinion understands the formula; nor did he say, 'This body is my body', which would agree with the way of thinking of the third opinion; but he said in a general way, 'This is my body', not using any noun as the subject of the statement, but only a pronoun, thus signifying the substance in a vague way, without qualifying it, and leaving it without any determinate form.

Hence: 1. The word 'this' does indeed point to a substance, but without saying anything definite about its exact nature, as we have just seen.[12]

2. The pronoun 'this' does not refer to the actual accidents, but to the substance which is contained underneath them. This was first bread, and later it is the body of Christ, which, although it is not informed by these accidents, is, nonetheless, contained underneath them.

3. The signification of this formula is thought of as coming before the thing it signifies by a priority of nature, in the sense that every cause is naturally prior to its effect; but it is not prior to it in the order of time, because this cause co-exists with its effect. And that is enough for the statement to be quite true.

article 6. *does the form of consecration of the bread accomplish its effect before the form of consecration of the wine is complete?*

THE SIXTH POINT:[1] 1. It seems that the form of consecration of the bread does not accomplish its effect until the form of consecration of the wine has been completed. Just as it is by the consecration of the bread that the body of Christ begins to exist under this sacrament, so it is by the consecration of the wine that the blood of Christ begins to exist there. If then the words of consecration of the bread were to take effect before the consecration of the wine, it would follow that the body of Christ would begin to exist in this sacrament without the blood. But that is an impossible situation.

2. Moreover, a sacrament that is in itself one is complete at one particular point; so it is that in Baptism, although there are three immersions, the first immersion does not produce its effect until the third immersion

sacramentum est unum, ut supra dictum est.[2] Ergo verba quibus consecratur panis non consequuntur suum effectum sine verbis sacramentalibus quibus consecratur vinum.

3. Præterea, in ipsa forma consecrationis panis sunt plura verba, quorum prima non consequuntur effectum nisi prolato ultimo, sicut dictum est.[3] Ergo, pari ratione, nec verba quibus consecratur corpus Christi habent effectum, nisi prolatis verbis quibus sanguis Christi consecratur.

SED CONTRA est quod, statim dictis verbis consecrationis panis, hostia consecrata proponitur populo adoranda. Quod non fieret si non esset ibi corpus Christi, quia hoc ad idololatriam pertineret. Ergo verba consecrationis panis suum effectum consequuntur antequam proferantur verba consecrationis vini.

RESPONSIO: Dicendum quod quidam antiqui doctores dixerunt quod hæ duæ formæ, scilicet consecrationis panis et vini, se invicem expectant in agendo; ita scilicet quod prima non perficit suum effectum antequam secunda proferatur.

Sed hoc stare non potest. Quia, sicut dictum est,[4] ad veritatem hujus locutionis, 'hoc est corpus meum', requiritur, propter verbum præsentis temporis, quod res significata simul tempore sit cum ipsa significatione locutionis: alioquin, si in futurum expectaretur res significata, apponeretur verbum futuri temporis, non autem verbum præsentis; ita scilicet quod non diceretur, 'hoc est corpus meum', sed 'hoc erit corpus meum'. Significatio autem hujus locutionis completur statim completa prolatione horum verborum. Et ideo oportet rem significatam statim adesse, quæ quidem est effectus hujus sacramenti: alioquin locutio non esset vera. Est etiam hæc positio contra ritum Ecclesiæ, quæ statim post prolationem verborum corpus Christi adorat.

Unde dicendum est quod prima forma non expectat secundam in agendo, sed statim habet suum effectum.

1. Ad primum ergo dicendum quod ex hac ratione videntur fuisse decepti illi qui prædictam positionem posuerunt. Unde intelligendum est quod, facta consecratione panis, est quidem corpus Christi ibi ex vi sacramenti, et sanguis ex reali concomitantia; sed postmodum, post

---

[2] 3a. 73, 2 [3] 3a. 78, 4 ad 3 [4] 3a. 78, 5 ad 3

[a] Remember that the sacrament, i.e. the *sacramentum tantum,* is the uttered words of consecration, and then, with them, the consecrated appearances of bread and wine, not just these last. And in the memory of our faith we always hear them being uttered.

has been completed, as was said above.[2] It follows then that the words by which the bread is consecrated do not produce their effect apart from the sacramental words of consecration of the wine.

3. Furthermore, in the very form of consecration of the bread there are several words, and the earlier ones do not produce their effect until the last one has been uttered, as we saw.[3] For a similar reason, therefore, the words of consecration of the body of Christ do not produce their effect, unless the words by which the blood of Christ is consecrated have been pronounced.

ON THE OTHER HAND, as soon as the words of consecration of the bread have been uttered, the consecrated host is shown to the people that they may worship it. Now this would not be done if the body of Christ were not there; it would be a kind of idolatry. Therefore, the words of consecration of the bread do produce their effect before the words of consecration of the wine are pronounced.

REPLY: Certain early theologians did say that these two forms, namely, of the consecration of the bread and of the wine, wait on each other in their activity; in such a way, that is, that the first one does not complete its effect before the second one is pronounced.

But this cannot be the case. Because, as we have already said,[4] for the statement 'This is my body' to be true, it is necessary, seeing that the verb is in the present tense, that the thing signified should exist as soon as the statement signifies it; otherwise, if we had to wait till some future moment for the thing signified, a verb in the future tense would be used, and not a verb in the present tense; and so the phrase would not be, 'This is my body', but rather, 'This will be my body'. The statement, however, actually indicates the thing signified immediately the words have been uttered. And therefore the thing signified, which is the effect of this sacrament,[a] must be straightway there; otherwise the utterance would not be a true one. And, moreover, this view conflicts with the ritual practice of the Church, which worships the body of Christ immediately the words have been pronounced.

We should then say that the first form does not have to wait for the second one in order to go into action, but that it produces its effect immediately.

Hence: 1. This would seem to have been the reason which misled those who held for the above-mentioned position. The right way to think about the matter is this—as soon as the bread is consecrated the body of Christ is made present as the precise result of the sacrament and the blood of

consecrationem vini, fit ibi e converso sanguis Christi ex vi sacramenti, corpus autem Christi ex reali concomitantia; ita quod totus Christus est sub utraque specie, sicut supra dictum est.[5]

2. Ad secundum dicendum quod hoc sacramentum est unum perfectione, sicut supra dictum est:[6] inquantum constituitur ex duobus, scilicet ex cibo et potu, quorum utrumque per se habet suam perfectionem. Sed tres immersiones baptismi ordinantur ad unum simplicem effectum. Et ideo non est simile.

3. Ad tertium dicendum quod diversa verba quæ sunt in forma consecrationis panis, constituunt veritatem unius locutionis: non autem verba diversarum formarum. Et ideo non est simile.

---

[5]3a. 76, 2
[6]3a. 73, 2

Christ is also there because it naturally accompanies the body; later on, through the consecration of the wine, the position is reversed and the blood is made present as the result of the sacrament, the body being found present because it naturally accompanies the blood; in this way the whole Christ is present under each of the species, as we saw earlier on.[5]

2. This sacrament is one in its completion, as we saw earlier,[6] to the extent that it is made up of two things, namely, food and drink, each of which has in itself its own completion; but the three immersions of Baptism are ordered to one homogeneous effect. And so there is no analogy.

3. The different words which are found in the consecration of the bread all concur to build up the truth of a proposition; the words of the two forms taken together do not do this. Hence there is no analogy.

Appendix 1

THE SACRAMENTALITY OF THE EUCHARIST

1. ALL OUR thinking is the seeing of the universal in the particular. Whether our thinking is concerned with things and their activity on the noumenal or on the phenomenological level, the mind rejoices in seeing the particular as an instance of the universal. On the phenomenological level we have the laws of physical science; on the noumenal level the unsophisticated no less than the professionally wise look for a world view, a comprehensive vision, a synthesis in which all things reveal their deepest meaning in their common obedience to a universal law. The theologian is *par excellence* he who sees the One behind the many; but his discipline also allows of restricted fields of contemplation where it is joy to gather a multitude of instances under some common formula.

2. The Christian liturgical celebrations, what the ancients called the mysteries of Christian life and we now more commonly call sacraments, do offer a possibility of theological contemplation in a special field, precisely because there is a formula of rich significance which all the sacramental celebrations can be found to obey. It is an impoverished sacramental theology that is content with the bare formula—an outward sign of inward grace. The full formula has two stages, namely the outward sign of inner and spiritual reality or event which is itself the sign of a further ultimate event within the deepest reaches of a man's inner, personal life of union with God. The use of this full, two-stage formula and the working out of its different applications in all the sacraments and in the Eucharist, both as sacramental sacrifice and as sacramental cause of grace, provides the particular exhilaration which goes with a genuine synthetic vision and makes one a theologian in this particular field.

To treat of the Eucharist outside this general field of sacramental vision would be a mistake. The profoundest theological understanding of the Eucharist in all its parts, the Mass included, is only to be had by remaining all the time faithfully within the range of these three together, *sacramentum tantum*, *res et sacramentum*, and *res tantum*. We have first the visible action or the visible elements before our senses, then there is the hidden reality which they immediately signify, and finally there is the ultimate reality to which this intermediate reality points and of which (in so far as it is signified by the outer sacrament) it is the sign. We can thus speak technically of the 'sign', the 'thing which is also sign', and the 'thing only'.

It is in connection with the sacraments which impress what is called a character (an indelible mark) upon the soul that this formula is commonly accepted by theologians. In baptism, confirmation and orders most theologians would gladly accept the formula and speak of the sacramental rite as

the 'sign only', of the character of baptism, etc. as the 'thing which is also sign', and of the gift of grace in the soul as the 'thing only'. It is a poor theology which would fail to see a progressive movement and which would think of the outer rite as indifferently regarding the character and grace as two unrelated things. The true view sees the rite as the sign and cause of the character, and the character (not apart from the rite) as the sign and cause of grace. To Thomists all this has the full reality of a contact with Christ; they are prepared to call it 'physical', in the Greek rather than in the modern sense of the term, to mean a real as well as a moral conjunction; his holy humanity is the efficient cause as well as the moral cause of the changes within our soul.

3. It is beginning to be recognized that in all the seven sacraments the character plays an important part as sign and cause of grace. This is clear enough in the case of the sacraments which actually impress a lasting character, i.e. Baptism, Confirmation, Orders. But it is now more clear that in the Eucharist itself, Penance, Unction of the sick and Matrimony, a modified character is communicated which is the sign and cause (not apart from the outer rite) of grace in the soul. This modification lasts for a greater or shorter length of time and can be the actual cause of grace when a sacrament (for example, matrimony) was validly but at first fruitlessly received.

But the character (with its modifications) is the sign and cause of grace because it is the touch of Christ on the soul. When the external sacramental rite is performed we are introduced into the presence of Christ the priest and sanctifier; he touches our soul, and the impress of that touch is the character. Through the rite he reaches out to touch us. The rite is over. But the touch endures. As touching us through the rite he causes grace. As still touching us when the rite is over, the going out of power from him need never cease. That is why we can always stir up the grace of our baptism, of our confirmation, of ordination. And as long as the modification of the character caused through the other sacraments lasts, Christ continues to touch us with a view to their specific graces and the current of grace can come alive.

So because of the character Christ is physically near the soul. If then the exterior rite is the sign of the character which is the impress of the touch of Christ, it is also the sign of Christ who through that touch (first mediated in and through the visible sacrament) conveys a current of life to the soul. The intermediate thing, the element which is 'thing and sign', is seen to be richer perhaps than we thought at first. It is not just a mark on our soul. It is an impress caused by a touch that lasts as long as the impress (and its modifications) endures. The 'res et sacramentum', the 'thing and sign', is the sign and cause of grace, because it is not just the impress of the touch of Christ, but the impress and the touch together.

4. It is when we come to the sacrament of the Eucharist that this last statement takes on a particular point and has a particular richness of meaning. If Christ himself enters into the zone of the 'thing and sign', of the thing signified by the outer rite, in the Eucharist he does so most fully, not merely

as present in the action of touching us and mediating grace to us thereby, or as allowing us to touch him and make our own the act of giving the body and the blood. These wonders are part of the realm of the 'thing and sign', of that intermediate world between what is happening under our very senses and what is taking place in the depths of the spirit where our life is deepening and our act of self-giving is the heart's heart of our Mass—the realm of the ultimate 'thing' signified. In the Eucharist the sanctifying Christ enters into the realm of the 'thing and sign', not merely as present in the exercising of his power or some activity, but as somehow 'contained' by the sense-phenomena of the bread and wine, as abidingly present as the very substance of the bread and wine themselves would naturally have been.

5. Here we have a unique presence of Christ in the world. It is real and 'physical' (or, let us say, metaphysical), but it is not natural. Only our faith can discern it. The sign of faith points to it and faith believes it. In the other sacraments and in the Eucharist itself as an act of sacrificial giving and at the moment of sacramental eating and drinking, Christ is present because contact is established between him and the soul, a contact that involves his exercising power. But when the sacrifice is over and even apart from the holy time of our partaking of the sacrificial food, he is there, permanently, under the veil of the accidents of bread and wine, not touching our souls as yet, yet as present under the appearances our very senses can touch.

So there is a touch. It is our touching the accidents that contain the body and the blood—the whole Christ. The idea of containing is an analogical one. The glass contains the water that fills it. The accidents of a substance contain the substance. There is a difference between these two. The first implies body circumscribing body. The second implies no circumscription of part corresponding to part. It is a sort of *spiritual* presence which involves no commensuration of quantity to quantity. The whole substance is equally present to any and to all of the parts of the containing accidents. So the accidents contain the whole Christ; he does not touch them, though they can be thought of as touching him. And we touch them.

6. The Christ whom we thus can always touch as long as the sacramental sign endures has come amongst us in this Bethlehem in order that from there he can reach out and touch our souls at the moment of Holy Communion. The '*res et signum*' is not just a '*res*'. It is a sign too; it points to a fulfilment in our eating it when divine strength issues from it into our souls and we are made one with Christ and with each other in love. That is the end, the *Thing* to which everything else is pointing. All other presences of Christ amongst us men—his presence in power, touching our souls and making that impress, permanent or fleeting, which is the character and its modifications through which he causes grace in our souls, his abiding presence under the appearances of bread and wine—all are ordered to that ultimate presence which is the *illapsus*, the descent of the Word upon the soul and with it the three divine Persons taking up of their abode within us.

7. That is what grace means. All sacramental grace comes to us deriving from the fulness of grace which fills the holy soul of the humanity of Jesus.

As filling his soul grace has its individuation, its particular way. It expressed itself through all the mysteries of the events that filled his life and through the mystery of his dying and rising again. Our grace is a sharing in the Christ-grace; our life is somehow configured to his. There is an *illapsus* of the Word upon the holy soul of Jesus, the soul that is also united hypostatically to that Word. We must be configured to Jesus in the very mode of our inner life. Our outer life must be the sign of his life and of his cross and resurrection.

8. What our outer moral life expresses, because at every moment in every choice it represents death and a resurrection, a renunciation and an entry into joy, our sacramental life expresses as well. The ultimate thing behind all the sacraments, the specific grace of the Eucharist, to which all the sacraments are ordered as their final end, is our sharing in the inner life of Jesus the man and our being configured to him who is the first-born of many brethren. Not merely is there an *illapsus* of the uncreated Word upon our spirit, but the Word comes upon us as having first and foremost come upon the soul of Jesus, and then upon Mary as the first to share his grace and to share it in a unique way. Thus we are configured to him as she was most excellently of all configured to him. That is the grace of the Eucharist because it is the ultimate thing at the heart of all our religion, at the heart of all our life of moral effort in this world. The Eucharist is the supreme sign of that ultimate gift. And between that sign and that gift is Jesus coming into his church—among his baptized people in the power of his transubstantiating action, in the physical reality of his still giving the body and the blood that goes with that action, and abidingly in that Bethlehem of the appearances of the bread and wine, that we may eat his flesh and drink his blood, to our hearts' content.

Appendix 2

THE PRESENCES OF CHRIST IN THE EUCHARIST

1. THE CHRISTIAN liturgy is the presence amongst his people of the risen Christ who died for them. He has entered into his Easter joy. There he abides. His people yet in time are still on this side of Jordan's wave. Not yet have they entered into their heritage. But even so, their leader, the new Moses, comes amongst them in a mystery. Veiled to their senses under the play of the sacraments, he is revealed to their faith; revealed as someone physically present and not merely as someone on the further shore. He comes amongst them really and not merely as the object of their thought and of their faith. This presence is not a natural one, but for all that it is objectively real and not merely subjective. Abiding always in his Father's presence, he comes mysteriously amongst us when any of the Christian sacraments are celebrated. That coming amongst his people is at the heart of all the seven sacraments and because power goes out from him we are lifted up into his holiness and of his fulness we do all receive.

2. But that grace-radiating presence is of avail only where there is faith. The Christian mystery is at once a sign of his presence and of our faith. The real presence of the risen Christ in the Christian sacrament is a gift offered to those who believe, a grace-filled visit from someone known and acknowledged to be Lord. The valid sacrament is always a sign of his presence; but if it be not also the sign of a faith reaching out to receive him, it is a lifeless presence that radiates no grace. Unless the risen Christ who died for us first dwells in our heart by faith, a sacrament, from which we should draw the waters of life, is like a fountain sealed.

Faith comes before sacrament. The case of infant baptism is unique; and even there the child is thought of as believing by the Church's faith. Faith comes before sacrament. We open our hearts to him and he is taken by an act that pierces the heavens. We are made one with him by faith and incorporated into the *Christus Totus*, the whole Christ of all those who are covered over with the glory of his merits, and whose sin is annulled and cleansed by that fire which is his blood. We are incorporated into the Christ who died for us and we make our own the strong cry of his blood. We are lifted up into the Christ of Calvary and made one with him in all his victory over sin.

3. Our faith looks up to the risen Christ and back to the Christ of time, of history, of the cross. The incorporation into Christ which is mediated to us by that faith is first and foremost an incorporation into the loving, adoring, meriting, propitiating Christ of the cross. We make our own his love of the Father, his adoration, his meriting, his propitiating. It is the loveliest part of our justification, of our being made holy—we are made holy by his holiness made ours. We are invested with the garment of his holiness, of

his propitiating blood. But the blood is also fire and it cleanses us through and through. We are made holy in ourselves, and our life takes on a character of meriting and propitiating. But all we have depends on him, derives from him; and if in one sense it can be said to fill up what is lacking, in a deeper sense it can add nothing to that primal fulness from which we all receive.

We are incorporated into Christ by our faith. Of course it is Christ who incorporates us into himself by taking the initiative and so drawing us to himself that he puts the faith into our hearts. And then the faith reaches out to him and draws him into our hearts. The fuller that faith is and the more loving, the more we are made one with him and the more we appropriate and make our own the power of his passion and the pleading of his blood. One involves the other; the psychological contact of faith involves the moral contact with all the moral worth of the loving Christ in his passion. Here are two *presences* of each one of us to our Lord—the psychological presence by which we are close to our redeeming Lord and to our risen Lord, looking back and looking up and forward; the moral presence by which we are covered with the glory of his redeeming act in time and make our own all the moral worth that went with the love for his Father when it glowed in his heart in time.

We are justified by faith, and, St Thomas will add, by the sacraments of faith. Faith is first and indispensable. When we make the various sacramental signs of faith, that basic justification will be reinforced and in the most generous way; the initial incorporation into the worshipping Christ will be deepened and enriched in ways beyond our calculating. That is God's arrangement. The sign of our faith will not be just a sign; it will bring with it (and through it) an enhancement of all that we had, a deeper union, a closer presence, a fuller life in God.

4. The sacramental signs of faith bring with them an enhancement of all that we already had. That means two things. First, an enrichment of all the soul's interior life of grace and a deeper involvement in all the current of worship that springs up always from the heart of Christ to his Father. Secondly, this is brought about because of the *real presence* of the worshipping, saving Christ, who comes amongst his people as their priest whenever any of the sacraments are celebrated. He comes amongst them as their priest, putting his priestly act of worship, which is his uninterrupted offering of the body and the blood, at their disposal, that they may appropriate it even physically, and make it the word that speaks their devotion and their love, and, more important, make theirs his devotion and his love.

In every one of the seven Sacraments the baptized people of God reach out to the risen Christ among them and touch (even physically, though not naturally) that priestly act of giving which lay at the heart of the Calvary event as a sacrifice. They touch it because of that mysterious faculty of contacting the risen Christ which was given them at their baptism, which links them up with Christ the priest, which is a door of entry into the court of worship where the risen Christ stands always before the Father. There he stands, continuing always till the end of time, as long as men on earth will

need it, that priestly act of giving the body and the blood, which made the Calvary act to be a sacrifice, and which was the heart of the sacramental sacrifice of the Cenacle, as it is the heart of the sacramental sacrifice which is our Mass. There are many masses, but the heart of them all is one and the same. There are many sacramental celebrations of various kinds, but at the heart of them all is the risen Christ present to his baptized people, a priest leading us in worship, into the holies, beyond the veil, offering—as long as men on earth can profit by this heavenly priest—the body and the blood.

5. The zone of Christian sacramental celebration is then a zone of worship. A worshipping priest is made really present to his people. Christ our *leitourgos* is amongst us who have been baptized into this worshipping community. In all the sacraments without exception there is this fundamental worship, into which we must also enter personally by our personal spirit of self-sacrifice; its moral worth we make our own according to the degree of our devotion. But the physical contact with the act of sacrificial giving of the body and the blood is always there, our physical presence to Christ our priest, the response of what is called the character of our baptism and of our confirmation to the character of priestly order.

6. This physical presence of Christ the priest amongst his people, his worshipping community, is brought about when in the sacramental celebration the ordained minister does something that makes Christ physically present to him, and then, dependently on that presence, present to the baptized person for whom he performs the rite. The character of Order, itself a further development of the character of baptism, has a certain active function in regard to the character of baptism. The ordained Christian can introduce the baptized Christian into the physical presence of Christ the priest, into which presence the ordained Christian has a power of entry that can never directly be taken from him and which he can exercise without dependence on any other. The baptized depends on the ordained. There you have the hierarchic structure of the Church. But at the end the initiate as well as the minister has an immediate contact with the worshipping act of Christ.

Each may have an immediate contact. Yet its significance is not always the same. The worshipping Christ may at the end be present to the ordained minister who actively celebrates the sacramental rite and to the baptized initiate into this zone of worship who outwardly plays a more passive part. But here we must distinguish between the sacramental sacrifice of the Mass and the celebration of a sacramental rite, the dominating purpose of which is the lifting up of man upon the plane of holiness in Christ. In all the sacramental celebrations there is the inner kernel of the worshipping act of Christ. In the Mass this is captured and enshelled (in that sign of sacrifice which is the twofold transubstantiation of the bread and of the wine) purely and simply for its own sake. The Godward movement of giving the body and the blood is made present to us in a sacramental shell that captures it for us, but is itself also a Godward movement of changing our bread and wine into that body and blood that are being offered to God. In this case

both ordained minister and baptized worshipper touch the kernel of Christ's giving with an equal immediacy, and for both it has the same significance of pure worship. But unless the ordained priest had first enshelled it in an act of transubstantiation, the baptized believer could never have grasped it with the hold his baptismal character enables him to lay upon it.

7. Only the ordained minister makes the sign of sacrificial giving which is the double act of transubstantiation; to him only is Christ directly present as the principal agent of transubstantiation. Christ uses his subordinate ordained priests and them alone as his instruments in the working of this miracle. But coming amongst his priests as transubstantiator, he comes simultaneously as offerer among his priests and his people, and to all as offerer is he equally really present. All, ordained and baptized, lay hold of the act of offering the body and the blood and are physically incorporated into Christ, the offering priest, at the moment of the Mass.

The transubstantiating act of which the priest alone is the instrument is no more salutary for him than for others in terms of real contact with Christ the offering priest. It is only his proper mode of contacting the priestly act of Christ. But contacting it thus first in the sacramental action, he mediates it to the baptized worshipper, who then contacts it himself, and with an equal sanctifying immediacy. There is dependence here, surely, but in the end they are all one, sharing with an equal immediacy in the priestly act of Christ the priest. The physical nearness is, at the end, the same; and the moral significance of that physical nearness is without any shadow of difference. From start to finish, it is pure giving, pure worship.

8. Apart from the moment of the Mass the real presence of Christ the priest in the other sacramental celebrations has differences that must be noted. For then Christ the priest comes amongst us, not only as Christ the priest nor only as using the transubstantiating action in the service of his priestly action; he comes as priest surely, in all the beauty of his worshipping act of giving the body and the blood, but then his action is the instrument that is being used to sanctify men, to take the baptized even further into the life of union with God. Then with the Godward act of worship is combined a current that runs in the other direction. Indeed, it runs so strong that we have to take thought to see the Godward movement it covers. Christ comes among his people, turned towards us, radiating life and grace; we do not always notice that he is turned also towards his Father. But it is so, and it is precisely the humanity of the worshipping Christ that is being used as an instrument in sanctifying men. That is why there is worship in all the sacraments. In the Mass, however, that worship is captured and made present in a way that does not divide our attention; the Godward movement is enshelled for us in a movement that is also Godward—the lifting up of our earthly bread and wine into the gifts of the body and the blood that are always before the Father's face—whereas in the other sacramental celebrations that Godward movement of worship is made present to us in a current of power that reaches from God to man.

9. It is because the presence of Christ the priest amongst us is now pre-

cisely as sanctifier that its significance is different for the liturgical minister and for the liturgical initiate. The minister mediates Christ the sanctifier to the initiate. But he himself is not sanctified thereby. The minister's sacramental function is purely causal. He and the sacramental rite he performs are the sign that Christ the sanctifier is physically present radiating holiness to the liturgical initiate. Christ is present to the minister as principal cause to instrumental cause, and dependently on this presence to the minister he is present to the liturgical initiate for whom the minister performs the sacramental rite. But Christ's presence to the liturgical initiate is as cause to effect. Dependently on his presence to the minister as cause using instrumental cause, he is present to the baptized initiate as cause to effect. The power of Christ is in the minister and in the rite; the effect of that power is in the baptized initiate.

Here there is a presence of Christ in sanctifying power, as in the Mass there is a presence through transubstantiating power. They are both real presences with different moral tones. To the human priest this presence is the presence of a power acting through his action (acting on the bread and wine or acting on the initiate); to the liturgical initiate, this presence in the sacramental rites other than the Mass is that of a power acting on him, while in the Mass it is a more mysterious presence, theologically less explored, not of a power, but associated with the power of transubstantiation exercised by the ordained priest.

10. Thus the presence of Christ to the believing Christian celebrating the mysteries of his worship is a rich and manifold thing. There is first of all the fundamental presence, the 'psychological' presence of Christ within our minds and hearts by the theological virtues. Then as a result there is moral presence to the saving Christ and our moral identification with him in all that he did for us by his living, dying, and rising again. Thirdly, there is the physical nearness of the baptized Christian to the risen Christ that takes place when the Christian sacraments are celebrated. Here we enter into the world of sacramental character, where ordained and baptized each play their part and where to each in different but corresponding ways the risen Christ approaches in all the beauty of his worshipping act that goes to his Father, and in all the power of his redemptive and sanctifying love. Here the character of the ordained minister of the rite plays an active rôle. He alone in the sacramental action is the agent used by Christ and is near to him in those causal terms. He alone is the instrument of sanctification as the instrument of transubstantiation. He mediates the real presence of the sanctifying and of the transubstantiating Christ. The baptized liturgical initiate plays a more passive rôle. But to him too Christ becomes really present, as someone whom Christ is touching with the *finger* of the sacramental rite, and in the Mass as someone who touches Christ—the offering Christ and his act of offering—with the *finger* of his baptismal character which is a sharing in the priesthood of Christ.

11. The notion of real presence, however, has not yet reached its fullest meaning. Real presence to minister, real presence to initiate, real presence

in the sacramental rites other than the mass, real presence in the Mass—all these, with the exception, perhaps, of the presence of the offering Christ to the baptized worshipper at Mass, can be explained by using the idea of principal and instrumental efficient cause. (The touch by which the baptized worshipper touches the offering Christ at Mass is, indeed, mysterious.) But the real presence of the body and blood of Christ (and of the whole Christ), under the sense-phenomena of bread and wine, reaches the very ultimate in the idea of real presence, though indeed the indwelling of God within the soul that believes and within the soul that sees him in vision goes far beyond it. For this is a presence of him who is pure act to spirit, and now we are discussing Christ in his humanity and his flesh and blood and ourselves as still wayfaring to heaven.

Under the appearances of bread and wine lie the body and the blood, as close to these appearances as was the substance of the bread and wine to the accidents before the change. It would be impossible to conceive a closer form of bodily presence. The accidents of the bread inhere in the bread and contain it. After the change they do not inhere in the body of Christ; but they contain it, just as really, just as closely, as they had contained the substance of the bread. There you have real presence at its fullest. And that is Christ's gift to us in the Eucharist. All love is communion. Christ's love must find expression in communion. Only a divine ingenuity could have devised that means of communion which is the real presence of the body and blood and of the whole Christ under the appearances of bread and wine, that we may get close to him in the bread of life and take it into our very hands and eat it.

Appendix 3

THE METAPHYSICS OF THE EUCHARIST

1. IN THOMIST sacramental theology the philosophical idea of physical instrumental cause plays a commanding rôle. And indeed this is only one field in which this idea holds a key position. In the general field of the relationship between the first cause and creatures in their activity, the theology of St Thomas sees the creature, the secondary cause, not only as a principal cause but also as an instrument in the hand of God. In the field of Christology it sees the holy humanity of Christ the man as God's instrument to produce miraculous effects and effects in the order of grace; also it sees all things held in existence by God using that self-same holy humanity as his instrument. Then again in the field of Biblical authorship it regards the inspired writer, who is the principal though secondary cause of his book in so far as it is justly regarded as his book, as also being the instrumental cause in so far as God is seen to be not merely the first cause of the writing (he is that in regard to every activity), but also its principal author. Finally, in the field of sacramental theology, it sees the minister of the rite and the action he performs as being the sign and physical instrumental cause of the sacramental character (and the modifications thereof) and of sacramental grace within the soul of the liturgical initiate.

2. The Eucharist is the supreme sacrament—to which all the others are ordered—their consummation and their crown. Here sacramentality is at its fullest and richest. Here we have a sign, not merely that Christ is with us in all the power of his sanctifying action, but also that he is amongst us in the power of his transubstantiating action, in the glory of his priestly offering of his body and his blood, and in an abiding way as the very source of our holiness under the appearances of bread and wine.

In the Eucharist it is particularly in the investigation of the presence of Christ as the principal cause of the transubstantiating action that the philosophical idea of instrumental cause is called upon to help our understanding about the mystery. In the other sacraments it is the presence of Christ as sanctifier at the moment of the production of grace in the soul that is theologically explained in the light of this theory. In the Eucharist, because Christ is sacramentally really present and as permanently as a substance is contained within the enfolding accidents, we can think of him as sacramentally present as sanctifier even before we eat the bread and drink the cup. Whether he—who is already sacramentally present as the very source of grace—actually uses the sacramental appearances of the bread and wine as his physical instrument at the moment when we partake of Holy Communion, is a moot point. At all events, in the Eucharist, as in the other sacraments, the theory of instrumental cause plays its part, certainly in the elucidation

of the presence of Christ as agent of the transubstantiating change which brings the presence of the adoring, offering Christ, in all the undisturbed glory of his offering that body into which the bread is being changed, of his offering that blood into which the wine is being changed. Christ is really, abidingly present as substance is contained within accidents; Christ is really but momentarily present as efficient cause using instrumental cause.

3. Theologies of a less realist complexion will, of course, admit that the effect of the transubstantiating action is a real presence of Christ; they will not always recognize, with followers of St Thomas, that the source of the transubstantiating action is also a real, though a fleeting, presence of Christ in the exercise of effective power. This goes back to a difference in Christologies. The spirit of St Thomas is a robust, physical realism—throughout this discussion the word metaphysical might be better than physical. There is another approach in which the psychological and moral values of the Christ-achievement are everything. Christ knows, Christ loves, Christ merits, Christ prays. That is capital. These values are not absent from St Thomas's theology. Indeed, they are paramount. But there are other exciting relationships to Christ. He touches us. And from the touch of his holy humanity power streams out. That was the situation in the days of his mortal flesh and indeed in those strange forty days of his visible, tangible, appearances amongst us. But now from where he is, on the other side of the veil, power streams out from him on to us, and at times it is a power that elevates us instrumentally and uses us. This is a touch, a real touch, not a bodily propinquity but a *spiritual* contact which dispenses with the need for local presence.

So it is that differences in Christology will involve differences in sacramentology too. If the man Jesus is seen as physically radiating power, our encounter with him in all the sacramental celebrations will take place on a plane of physical realism as well as on that of faith and of moral value. So it is that the view of the sacred humanity being used always by the Blessed Trinity as the instrument in the production of grace and of other effects finds a natural corollary that it is also used in the Eucharist as the instrumental cause of the miracle of transubstantiation and in the production of the sacramental effects. And as such it has as a subordinate instrument the liturgical celebrant and the sacramental rite at the moment of the transubstantiating action. The priest and the faithful with him encounter the high-priest of their oblation at the moment when that high-priest is using his subordinate, his representative, his vicar, to change the bread and wine into his body and blood. That is the mode of his coming amongst them in all the glory of his priestly giving; he will remain amongst them, abidingly, in all the reality of his body given and his blood poured out, in another mode of presence that results from that.

4. Let us look at the metaphysics of instrumental causality. God is the first efficient cause and the ultimate final cause of all that is. He is also the supreme pattern or exemplar cause of all. He is pure being. The shadow of limitation falls on the being of all others. He is existence. They have exist-

ence. He cannot not be. They can not be. Every moment of their existence can be seen as a coming into existence. Yet things too are causes. In a true sense they have effects and bring other things into being. There is in their nature a power in some way proportioned to their effect. A father generates his son. He is a true cause, a principal cause, although only a secondary cause, because all that he has he has from the first, the transcendent, the metaphysical cause. The whole order of physical causes has a metaphysical background or underground which supports and causes it. Causes in the physical order are secondary causes, and there is a first cause that causes their very causality, yet so causing it that it is genuine causality, and in the case of voluntary agents so causing it that it is free. Here we touch on the analogical participation of creaturehood in the uncreated.

So created things in their own way exercise a genuine causality. Yet when we look at created causes themselves we observe that sometimes they act with a certain independence within their own secondary field as principal causes, and sometimes they are merely instruments being used by a principal cause. For instance, I am a principal cause of my thinking now, and of my writing on this paper; but the pen in my hand is an instrumental cause of the writing. The writing flows immediately from the pen, but only as guided by my hand and mind and thus heightened to share in a power and movement deriving from hand and mind. All the same the pen contributes its own quota to the total effect, the black lines that are being guided, yet only because it is triggered into action and held in action by my hand, and ultimately by my mind and will. So it is that in every instrument we can distinguish between the natural power of the instrument and the instrumental power geared to a higher effect, a causality that is transiently communicated to it when actually being used by a higher cause. The higher cause elevates the instrument in using it, and simultaneously sets in action both its normal power and the communicated power. Acting thus in harmony the joint effect is seen to be one, although we can distinguish the strands of reality in the effect that derive properly from the principal and from the instrumental cause.

Sometimes the part played by the instrument is less obvious. What it properly contributes to the total effect is not quite like the black lines on the paper which are formed into intelligible characters by the hand that holds the pen and the mind that guides the hand. Rather it contributes to the total effect by just being itself and perhaps just by acting within its own proper field; but in doing so it modifies the action of the principal cause and gives it a direction which it would not otherwise have had and which perhaps it needed in order to act at all. The water of baptism acts on the body of a person; the power of causing grace which is in the sacrament acts on the soul of a person.

Thus it is in the transubstantiating action. The human priest utters the words of consecration in the person of Christ. He pronounces them over the bread and the cup that are before him. At that moment he becomes a sacramental sign. He is the sign of the transubstantiating Christ. But he is

the veil, the envelope of the transubstantiating Christ who is really present to him. Christ who is locally in heaven is in real and spiritual contact with his priest at our altar at some point of this tiny planet. This is a contact that bridges distance in place, and needs no local proximity of Christ to his priest. It is in an exercise of power that uses the priest on earth and his human activity in the sacramental rite that the transubstantiating Christ becomes present at the moment of the changing of the bread and wine; as a result of this he becomes present in another, a more abiding way. He becomes present abidingly under the consecrated species because he was first present fleetingly to the consecrating priest.

5. It is the character of priestly order that marks the priest as the instrument of Christ. The priestly character is an instrumental power. But it is a special kind of instrumental power. As a rule an instrumental power is only found in an instrument when it is actually being used by a higher cause. But the human priest enjoys the permanent possession of the power of transubstantiation and he becomes the actual instrument of the transubstantiating Christ whenever he wills. There is an analogy to this in the very humanity of the transubstantiating Christ itself. That very humanity becomes the channel of the power of Trinity using it as its instrument whenever Christ as man freely wills that it should. And now we find the humanity of Christ's priest on earth becoming the subordinate channel of the power of the Trinity, subjected to the humanity of Christ, whenever Christ's priest on earth freely intends that it should.

When the ordained priest freely co-operates with Christ the priest he becomes the actual instrument of Christ the priest. This is true when he celebrates the sacramental rite that signifies and causes grace in the soul of the initiate, as, for example, in Penance. It is also true when he celebrates the mystery that signifies and causes the change of the bread and wine into the body and blood. In exercising his own natural activity, in pronouncing the words of consecration over the Eucharistic elements, or in making any other of the sacramental signs, he channels in a particular direction the action of the principal cause who is Christ. It is this bread, over which he is now uttering these words, that is changed. It is this person with regard to whom he is now celebrating this rite who is the recipient of the divine influence that floods the soul with grace. Thus there is, as in the exercise of all instrumental causality, an activity on the part of the instrument (or, at least, a being itself), that renders a service to the principal cause.[1]

6. In the sacramental world Christ uses his human priest as his instrument both in the exercise of his power of transubstantiation and in the exercise of his power of sanctifying souls. He comes among the baptized through his priest. But whether he comes as sanctifier or as transubstantiator, he comes always as offerer. There is offering as well as sanctifying. There is

[1]The case of the image in the *phantasia*, which is the instrument of the *intellectus agens* in causing a *species* in the *intellectus possibilis*, is an example of an instrument rendering a service to the principal cause just by being what it is.

offering as well as transubstantiation. And when it is found within the envelope of the double transubstantiation, we have the sacramental sacrifice of the Mass.

So the idea of physical instrumental cause throws a flood of light upon the way the sacraments in general convey grace to the soul and upon the way Christ is said to be the principal offerer in the Mass. Because a higher cause is really present to the lower cause it uses as its instrument, Christ is really present in all the sacramental celebrations, whether they are concerned with the sanctification of man or with the unique and singular consecration of the Eucharistic elements. This real presence is not as intimate and abiding as the real presence of the body and blood of Christ to the accidents that contain them. But it has something which the more abiding presence has not got. It is a presence immediate to us. Christ as cause touches the priest who is his instrumental cause.

When the priest is the instrumental cause of grace, Christ as principal cause touches the soul of the liturgical initiate as a cause touches an effect. When the priest is instrumental cause of transubstantiation, Christ the offerer is put in touch with the soul of the baptized worshipper who with the priest is offering the Mass. In the more abiding presence of Christ under the consecrated elements, we may indeed, even locally, touch the species, but it is the species that touch Christ. This is the mysterious, analogical, touch by which accidents contain the substance to which they refer.

7. This is that real presence of Christ to which the words 'real presence' in Eucharistic theology primarily refer. It would be a pity if the historic controversies about this real presence were to make us think that it was the only real presence to be discussed. Indeed, it was perhaps because of the polemics concerning this real presence in the host at the time of Berengarius and from the sixteenth century onwards that theologians forgot to notice that in all the sacraments and in the sacramental sacrifice there was another real presence, less wonderful indeed, but at the heart of the matter and the key to its full intelligence.

8. The real presence in the host does, however, come to the very ultimate in the possibilities of real presence. True, we do not touch the Christ within the host; nor does he touch us, except at the time of sacramental eating. But our very local nearness to the host which is as close to him as accident is close to substance—a nearness which is most intimate at the moment of communion—is the ultimate expression of divine love in our regard. We eat him really, though not naturally—that would be horrible; we eat him really, but sacramentally. There could not be a closer sign of our being made one with him in love.

9. This real presence is explained in terms of substance and accident. On the philosophical level St Thomas will exploit the riches of Aristotelean metaphysics. But the basic idea of his treatise is an insight of unsophisticated thought. We are using it in ordinary life all the day long. It corresponds, to some extent, to the difference in our powers of knowing, the difference between our intelligence and our senses.

Our senses are confronted by the appearances of a thing; our intelligence touches the thing itself that exists, reaches it as an existential ground of being for all the surface qualities that affect it. Some of these qualities derive from the inner core of its being and reveal to us something of the inner nature of the thing. All our knowledge begins with the shock of sense-experience. Then we penetrate by our intelligence towards the mystery of the thing as an existent and we also gain some intellectual knowledge of its meaning as essence. The distinction then between the heart of a thing and its surface qualities, the noumenon and the sense-phenomena, the substance and its accidents, is really a familiar one and part of the everyday working of the human mind.[2] There are, of course, sophisticated thinkers to deny it; they are those who will deny that there is any fundamental difference between intellect and sense. Catholic theology and, indeed, Catholic dogma is for ever wedded to what is the implicit metaphysics of the ordinary man; the real presence of the body and blood, and of the whole Christ, in the Eucharist is to be intellectually grasped in terms of the distinction between, and the presence to each other of, a substance and its accidents.

10. In this, however, as in other fields, the theologian's philosophizing about the mysteries of faith has led to developments. In the mystery of the Word incarnate, for instance, the theologian sees what had eluded the mere philosopher; he sees that personality and individuation are not to be identified. Here, too, in the Eucharist, he sees that an accident's *containing* the substance to which it refers is not to be identified with its *inhering* in it. The pure philosopher would hardly have thought of this distinction at all. For him the inhering would be the containing. The theologian who at first saw the quantity of the bread inhering in the bread and thus containing it, now sees that same quantity no longer inhering in any thing at all but actually containing the whole Christ just as really as up to the change it had contained the substance of the bread.

This *containing* would seem to be a relationship—to belong to the Aristotelean category of what are called predicamental relations. But it is not just a relationship; it is emphatically a relationship of containing. It is not just a relationship to the body and blood of Christ who is in heaven, a reaching towards him, a sort of yearning for him. Such a relationship would hardly be the explanation of a real presence. The ultimate explanation of the real presence of Christ in the Eucharist is a relationship between the accidents of bread and wine and the body and blood of Christ. But it is a relationship of containing. Cajetan, the illustrious sixteenth-century commentator of the *Summa*, constantly spoke of it as a relationship to Christ as contained, and Pius XII, in an address to the first international liturgical congress (1956), found it salutary to repeat this teaching. The Eucharistic species are no empty envelope addressed to Christ in heaven. The Christ who is locally in

[2]The division 'substance and accident' is commonly equated with that between 'thing and appearance', yet strictly speaking 'accident' is a metaphysical category, perceived and applied only after that of 'substance'.

heaven is really contained, although not naturally, but sacramentally, *within* the sacramental species.

11. Another matter in which the demands of his faith have led the theologian further than the philosopher in metaphysics concerns the way in which quantity affects a bodily substance. The philosopher will see substance as in place, and as extended in place. He will see the accident of quantity or extension as putting part of the thing outside part, and all this in reference to the part outside part of the encompassing place. But the theologian believes that the whole Christ is contained by what was the quantity of the bread. He knows that this quantity does not inhere in Christ, does not in any way affect him; its sole function is to *contain* him and, as thus purely and simply contained, to relate him to the place that encompasses the quantity. But the Christ contained within the quantity of the host, really present in this unique and sacramental way, this way in which substance is contained by quantity, has himself his own connatural quantity. Here is a great danger of misunderstanding the situation. Because the extended Christ is underneath the quantity of the bread, we are in danger of thinking of him there as in a place, in the same way the quantified bread and now the quantity of the bread is filling the place that encompasses it. The extended Christ underneath the quantity of the bread is not there as filling a place. He is there just as the substance of the bread was before it was thought of as inhered in by its quantity and extended by it in place. He is really there in a unique manner; he is contained, in the unique way accident contains substance before it exercises inherence in it; that is all. Let us attempt to make this clearer. The Christ thus contained who himself is quantified, extended, and has substantial parts outside parts, does not, as it were, flow into a point. He is related to each part of the quantity of the bread that contains him as the centre of a circle is equally and completely related to any part of the circumference. He is there *per modum substantiæ contentæ*, yet what quantifies him is his own quantity, which is without direct reference to a place encompassing the quantity of the bread. The quantified Christ is really there, but not as a quantified substance is normally related to an encompassing localizing quantity, but purely and simply as a substance is related to a quantity that is purely and simply containing it. Thus Christ in the Eucharist is quantified, but not in relation to any encompassing, localizing quantity. So it is that the theologian realizes that quantity does not always extend a thing in place. He sees quantity as exercising two degrees of function. First, it extends a thing in itself; then it extends it in a place. Thus for the second time he is led further than the philosopher. Quantity and the other accidents contain before they affect their subject; quantity extends a thing in itself before it extends it in place. And in both cases the separation of these functions is established in the Eucharist.

12. The real presence of Christ in the Eucharist, completely transcending any mode of natural presence, is brought about by the changing of the bread and wine into the body and blood of Christ. The idea of changing has, of course, to be used most cautiously. Here we have a unique situation in

which the idea of changing is verified in an utterly unique way. Absolutely nothing is done to the body and blood of Christ. Whatever happens makes Christ present not because of something done to him, but because of something done to something else. No real change, even of the slightest kind, is made in the body and blood of Christ. He is made to be really present because of a real relationship between the consecrated appearances of bread and wine and his body and blood. On his side it is a mere relationship in our mind; we see him as related to what is really related to him. The presence is a real presence not because of any added reality or any change in Christ; it is because the consecrated species are now exercising the real relationship of containing, no longer in regard to the substance of the bread but in regard to the body and the blood, which have succeeded as if they were just substance, to the substance of the bread and wine.

13. Any idea then of bringing Christ in under the species, of bringing him down on our altars (the 'Adduction Theory'), is foreign to St Thomas's mind. Christ is there not because he has been brought down, although for theologians of the Scotist school this will seem to be a fair way of describing the situation.[8]

If we do not bring Christ in under the species, simultaneously annihilating the substance of the bread, in order, as it were, to 'make room' for him, should we then say that we produce him out of the bread? In a sense the word 'production' is less unhelpful than the word 'adduction'. At least it excludes the idea of adduction and makes us realize that it is the bread that is changed and not Christ who is changed. And it also has not to fall back on the idea of annihilation, which no one really likes ever to attribute to God. For this reason, perhaps, a respectable Thomist like Billuart could allow himself to speak of 'production' in this case. But when all is said, it is an unhappy term. To produce the body of Christ out of the bread too strongly suggests a substantial change which leaves as substratum the primal matter of the bread. St Thomas shows that the Eucharistic change is certainly not that. We are left then with the vague word 'change', '*conversio*'. What it should suggest to us here is the total passing over of the complete reality of the substance of the bread (matter and form; essence and existence) into the reality of Christ's body which is in heaven: but in such a way that, as a result of this passing over, the accidents are not left hollow symbols of Christ in heaven, but are filled as really containing him who is locally there, yet also here, non-locally, non-naturally, really, uniquely, sacramentally, miraculously, *per modum substantiæ*. We could imagine a passing over of the reality of the bread into the reality of Christ's body, leaving the accidents an empty envelope. It would be a transubstantiation. But it would not result in the real presence of Christ in the host. It would not be the Eucharistic transubstantiation which our Catholic faith believes.

---

[8]Note how in theorizing about the sacrifice of the Mass, any idea of really doing anything to Christ is excluded from the Thomist field of view.

Glossary

accident: logically, as a predicable, a quality that is not of the very nature of its subject. Metaphysically, as a predicament, one of the nine categories of being other than substance; it naturally clings to substance in order to be real and enriches substance.

act or actuation: the positive contrast to potentiality or indeterminateness. An analogical concept.

change: the passage from being something in potentiality to being it actually.

character: the technical term for the seal or indelible mark left on the soul by the sacraments of Baptism, Confirmation and Orders. It enables its holder to take part in Christian worship.

creation: the bringing of a thing into being from no pre-existing material.

essence (created): the potential principle of the realness of a created thing.[1] This element is also a meaningful pattern.

existence (created): the actuating principle of the realness of a created thing.[1] Not to be conceptualized in a formula.

form: in philosophical physics, the determining principle of a thing which shapes the material. See *matter*. In sacramental theology, that part of the sacramental sign which gives point to its significance; the part of the sign which is the words spoken.

image: a sign of something, but not an empty sign. It *contains* (in varying degrees of *containing*) that of which it is the sign.

instrument: a subordinate cause elevated above its nature and applied to an effect above itself by a principal cause in the power of which it is moved.

latria: the worship given only to God.

matter: in philosophical physics, the basic indeterminate element which is determined by forms which make things to be this and that (substantial forms), and then to be thus and thus (accidental forms). In sacramental theology, the indeterminate element of the sacramental sign; it needs to be given a precise point of meaning by the determining part, or form. The bodily part of the sacramental sign (water, bread, wine, oil) and the action of using it.

potentiality: the capacity to receive an actuation or a determination of being; also to become or be changed. An analogical concept.

primal matter: as it were the ultimate *stuff* of material things; more accurately the substantial potentiality in all bodily things.

quantity: the first and most characteristic accident affecting all bodily substances. It makes the thing have parts outside parts, both in itself and in reference to the parts of the place that contains it.

species: logically, a determinate thought-pattern which embraces the full

---

[1]Here the ideas of potentiality and actuation are used by analogy. They do not quite coincide with these ideas as used on the plane of essential perfection, where we first found them. The analogy is that potentiality is seen as a principle of limitation.

meaning of the individual capable of existence. Metaphysically, the inner nature of a thing—its kind. Used also for the outer form of a thing which reveals its inner nature. In the Eucharist, the sense-phenomena, the appearances of bread and wine.

subject: what underlies accidental change—the substance. What underlies substantial change—primal matter.

substance: that which exists without needing any created ground of its being in the way an accident does. The heart of a thing underlying the sense-appearances.

substantial form: the inner determining element of a substance which actuates the sheer potentiality of the primal matter, makes the thing to be what it is and is the spring of its existence.

transubstantiation: the change of the whole substance of the bread into the body of Christ and of the whole substance of the wine into his blood, only the accidents of the bread and wine remaining.

truth: in sacramental theology (and indeed in a wider context), the thing that is pre-figured, the substance that casts its shadow backward into time.

Index

A

B

C

D

E

F

G

H

I

J

L

M

N

O

P

R

S

T

U

W

20950715R00148

Made in the USA
Middletown, DE
13 June 2015